THE THEATRES OF GEORGE DEVINE

THE THEATRES
OF
George Devine

IRVING WARDLE

JONATHAN CAPE
30 BEDFORD SQUARE LONDON

FIRST PUBLISHED 1978
© 1978 BY IRVING WARDLE
JONATHAN CAPE LIMITED
30 BEDFORD SQUARE
LONDON WC1

British Library Cataloguing in Publication Data
Wardle, Irving
    The theatres of George Devine
    1. Devine, George 2. Theater – Great Britain –
    Production and direction
    I. Title
    792'.0232'0924   PN2598.D/
    ISBN 0-224-01415-3

PRINTED IN GREAT BRITAIN
by W & J Mackay Limited, Chatham
On paper supplied by Grosvenor Chater and Company Limited.

For John Lawrence

CONTENTS

ILLUSTRATIONS

PREFACE

WHEN he was running the Shakespeare Memorial Theatre in the 1950s, Glen Byam Shaw made a hobby of collecting photographs of his Stratford colleagues. Not autographed star portraits, which would hardly have been of any interest to a man in Shaw's job, but pictures of Britain's leading actors as children. It was a gallery of the great pretenders before they had learned the art of pretence.

Among the collection was one studio portrait of a dumpy little boy of about six. He stands uncomfortably in his best clothes with a toy train (property of the photographer) carefully arranged at his feet, and his moon face creased into an unconvincing smile. It is not a happy picture. To Anthony Quayle, Shaw's co-director at Stratford, it seemed to be saying, 'I know I look awful, but I hope you like me.'

There are other, better known pictures of George Devine. There is the portly and ambitious young President of the OUDS who catapulted himself from Oxford to the West End stage in the early 1930s. There is the drama school teacher from whom two generations of students learned everything about comedy from Farquhar to farting. There are long-remembered performances, like his pre-war Andrey in *Three Sisters*, and his post-war Antrobus in *The Skin of Our Teeth*. And, much the best known, there is the Devine of the English Stage Company; a role for which he shed his Falstaffian skin and emerged as the craggy patriarch of Sloane Square. After his death in January 1966 some of his old friends held a memorial meeting on the stage of the Royal Court Theatre. In age they ranged from Edith Evans, who had played in Devine's Oxford *Romeo and Juliet*, to John Osborne, Devine's first great discovery for the

ESC. Over thirty years of stage history, and again the pictures
did not add up. To Edith Evans he was still 'Georgie', the
lovable junior. To his ex-students and to the Royal Court
writers he was a father figure. Also in the audience were old
friends from other periods of his life, some from his Oxford days
who left the meeting before it was over, unable to recognize the
man they knew from anything that was being said.

Devine was, and remains, an elusive personality. At the Royal
Court he famously ran an organization which restored the
theatre to the forefront of British artistic life, but he did so without acquiring much personal glamour. While other people at the
Court were making their reputations, he was minding the shop.
And although he won deep respect during his lifetime, it was
more as a force for the good than for any specific area of work.

Since his death the impersonal mask has hardened. For those
who detect a new age in the British theatre, Devine ranks as its
patron saint. His career is seen as a monument to the good grey
virtues of team spirit and selfless endeavour. I have heard playwrights describe him as a plank over which they were able to
walk. He let down the drawbridge, he opened the door, he
smuggled out the keys to the citadel. Devine metaphors generally
imply some humble military role, suggesting that his justifica-
tion lies in the chances he gave to other men. And when you look
back to the earlier phases of his career, it is the same story. He is
always sunk in some collective venture from which you can
only fitfully disentangle his own contribution.

Such, of course, is the general nature of theatrical work,
belied by theatrical biography's pursuit of flamboyant individuals.
The division of the field into thoroughbreds and cart-horses
makes no sense in Devine's case because he was not particularly
interested in winning. He cared less about succeeding in the
theatre than about helping the theatre to succeed. He immersed
himself in other people's affairs. He largely effaced himself when
he had a company of his own. But if you follow the record of his
associations through from the time of Komisarjevsky to the Royal
Court, what emerges is the story of the English theatre's repeated
efforts to renew itself. Any account of his career will also be an
account of how the theatre changed in his lifetime. To the
extent that it now takes subsidy and the company ethic for
granted, that it opens itself to Continental art and modern
British life, it owes ground rent to Devine. Not only to him, of

course, as the story developed like an Olympic relay with the torch repeatedly changing hands, but Devine is exceptional because he stayed the course longer than anyone else, and because it was his torch that finally lit the bonfire.

That was in 1956, already quite a long time ago, and theatrical memory is short. Devine has not been forgotten but he has been 'placed' in a way that stifles curiosity. Having walked across him, the breakthrough generation put him on a pedestal. Even Lilian Baylis, that other great theatrical parent-figure, is more alive in the public imagination from pre-war memories than the grizzled sagacious Daddy who figures on the brochures of the George Devine Award like an advertisement for the judicious pipe-smoker.

Devine was interesting in a way that none of the posthumous metaphors acknowledge. He was not a docile plank, or an obliging little turnkey, nor was he a serene elder statesman of the theatre lending a sympathetic ear to the young. Under all the masks he wore there was the one constant element of incurable dissatisfaction: dissatisfaction with himself, and with the theatre to which he had committed his life. I met him only three times and always for formal reasons. I can look up what he said, but the remark that stuck in my memory was one he delivered out of the blue as we were crossing the road: 'I do believe intensely in the creative value of struggle.' I understand the passion he put into that statement rather better now than I did at the time, and one thing that clarified it was the picture of that little boy with the sickly smile. Chronology apart, it is a good place to begin.

I.W.

ACKNOWLEDGMENTS

M Y thanks are first due to Giles Gordon for persuading me to write this book; and to Jocelyn Herbert who entrusted me with letters, documents and photographs relating to Devine's work from the 1930s, and who found time for repeated interviews and readings of a manuscript considerably bulkier than the present text. My deepest debt is to her.

George Devine was a man with many good friends, and they have extended their generosity and kindness to his biographer. One example is that of Sir John Gielgud who gave up an afternoon to talk to me at the end of a week in which he had lost two of his oldest friends and suffered a severe head injury. I must record my gratitude to him and to the following colleagues and members of the Devine circle who wrote or talked to me and from whose recollections the story has been reconstructed: Sir Donald and Lady Albery; Juliet Aliston; John Allen; Ande Anderson; Lindsay Anderson; John Arden; Dennis Arundell; Dame Peggy Ashcroft; Alan Bates; Peter Bayne; W. R. G. Bell; Sir Lennox Berkeley; Peter Best; Yolande Bird; John Blatchley; Stuart Burge; James Cairncross; K. Carter; Lord David Cecil; M. D. Chater; Lord Clark; David Cregan; the late Sir Peter Daubeny; R. Kingston Davies; Nigel Dennis; William Devlin; John Dexter; Doreen Dixon; Frances Doncaster; Stephen Doncaster; Patrick Donnell; Denis Dowling; Peter Duguid; Frank Dunlop; Laura Dyas; Michael Elliott, W. E. Escritt; the late Charles Fenby; William Gaskill; Peter Gill; Eric Gillett; George Goetschius; Marius Goring (who also supplied me with documents on the origin of the London Theatre Studio and recordings of Michel Saint-Denis); Dora Grant; R. A. D. Grant; Sir Alec Guinness; Michael Halifax; George Hall; Tom Hammond; Lord

Harewood; Margaret Harris; Rex Harrison; Michael Hastings; Dr John Henderson; Professor Hugh Hunt; Clare Jeffery; Ann Jellicoe; Keith Johnstone; Harriet Jump (Devine); Leslie Kark; Charles Landstone; Basil Langton; Sir Denys Lasdun; Oscar Lewenstein (who also allowed me to read the minutes of the English Stage Company's Management Committee); Christopher Logue; Val May; Keith Michell; Dr Jonathan Miller; Harry Mills; Professor John Mitchell; Yvonne Mitchell; Helen Montagu; Lee Montague; Charles Monteith; Elizabeth Montgomery; Beecher Moore; Lord Olivier; Lady Olivier (Joan Plowright); Anthony Page; Litz Pisk; the late Professor John Plamenatz; Giles Playfair; Greville Poke; Anthony Quayle; W. Ramsden; Sir Terence Rattigan; Sir Michael Redgrave; Llewellyn Rees; Tony Richardson; Pieter Rogers; Vera Russell (Lindsay); Suria Saint-Denis (Magito); Athene Seyler; Glen Byam Shaw; N. F. Simpson; Frank Singleton; Christine Smith; Nicholas Smith; John Southworth; Edmund Tracey; J. C. Trewin; Norman Tucker; Kenneth Tynan; Peter Ustinov; C. H. P. Verrinder; Sir William Walton; Arnold Wesker; Dr T. R. Williams; Angus Wilson.

I am also grateful to Anne Jenkins and Sue Rolfe for allowing me to usurp their office space at the Royal Court Theatre; to William Rees-Mogg and John Higgins for giving me time off to write the book; and to my wife, Elizabeth, for her help in revising it.

It will be obvious to every theatregoer that my treatment of the English Stage Company suffers from one glaring omission; namely any examination of Devine's friendship with John Osborne. When I approached Mr Osborne, he declared an emphatic lack of interest 'in providing copy or helping in the compiling of a book about George Devine. My relationship with him spanned some ten years and I regard it as a private one.' Naturally I regret this decision, and can only hope that one day Mr Osborne will complete the story himself.

1

⚜⚜⚜⚜

THE DEVINES

As a man, George Devine considered that he had been deprived
of childhood, and you would suppose as much from the holiday
snaps of a stolid bespectacled schoolboy labouring away at sand-
castles in a hot suit. He looks solitary and ill-at-ease with his
body. At the time of the Byam Shaw photograph he was living
with his parents in Lucas Square, Hampstead Garden Suburb.
His father was a clerk in Martin's Bank. His mother was insane.
And their precarious domestic life was at the mercy of her fits of
hysterical anger and black inertia: not to mention the times
when she would leave home, sometimes taking young George
with her.

The first time this happened was shortly after his birth on
November 20, 1910, when the couple were living in Hendon.
According to Devine, this must have been within the first year
of their marriage, as he claimed to have been conceived on the
wedding night, after which his mother turned to his father and
said, 'You must never do that again' – thus severing conjugal
relations for good. No record survives of how they got through the
following year. But the sexual shock seems to have turned Mrs
Devine unalterably against her husband, and the birth of her
son only intensified this antagonism. She fastened on to the child
with a jealous possessiveness that excluded the father. She had
been brought up, so she said, to believe that she was 'not like
other girls', and marriage had insulted that belief. From physical
disgust, she went on to convert her husband into an enemy.
And when the strain of sharing the same roof with him became
intolerable, she snatched up the infant George and bolted.

The family eventually traced her to an isolated house in the New
Forest and persuaded her to come back. Her husband, meanwhile,

had moved from Hendon to the Garden Suburb, perhaps with some faint hope of repairing the marriage by this change to a slightly grander address. As for the New Forest interlude, one can only guess at its devastating effect on the boy. To be walled up in a lonely woodland cottage with a mad woman, even if she is your mother, is the stuff of some horrible fairy tale. If Mrs Devine suffered a trauma on her wedding night, she passed on the damage to her son. Often, when he was too small to get up himself, he would be left in bed all day. According to Devine's daughter, Harriet, his mother would spy on the milkman through the window. 'She used to say, "He's in love with me. He's come to see me. He is the Prince of Wales, but of course he won't say so".' It was an episode he tried to blot from his memory, rarely discussing it even with his daughter or his closest friends.

By the age of five, Devine was back with both parents at their new house and attending a nearby kindergarten, which gave him some chance to escape the domestic gloom and make a few friends of his own. One of these was Frances Doncaster, the daughter of the Old Vic designer Wilfrid Walter. A year younger than Devine, she was much impressed by his protective manner on their ten-minute walks to school. During thunderstorms he would steer her firmly down the road well away from the trees, saying, 'It must be exactly in the middle.'

At that time, Hampstead Garden Suburb was not the faceless area it is now. It was a good place to live, especially for children: a planned garden suburb existing as a unit quite separate from Golders Green. Its character was semi-rural. Butchers' carts called twice a week. Side by side with the new squares, the old farms were still there. And the district connected with the Heath extension without touching any main roads. It attracted the kind of residents who were flooding out to Span developments in the 1950s. Among Mrs Doncaster's neighbours were Collins Baker, the Keeper of the National Gallery, and J. B. Manson, subsequently Director of the Tate. One of the local preachers was the brother of the actor-manager Arthur Bourchier. There was a thriving community centre seething with amateur weavers and drama groups.

None of which was of any help to the Devines who, character-istically, had picked a dud square to live in. Lucas Square was an isolated collection of semi-detached houses full of old ladies, one

of whom regularly laid an extra place at table in case the Lord
dropped in for tea. There was no walking on the grass in Lucas
Square, and children never wanted to play there. Occasionally
Mrs Doncaster would nerve herself for a visit to see young
George Alexander. She remembers his house as a black cavern
with heavy mahogany furniture and no trace of flowers or
colour. But she rarely saw the inside of it as the Devines gave no
parties and shut themselves off from their neighbours. She spent
most of her time in the garden with him where their favourite
game was playing houses. George always took charge of these
games. His mother would sometimes bring them tea in the
garden, but 'something always went wrong. I always seemed to
go home in disgrace for some reason or other. Always *her* deciding something was wrong. There was always the sad pale face of
the mother.'

Her first memory of Devine's interest in the theatre is another
disaster story. One afternoon she found that he had curtained
the porch with a dust-sheet and arranged candles as foot-lights
on the two steps down to the garden. When she arrived, he lit
them; and that was the end of the show as the curtain caught
fire and blazed up to the top of the porch. Inside was a cage of
birds, the cherished property of Mrs Devine. 'I remember her
screaming: "Oh my poor little birds, my poor little birds!" I
was sent home feeling terribly guilty and George was sent to
bed.'

Nor did he have much fun with other children in the area.
Mrs Doncaster remembers no other friend he made. There was
never anybody else in the garden; and at school he never became
part of a group. It was, she says, a 'sporty philistine place where
you had to be good at everything'. She thinks Devine hated it as
much as she did. As he was short-sighted and bad at team games
he became a natural target for a gang who used to waylay him
to jeer about his father's limp, and beat him up. George Devine
Senior was regarded as an amiable unfortunate on account of his
peculiar wife and of the bad leg on which he was observed
stumping home to her every evening. Young George endured
these ambushes with stony detachment. 'Then his mother made
things worse by lying in wait for the attackers and shrieking
"How dare you tease my little boy about his poor father who
fought for you in the war?"' (Another source ascribes Mr
Devine's disability not to enemy action but to having put his foot

down a rabbit hole.) George became even less popular at school after this.

As for his father, it must have been a novel experience to be publicly defended by his wife when her usual habit was to vilify him in her son's hearing and treat every small gift or endearment as enticement to sharing his detested bed.

Mr Devine's baptismal name was Giorgios. He was one of seven children of an Irish-Lancashire father and a Greek mother. The wife he had the bad luck to marry, Ruth Cassady, was a Scots-Canadian girl. So his son was the product of five nationalities.

George Devine, the subject of this book, was not a family-minded man. When he grew up, he preserved some contact with the people who had been kind to him in childhood, but he had no interest in blood-ties. After his father's death in the 1920s, he fell out of contact with his relatives and treated the theatre as his family. To his Oxford friends he played the part of a self-created character with a mysterious background, and when he mentioned the Devines at all it was to tell funny stories about eccentric uncles.

An account of this enterprising and slightly dotty clan is nevertheless relevant to his adult life. There are two reasons for this. First, not only his early childhood but also his boarding school education took place inside the Devine family. Secondly, for two previous generations the family had been possessed by reformist ideals which George Devine inherited and applied to an area of society from which some of his godly forbears would have recoiled.

His grandfather, Henry Devine, began in the Manchester office of a Greek shipping merchant and quickly established himself in the cloth trade after marrying the boss's sister. But as soon as he achieved prosperity he turned from practical affairs to philanthropic schemes. He seems to have been a born missionary who mistook himself for a businessman. And when his good luck ran out in the cotton slump of the 1870s, he divided his remaining capital between his elder sons and emigrated to Greece, where, after his wife's death, he spent his last years preaching to peasants in the hills outside Athens.

The pattern of business and philanthropy recurs in the lives of his sons: at least with the two of them who meant most to George Devine. They were all given Greek names which they subsequently anglicized, with the exception of the untranslatable

Minos. Minos was the obvious success among them and the least typical of the family. He was a career clergyman who took an Oxford degree in theology and went on to a series of Congregational pastorates before making an astute move to the Anglican church. This led to his appointment as Vicar of St Peter's, Vere Street, one of the sleekest livings in Central London, where he remained for seventeen years. One of George Devine's stories was that his uncle, as a young man, married a member of the congregation who told him after the wedding: 'Don't think you're going to touch me: I only married you to get a front seat in the church.' And that when his wife died, the elderly Minos promptly married a young girl and within a month had 'fucked himself to death'.

Of the other uncles, Alexander was probably more important to the young George Devine than his own father, as he took charge of the boy's education, both as a headmaster and as a wickedly experienced man of the world, from his prep school days until he went up to Oxford.

Lex (as he was known to his family and pupils) may not rank with the educational pioneers of the century but he can certainly claim a place with the great independent school eccentrics. Sparing no time to feather his own nest, he embarked on good works right from the start. As a cub reporter covering police courts for the *Manchester Guardian*, he was appalled at the treatment of young offenders and decided that the waste could be stopped if only these gangs of 'scuttlers' (*fin de siècle* skinheads) had a place of their own. In the grip of this obsession, he turned it to a roaring success with a series of working lads' clubs, supported by the gentry, which achieved their social zenith when Lex snared a royal – Prince Albert Victor of Wales – to unveil a brass tablet at his new club in Oldham. As it was rumoured that the morning coat and grey top-hat he wore for the occasion had been bought with club funds, this high point of Lex's empire also brought the first rumblings of its collapse. Downfall followed in 1890 when his committee put Lex on the spot for paying club cheques into his own bank account.

He still saw himself as the bad boys' friend, but having failed with the poor he now decided to try the rich. Without any educational credentials, he managed to promote himself from warden of a resettlement centre into head of a boarding school. Salisbury Grange, Edmonton, was its first address, and from here, Lex broadcast his appeal to the headmasters of Britain: 'Don't expel your bad boys. Send them to me.' The result was a stream of recruits from Harrow, Clifton and Rugby; and within a year, the need to move to larger premises at Mitcham.

Through this contact with Grade A rejects, Lex stopped idealizing public schools. Perhaps it was not the boys that needed reforming but the system. To put this to the test he took over a 160-acre estate at Enfield called Clayesmore and set the new policy in motion by ordering the Mitcham boys to report to him on foot. The march took them five days. On arrival, they found that the rules had changed. They were no longer in a reformatory but back in a boarding school with other ordinary boys. Lex was taking no more hard cases. He wanted to put Clayesmore on the map as a great public school, and could not afford to have the place regarded as an educational Australia where the system dumped its waste. Abbotsholme and Bedales had lately been founded; and he wanted his institution bracketed with them as 'the ABC of educational reform'. This task occupied the rest of his life, and we shall leave him at it until the arrival of his nephew at Clayesmore twenty years later.

Lex's younger brother George also made a start as a social re-former, but in his case good works rested on a solid base of material security. He came down to London in the early 1890s to take a job at Cocks Biddulph's Bank in Whitehall, and he re-mained a banker to the end of his days. Philanthropy was a spare-time activity.

In London, he was taken under the wing of his bank manager who did what he could to supply him with a substitute family. But before long, George was looking round for a flock of his own to look after, and he found one ready-made at a House of Charity in Soho Square, where he worked as a volunteer fund-raiser and later as superintendent. He then founded a boys' club in Great Peter Street, Victoria, with the idea of giving local boys an alternative to the streets and the company of drunken parents. Unlike Lex's highly disciplined establishments, the place was run on a fun principle and went in for games, shows and weekend hikes.

Among the people to whom he was introduced by his manager were a Clapham family, the Searles. Mr Searle was a headmaster and the father of two little girls who adopted George as an

honorary uncle. Dora, the younger of the two, kept in close
touch with him until he married, and remembers some of the
club shows he put on for the boys: musical entertainments,
sketches by George, and aquatic melodramas in the Westminster
Baths. 'As a kid of seven, those were the plays that used to strike
me so much. He wrote them himself. And he'd have Neptune
on a raft in the middle of the pool; and the boys drowning and
being saved.'

The uncle-niece relationship persisted for some fifteen years
until Dora's engagement in 1910; at which point George faded
from the scene and shortly afterwards announced his own marriage to Ruth Cassady. He then disappeared into the black hole
of Lucas Square. The reunion came at the end of the war when
George needed help. He and his wife had separated, and there was
no one at home to look after his son. Dora (now Mrs Grant), took
young George into her family during the holidays and encouraged father and son to treat her house in Merton as a second
home. With that, the friendship returned to something like the
old pattern.

The difference, of course, was that he was no longer an enthusiastic young man, but a middle-aged bank manager with
an unhappy private life. This was the father young George
Devine knew. What was he like? At Merton, he settled into the
role of resident clown. He was a short fat figure who walked
with a limp (one foot had been amputated). He collected butter-
flies and played long-distance chess. He 'laughed at absolutely
everything', and his arrival, pince-nez glittering through a cloud
of cigar smoke, meant that silly things were going to happen. He
would secretly doctor the drinking water; or appear in the garden
with his hat on back to front, wearing a false beard. 'I remember
him saying to the boys, "Laugh. If you can't laugh with something, laugh at it!" And they'd all go "Ha, Ha, Ha," to tease
him.' One person who did not laugh was young George, who
would look on in solemn bewilderment at the mirthful scenes on
the croquet lawn. Evidently it had never struck him that his
father was a funny man. In his element when surrounded by
other people's children, perhaps he was out of his depth in caring
for a child of his own. The subject came up once in a conversation
with Dora Grant:

> Old George and my husband had gone off with the boys, and I
> stayed behind to look after young George. We had a bathe and then

he came and sat by me near our tent. And, to my surprise, he started talking. He was not a talkative boy: he would ask questions, but he wasn't one who opened up on his own. He only spoke when he was spoken to. But he started talking about his father. He said, 'What sort of a man has my father always been?' or some such words. And I started telling him about how sweet he'd been to us as children. He said, 'Do you like him?' I said, 'Oh yes.' Then he said, 'Was he ever cruel or anything like that?' 'Oh no.' Then he said, 'My mother says he's a cruel man.' So I could tell he wasn't exactly in touch with his mother. I said, 'George, I don't know anything about your mother, but I will answer you that your father was a marvellous man in the way he looked after those boys, and you'll never tell me that he was cruel to you.' And he said, 'No. I think you're right.'

Clayesmore, by the time George Devine got there in 1919, had moved on again: first to Pangbourne, and then to Northwood Park, a 250-acre estate on the Hampshire Downs. Lex, too, had been on the move. When bailiffs swooped on his Pangbourne premises he climbed a tree and took photographs of his disappearing furniture. Then, so he said, he pawned his watch to pay the rail fare to Yorkshire where he charmed £2,000 out of a wealthy sympathizer. On his return, he pasted the photographs into an album with the caption, 'An incident in the history of the school', and reopened Clayesmore as usual at the end of the holidays. That was back in 1904. Two years later he was covering the Olympic Games for the *Daily Chronicle* and in 1913 he went out again as the paper's Balkan War correspondent. He returned with a new mission. Henceforth, second only to the survival of Clayesmore, was the cause of Montenegran independence. As in his Manchester days, he was stirred by the sight of an underdog, and he saw Montenegro as the underdog of Europe. During the war he engaged in Continental relief work for the country's scattered refugees; and for this and other services, he was appointed Minister Plenipotentiary in London by the exiled King Nicholas. Clayesmore itself became a semi-official Montenegran base, taking in the children of exiles and giving hospitality to outlawed patriots like Stepan Radić, the leader of the Croatian peasant party, who was later assassinated in the Serbian Parliament.

Under its surface eccentricities, though, Clayesmore had settled down into a fairly conventional school. Manual labour ('Every boy must dig') remained a corner-stone of its policy, but the reformist zeal had ebbed away. When Lex founded his school in 1896 it had no rules; by the 1920s it had acquired the full apparatus of a house system, prefects, and beatings for petty offences.

What remained remarkable about the place were some of the wildly improbable schoolmasters whom Lex had taken on. One of these was the Count di Balme, a former colonel in the Italian cavalry who had taught at the crack Tor di Quinto cavalry school in Rome. Another was Captain Desmond Coke, the satirical novelist who had made his name with *Sandford of Merton* and the immortal line: 'All rowed fast but none so fast as Stroke.' English was taught by George Scott, who had been brought up in St Petersburg and imprisoned by the Bolsheviks on a spying charge. Scott spoke four languages, played the violin, and went on tremendous binges after which the boys sometimes had to put him to bed. He had, according to Devine's contemporary John Plamenatz, 'a broadening effect'.

But for sheer improbability, the headmaster topped the bill. After his crusading youth, Lex expanded in his middle years into a feudal grandee who ran his territory unencumbered by any board of governors. Although there was never enough money to buy Northwood Park, he always smoked the best cigars, drank the best brandy, and imported a French cook who prepared meals for him alone. Every Thursday he went to London for a night at Claridge's, where he kept up an international social life.

Inside the school he shared his fantasy life with the boys at a weekly event called the 'levee'. This was a Sunday-night party in his study for about thirty boys who turned up in pyjamas, usually discovering the headmaster improvizing at the pianoforte. Under the Montenegran crown and crossed swords and by the light of one shaded lamp, Lex would then deliver thrilling reminiscences of his past adventures, some of which his audience later found to be stories by Wilkie Collins and Annesley Vachel. Sometimes he would arrive in a darkened dormitory and invite the boys out for a swim: 'I'm no ordinary schoolmaster.'

John Plamenatz recalled him forty years later as:

Less given to moral disapproval than it was almost conceivable that a headmaster could be. When we were alone with him he would tell us about the things that people did which were sometimes quite scandalous. He was unexpectedly not shocked by things – such as vagueness about money, and certain kinds of lying and tricks –

which other people would think contemptible. He was not a gentleman. He had a natural charm: a beautiful smile, and pleasant ways
of holding his head and teasing people. He could coax and cajole
people. He could speak angrily or lovingly. There was a great deal
of flirtation in his manner. He was a very emancipated person.
English people are said to have difficulty in expressing their feelings:
he had none. I think George Devine probably did have.

George Devine remained an inconspicuous schoolboy until his
last years at Clayesmore, and even then he struck people as the
temperamental opposite of his expansive uncle: a withdrawn,
well-behaved boy who made no close friends and who did his
best without being particularly good at anything. At prep school
he seems to have had his work cut out to fit in with the system
which began with an early morning run and a nude plunge into
an unheated pool. Games were an ordeal to him. He was heavily
built and short-sighted; and his reactions were slow. However, he
got through without being bullied for being a physical misfit or
for being the headmaster's nephew. Academically he was something above the average in a below-average school. More important, he looked old for his age. To his contemporaries, George
Devine never looked young. It was not only a matter of looks,
but of prematurely formed character. Older people, says Plamenatz, 'preferred his opinions and judgments. George's background had made him cautious and watchful, but he'd also
developed a strong sense of humour and perception from his
childhood. He knew more about life than any of us. He was
terribly good as a reporter.' As a prefect, he was good at managing
people without bullying, and by the time he was made School
Captain in his last year he ranked almost as one of the staff. Like
the other Devines, he became a man who got on well with
children. Lex was popular with his boys. So was George's father,
who frequently popped up in their midst to tell tall stories and
conjure threepenny bits out of the trees. And so was George,
even to those who found him solemn.

Finally, there was the theatre. Clayesmore put on two shows a
year: a play in one term and a concert in another. In middle age
Devine told an interviewer that he had wanted to go into the
theatre 'ever since I was a tiny tot', but there is no evidence that
he set the Clayesmore stage on fire. According to A. L. Kark,
another pillar of the school's fine arts society, he began by performing 'terrible monologues' in the dark with a red and green

torch. Then there were Gilbert and Sullivan shows and the annual concerts where he went in for music-hall numbers and burlesque turns. In the plays he appeared as Drinkwater, the Cockney convert in Shaw's *Captain Brassbound's Conversion*, and as Lingley, a greedy businessman in Sutton Vane's *Outward Bound*, on which the *Clayesmorian* commented 'Devine knows more about the stage than anyone else at Clayesmore and consequently made himself too much "at home" on it.'

Whenever his name crops up in the school magazine – debating on censorship, co-directing with Scott – he sounds like an ideal candidate for the National Youth Theatre: a reliable all-rounder with plenty of team spirit, but not much of a performer compared with Kark or the magnificent Wheeler major. Whatever his stage ambitions, he seems not to have confided them to his uncle, with whom he had developed a close relationship involving career plans that had nothing to do with the theatre. The relationship dates from Devine's mid-adolescence when his father removed him from the care of the Grant family and allowed him to take his holidays abroad with Lex. Showing boys round Paris was one of Lex's specialities, and Devine would return from these trips primed with curious information well outside examination requirements. Whatever master-pupil taboos were set aside when they were installed in the rue de Castiglione, it is clear that Devine's attachment to France – one of the great strengths of his working life – pre-dates the Continental theatrical contacts he made in his twenties.

All this (plus his father's death) strengthened the pact between the headmaster and the school captain; though he was fully aware of Lex's blind spots and romantic absurdities, and would mimic them affectionately. There were basic similarities between them. Temperamentally Devine, no less than his uncle, was a teacher. Both sided instinctively with underdogs. Both were institution men who retained a strong appetite for outside experience. Both substituted instititutions for family life. Lex was childless and well into his seventies. He had created the school and run it as a one-man show, but now he was looking round for an heir. Here was the final bond with his nephew: for when Devine left for Oxford it was with the prospect of inheriting Clayesmore and taking over the headmastership.

Devine went up to Oxford in October 1929. For the next three

years he was officially a Commoner reading modern history at
Wadham College. But the story of his Oxford career is of a
growing split between his official and unofficial life, finally so
wide that he left the university one term early without taking his
finals.

The original plan was clear-cut: to get a good degree and then
return to Clayesmore armed with the qualifications to justify his
succession. His future was mapped out, and it did not include the
theatre. It did not take long for Oxford to upset this comfortable
scheme; and the school captain changed into a juvenile actor-
manager swinging Lex's silver-topped cane and furnishing his
guests with monogrammed ashtrays Lex had collected from some
of the best hotels in Europe.

The Oxford Devine was a hard figure to miss. A street snap-
shot showing him with Peggy Ashcroft tells it all – the immense
brown overcoat, the muffler (which he wore all the year round),
the stick, the authoritative stride. But he did wear a different
face for different people. Two of his closest friends, Peter Best
and Henry Blyth, had nothing whatever to do with the theatre.
Devine shared tutorials with them, and in his third year he invited them to share a cottage with him in Bath Place. To Peter
Best the most important thing about him was his kindness and
the fact that he was always ready to forget theatre politics and
listen to someone else's problems.

Another friend was the late Charles Fenby, then Editor of the
Oxford Mail. To Fenby, and to members of the OUDS, Devine
was called 'Scatters' – a nick-name unknown to his friends in
Bath Place. It was bestowed on him by the *Cherwell*'s nonsense
society column, after the Edwardian rake 'Scatters' Wilson, and
it was a good name for the Devine whom Fenby knew. The two
were regular poker players, but they played to their own rules,
throwing bad hands away or tearing the cards up, so that they
were always left holding four aces. Devine also had a taste for
character parts, usually aggressive ones. He would appear on the
doorstep twirling his cane, and then prod Fenby in the stomach
with it and roar, 'What! Shall we have incisions, shall we im-
brue?' Ancient Pistol was one favourite. Another was Groucho
Marx. Once they raided Fenby's digs while a party was going on,
dumped the entire contents of Fenby's bedroom in among the
guests and then vanished into the night. The Marx Brothers
'seemed to us the greatest performers there'd ever been because

they acted out this fantasy life which we had imagined ourselves.'
There is not much kindness in Fenby's picture. Rather it shows
Devine as a victim of turbulent moods, sometimes repressed into
taciturn brooding, sometimes exploding into uncontrolled rage.

For a publicity-conscious undergraduate Fenby was an extremely useful acquaintance – and Devine, however selfless in
his later career, was certainly ambitious at this stage. But no
such calculation seems to have entered into the relationship. He
knew where he wanted to go, and the contacts he cultivated were
with people who might share the stage with him or give him
parts: not with publicists of the Oxford playground.

With the original prospect of returning to Clayesmore he
made an orthodox beginning: passing the History Prelim
examination in his second term (Hilary 1930), and setting off
with Best and Blyth on the round of libraries, lectures and
tutorials for which they turned out two essays a week. Lord
David Cecil recalls that his tutorials with Devine 'generally involved interesting and stimulating talk about literature and, of
course, especially about the drama. His personality was distinc-
tive: he looked older than the average undergraduate, and
seemed older too; mature, responsible, even a little fatherly. He
coupled this with a lively responsive mind and a warm likable
friendliness. I would like to stress what a strong impression
George left on his old tutor – much stronger than most pupils
did. It changed the relationship of tutor and pupil into that of
friend and friend.'

Meanwhile, Devine was impressing these same qualities on the
committee of the Oxford University Dramatic Society. He joined
almost on his arrival at Oxford: not a difficult thing to do as the
OUDS in those days was open to any undergraduate who could
pay for membership. To many of its members it was simply a
dining club, but to get on in the Oxford theatre it was necessary
to join. This applied equally for Devine, who had no prior
theatrical connections, and for his rival Giles Playfair, whose
father Nigel had recently been knighted for his work at the
Lyric Theatre, Hammersmith. The OUDS offered a direct route
into the profession. Another contemporary, Hugh Hunt, describes it as the only means by which an undergraduate actor
could get his foot on the ladder. 'You got into the profession on a
higher rung because you met people. In those days, personal
introduction was the most regular way in.'

For someone in Devine's position, the importance of a career in the OUDS was far greater than it would be today. Not only did the society maintain a continuous existence in its spacious George Street premises: it also worked in direct association with the professional theatre. Membership excluded girls; and on the occasions of the two big annual shows (a February production at the New Theatre, and an open-air production in the summer term), professional actresses came in to play with undergraduate casts. They were not paid: but, as Giles Playfair says, they were 'put up and loved'. It was also usual to engage visiting directors, who generally did receive a fee. On these modest terms, the OUDS was able to attract some of the brightest stars of the time. What they got out of it was prestige. Oxford was news to theatre critics no less than to stunt reporters. It was also a number one touring date, and the big names on the New Theatre bill could often be prevailed upon to grace the OUDS dining room. Other regular visitors were critics like W. A. Darlington of the *Daily Telegraph* and Charles Morgan of *The Times* who would drop in for lunch at the President's table and discuss the choice of future plays and guest artists.

The President when Devine joined the society was Brewster Morgan, an American who himself claimed to have been a pupil of Reinhardt. Contemporaries remember him as an undergraduate magnifico who entertained on an alarming scale and went around accompanied by a bodyguard of admirers.

While Morgan was rehearsing his outgoing *Macbeth* Devine and Playfair embarked on their rival bids for the presidency, culminating in a briskly fought election campaign in the spring of 1931. This was a stirring chapter in Oxford politics featuring two beautifully contrasted contenders. Devine arrived as a theatrical outsider; Playfair had been immersed in the theatre from childhood. Devine had a clear idea of one thing he wanted to do; Playfair had numerous objectives. Devine was happy to further his interests by joining the establishment; Playfair saw himself as an independent rebel.

For the first year, Devine lay low, stabilizing his position in the club and cultivating the friendship of its incoming President and Secretary, Peter Bayne and Lionel Hale. Playfair, meanwhile, was seeking to repeat Gyles Isham's hat-trick of becoming President of the Union and Editor of *Isis* as well as President of the OUDS. Rebuffed by the first two, he did get a part in

Morgan's *Macbeth*, but only to antagonize the committee by denouncing their director as a charlatan.

June was approaching, and with it the OUDS commemoration-week play. Devine was not short of other allies in the club. One of them, Dr T. R. Williams, says, 'he advanced *fast*. He made a big impact very quickly. He looked and behaved like a man among boys; and it seemed inevitable to us lesser mortals that this chap would become President.' The show was *Twelfth Night*, directed by Gyles Isham in the Fellows' Garden of Queens. Jessica Tandy played Viola and Hale Malvolio. Playfair, to his great surprise, was invited to play Sebastian. Devine, whose moment had now arrived, sailed through his audition and got Sir Toby.

Although his stock was rising, he had no immediate prospect of succeeding Bayne, the standard procedure being for the Secretary to step into the outgoing President's shoes. Hale's election seemed a foregone conclusion. Then, of course, there was Devine's Clayesmore plan which hinged on getting a good degree. Somehow, he continued to get through the inescapable minimum of academic work, but by his second year he was practically living in the OUDS club. After breakfast he would crash through whatever tutorial preparation was required, go to the OUDS for lunch and stay there for the rest of the day, getting back around midnight to pour his accumulated worries into the ear of Peter Best.

The situation was abruptly resolved by two events during the winter vacation. First was Hale's disappearance from Balliol. Then, on Boxing Day, Lex died and the facts of the Clayesmore inheritance came out. Briefly, there was nothing to inherit. Despite Lex's grandiose plans for the school he had never managed to buy Northwood Park, and his death revealed Clayesmore as yet another castle built over a financial chasm. The school migrated to a new address in Dorset, and all Devine received was a personal legacy.

Thus, when he came back to Oxford for the spring term of 1931 he was able, for the first time, to apply himself single-mindedly to what he wanted; which, for the time being, meant vanquishing Playfair.

The contest began on level terms with the OUDS production of Flecker's *Hassan* at the New Theatre in February. This was the society's big annual show, as one might suppose from its staggering cast list. Peggy Ashcroft and Thea Holme came in to play Pervaneh and Yasmin: undergraduates in the company included William Devlin, Hugh Hunt, Raymond Raikes, Frith Banbury, Terence Rattigan and the future M.R.A. supremo Peter Howard. Against this competition, Playfair and Devine secured the parts of Hassan and the Caliph. Devine was now on the OUDS committee: Playfair, to equalize, says, 'they only did *Hassan* because they thought I could play Hassan.'

The show was officially billed as 'produced by Gibson Cowan under the personal supervision of Basil Dean'. This meant that the rights of the play carried Dean with them as a package deal (he had directed the 1923 premiere), but that he delegated the work to his stage manager. Devine almost missed the show. On vacation in Paris he had picked up an infection and throughout the six weeks of rehearsals he was disappearing for injections at the Radcliffe Infirmary and provoking groans of 'Where's Devine? He ought to be on the divan.' This must have been even more painful than the treatment, given the Stakhavonite methods of Dean's stage manager who rehearsed his cast for twelve hours a day irrespective of university rules. The London critics then dropped like a ton of bricks on the undergraduate playing and laid the blame on the luckless Gibson Cowan. To Terence Rattigan, too, it was a 'shatteringly awful faux-Basil Dean production'. But the two rivals emerged with honour. Oxford welcomed Playfair like a returned prodigal and, Lord Birkenhead, in *Isis*, went overboard for Devine. More to the point is the impression his Caliph made on the rest of the cast. Devlin says it was 'suave, professional, assured'; Ashcroft calls it 'marvellous'. Even Rattigan allows that he played the part 'very well'. According to Ashcroft and others he was helped by the foreignness that already marked his Oxford manner (some people thought he was a Jew), a quality that made him appear alien as well as older. Peter Bayne says 'the most remarkable thing about his performance was the imagination which it showed. He had seen people who had various of Sir Toby's characteristics but I don't think that he had ever seen a monarch or indeed a very powerful man, and yet he invented one that appeared entirely authentic.'

The last *Hassan* rehearsals took place in the shadow of the election, and before the opening, Bayne informed Playfair that his committee had decided to nominate Devine as the next

President. Playfair took this as an invitation to battle with the OUDS establishment. The annual OUDS presidential election was generally a quiet affair. The outgoing administration would nominate the next year's officers who would then be adopted without opposition. Playfair cast a spanner into these gentlemanly works by instituting a counter-nomination on his own behalf which split the Committee in half. His youthful account of the campaign in *My Father's Son* gives a lurid picture of Italianate intrigue.

Each side had its own election machine. Canvassers tramped the streets and scoured the colleges to drum up support. Devine canvassed Peggy Ashcroft with success: Thea Holme came in on Playfair's side. The OUDS Senior Librarian joined forces with Playfair: Devine netted the Senior Treasurer. The two undergraduate papers also took opposite sides. Lionel Hale (who had retained his editorship after going down) pushed Devine's claims in *Isis*: Playfair, a regular contributor to *Cherwell*, was championed by its editor, H. J. D'Avigdor Goldsmid. The fateful Sunday morning dawned. Fleets of cars were dispatched to bring members in to the poll from outlying parts of Oxford. Other members arose from sick-beds and shuffled along to George Street through the February weather to hear the result of the count: Devine 48 votes, Playfair 45. The result still rankled with Playfair forty years later.

Devine enjoyed the office of President socially as well as theatrically. He liked entertaining and being entertained. He had a gift for easy extempore speech which impressed those who came to the club's Saturday suppers. To the overcoat and cane were now added a bow-tie, a wide-brimmed black hat and a cigar. Lex would have approved. But in spite of his actor-manager wardrobe, he was noticeably cool about stars and reserved his main admiration for experimentalists like the emigré director Komisarjevsky. 'His appearance and affectations may have been from the du Maurier generation,' says Peter Best, 'but not his ideas.'

Meanwhile, installed in Bath Place opposite the Holywell Music School, he had another base for cultivating useful friends. The cottage was regularly thronged with touring actors from the New Theatre who turned up for drinks or pre-lunch parties, and sometimes took over the spare bedroom. Devine was a modest entertainer by Oxford standards, but Bath Place was not cheap;

nor was the cost of dining at the President's table. He was hard up. On one occasion Uncle Minos arrived in Oxford to preach the University Sermon. Devine kept well away from that, but he had lunch with his uncle and asked him for a loan: to which Minos replied, 'The Devines do not borrow' – which must have sent Lex spinning in his shroud.

OUDS activities did not consist solely of social life and the two big annual productions. The first event in the society's calendar was a ribald revue known as the Smoker; and before the incoming President could start moving into glittering professional circles it was his task to produce one of these rowdy, filthy, hard-drinking evenings. The OUDS also put on an annual programme of undergraduate one-act plays.

Given Devine's later devotion to the art of slapstick and the promotion of new writers, one would have expected him to make full use of these two events: but there is no evidence that he did. Bayne has vague memories that his revue, *Always a Little Further*, 'showed a talent for farce', but what people really remember about the Smokers are Osbert Lancaster's mock lectures and Terence Rattigan's feline contributions under the soubriquet of 'Lady Diana Coutigan'. The one-act shows present a similar blank. On holiday at Fonthill the year before, Devine and Peter Bayne had collaborated in writing a one-act thriller called *In the Very Room Above This*: it was set in a pub, and the main interest was in developing a plot in the midst of typical conversation round the bar. Much to the authors' indignation, the OUDS committee turned the piece down. Subsequently, Devine had the distinction of rejecting a work by Rattigan, who bore no grudge. 'I'm sure he was right. It was a highly experimental piece, rather in the vein of Constantin's effort in *The Seagull*. He was very kind. He said: "Some of it is absolutely smashing, but it goes too far." It did.'

Contemporary memory has nothing more to offer on these two events, and my suspicion is that Devine had small interest in such diversions within the Oxford rock pool: as also appears from the fact that he cancelled the Members' programme for the Michaelmas term and substituted a full-scale production at the Oxford Playhouse. This was a performance of Chekhov's *Ivanov*, with Devine directing and playing the lead in a big black beard. It opened to a thin house including Dr Williams who says, 'I never laughed so much in the whole of my life. I literally fell on the floor, rolled on the floor in agony with laughing so much. It's a comedy and they all put beards on and played it as tragedy: they didn't understand Chekhov in those days.' Devlin, who played Borkin, agrees. 'Very rushed, no chance of proper rehearsal with clothes and props: bashing away at the audience, what there was of it. My only clear recollection was the climax where Ivanov draws his pistol and shoots himself. Unfortunately, it wouldn't come out and George blew a nasty hole in his trousers. We drowned our sorrows in a good deal of drink.'

As Chekhov had only lately begun to filter into the British repertory, it was not surprising that Oxford got this piece wrong. Fagan had given *The Cherry Orchard* its first British public performance at the Playhouse in 1923. But if Devine had anything to emulate it was the work of Komisarjevsky's little theatre in Barnes which, during its one year of life from 1925 to 1926, had staged pioneer productions of Chekhov, Gogol and Andreyev: *Ivanov* was among these. Komisarjevsky was also well known to the OUDS for whom he had directed Romain Rolland's *The Fourteenth of July*. That was before Devine's time, but evidently he knew Komisarjevsky's work as he told Bayne how greatly he admired it and questioned him about the Romain Rolland production in which Bayne had played. Komisarjevsky himself lists this as one of a series of productions in which he experimented with 'dynamic lighting'; a subject of interest to Devine who was already learning his craft as a lighting specialist. The link with Komisarjevsky became an important factor at the beginning of Devine's post-Oxford career.

The Playhouse *débâcle* was followed by the one OUDS show of Devine's time that has gone down in theatre history: *Romeo and Juliet*, which John Gielgud directed at the New Theatre in February 1932.

Inviting Gielgud was Devine's idea, and it was an astute move. Gielgud, with ten years of classical work behind him and a big commercial career just opening up, was emerging as the dominant London star. He had already appeared in three productions of the play. but, at the age of twenty-eight, he had never previously directed – so, in that sense, Oxford was offering him a chance.

Accompanied by his committee, Devine went to London during the Christmas vacation and tackled Gielgud in his dressing room at His Majesty's Theatre where he was playing in the long-running adaptation of Priestley's *The Good Companions*. The OUDS President impressed Gielgud as 'rather ungainly and gross. Very greasy, spotty, and unattractive. But he had great humour, great charm; and he was immediately very intelligent.' Gielgud was sufficiently tempted by the invitation to talk the management round to approving a simultaneous out-of-town engagement.

Soon after Christmas, Gielgud came down and cast the play: 'casting' being the outcome of delicate negotiations between the director and the committee. Gielgud saw and approved Christopher Hassall for Romeo. He did not think much of the heavyweight bespectacled President's chances as Mercutio. But that was the committee's choice. Devlin played Tybalt. Hunt doubled as Chorus and the Friar, and Rattigan appeared among the maskers. Ashcroft returned as Juliet, and Gielgud enlisted Edith Evans as the Nurse.

He also nominated three unknown girls as his costume designers. Devine, who saw no reason for ditching the Society's regular designer, put up strong opposition to this but gave in when Gielgud showed him some of the girls' drawings. He then visited them in their Kensington workroom and offered them the job. '"Oh yes, we'll do it"', one of them recalls: 'and we rushed out and hired a couple of people to sew for us. But we did most of it ourselves. That was really how we started. Before that we'd been making fancy dresses for the shops at Christmas.'

The speaker is Elizabeth Montgomery, and her two partners were the sisters Margaret and Sophia Harris. Better known as the firm of Motley, the trio had first met as students at a small Chelsea art school. They came from genteel homes in Kent and they had no stage experience beyond their weekend trips to the Old Vic from which they produced character drawings of the 1929–1930 company. Many of these they sold to the actors, 'who used to say, "Can you wait till pay-day?" Then we were given the three guineas.' Gielgud, always on the alert for new talent, was enthusiastic, and when the Oxford *Romeo* put him in a position to help, he gave the 'three silent and retiring young women' the chance they needed. This was the beginning of a great working partnership, and a crucial event in Devine's life.

Gielgud had just over a month to rehearse the play; and according to Devlin he 'really *taught* us rather than produced us: the right method for intelligent undergraduates with flexible voices. Quite unconsciously, Gielgud has the effect of a headmaster on his companies; at least for me and possibly for George Devine, as we had both literally been his pupils.' The cast also received doses of professional discipline from Edith Evans who was apt to drop on late-comers with crushing disapproval and who marched the company briskly to Godstow and back when rehearsals finished early.

Off-stage, the OUDS was again in the grip of election-fever. Devine, following standard procedure, was running his Secretary Hugh Hunt for President. Playfair, returning to the battle, was canvassing support for a candidate of his own. And on the day of the election his forces converged on Bath Place with the aim of kidnapping Hunt: a move which Devine foiled by smuggling Hunt into Peter Best's bedroom. Gielgud, disappearing every afternoon in a puff of smoke, saw nothing of this, but the ladies in the company were kept busy soothing the rival factions. Devine had a strong ally in Ashcroft: it was also at this time that he was drawn into intimate friendship with the Motleys.

The production, as Gielgud describes it, was a first sketch for the famous version he directed three years later in his New Theatre season, alternating with Olivier as Romeo and Mercutio. His starting point at Oxford was to apply the still novel Shakespearian methods which he had absorbed from Harcourt Williams's régime at the Old Vic. Williams was a disciple of Granville Barker; and his mission at the Vic was to carry Barker's stylistic reforms into the stronghold of popular Skakespeare. This meant a purge on Bardic rhetoric, continuity of action, and the principle of designed production. Williams was energetic in his pursuit of the first two; but the third lay beyond his powers as the Vic's miserly budget did not stretch to designing every production afresh, and most shows were set and costumed out of the theatre's dingy existing stock.

At Oxford, Gielgud had the resources to carry out all three points of the programme. And he had ideal partners in the Motleys who already saw costume as an integral part of stage character, and specialized in creating stunning effects with the humblest materials. Décor for *Romeo* was shared between them and Anmer Hall's designer, Molly McArthur, who supplied the set. This was a triple-arched affair, backed with drapes and a central raised doorway. It was cheap; and, as Gielgud recalls, it had the advantage of simplicity and speed. But, even from faded old photographs of the show, there is an immediate contrast between the cut-price background and the figures on stage who seem to have emerged from a quattrocento painting.

Gielgud took a night off from *The Good Companions* to see the opening on February 9, and 'nearly died with anxiety and mortification when the curtain fouled, causing a two-minutes' wait towards the end of what should have been a non-stop production'. Otherwise it was a triumphant occasion; and at the end of its week's run, an unheard-of thing for the OUDS, it had made a profit.

The Times greeted the show as the society's 'best balanced and most satisfying performance of recent years'. Honours were spread about between the Oxford amateurs who had 'cared to speak verse again' and the two actresses; not to see them was 'to miss a part of the history of this play'. Devine 'whose Mercutio makes not very much of Queen Mab, does not shine in his set speeches, but, give him dialogue and action and feeling directly responsive to action, and he will vitalize the stage with them, his treatment of Mercutio's death being particularly distinguished'.

Confirming this impression forty years later, Lord David Cecil describes the production as 'easily the best performance of the play I have ever seen: straightforward in interpretation but fresh with youthful lyrical rapture, so that it seemed at once wholly in tune with Shakespeare's intention and yet as if it had been written yesterday'.

Bronson Albery brought the production to London where it was given a Sunday-night showing at the New Theatre in aid of Lilian Baylis's Vic-Wells Fund. Hugh Hunt was delegated to hand over the box office take to Miss Baylis at the end of the performance. 'I told George Devine that as he died half way through the play and I had no pocket in my gown as Friar Laurence, would he please put the cheque in his pouch, and I'd hold my hand out for it at the right moment. The cheque was duly made out, and Lilian Baylis duly appeared on stage in the M.A. gown and hood in which she was very fond of parading. In the middle of my speech I held out my hand, but nothing came in because George had forgotten all about it. I had to mime this business of giving her the money, and Baylis wasn't having that at all. "Come on, dear," she said sarcastically, and quite loud enough for the front rows to hear, "where's the cheque?"'

Mercutio was Devine's passport to the London stage, and as

Devlin says, it was a calculated risk. How did such an earthbound actor succeed in such an airborne role? Gielgud recalls 'this big Greek boy who was suddenly remarkably good in a part I hadn't thought he would be very good in'. But as to detail, all he remembers is that Devine fought quite well. For Terence Rattigan, 'George was miscast, but pretty damn good all the same. I was one of the "gallants" in the Queen Mab scene so I could and did observe him in that impossible "aria" very closely indeed. I was sure he was going to make a great actor. Well, I was wrong.' To Ashcroft, he was 'dangerous and quick-witted: he had a lightning mind'. To Lord David Cecil, the 'lightning-flash quality' was precisely what he lacked. Piecing such impressions together, I can imagine only one way in which he can have succeeded in the part: namely, by capitalizing on his physique and making Mercutio the old man of the gang. In the photographs he cuts a slouching, middle-aged figure in contrast with the trim juveniles. Among their boyish, unformed faces, he stares out with cold composure. His delivery is described as dry and sardonic. 'He was an aggressive actor.' 'He had a harsh abrasive voice, as if he had a tie over his nose.' This sounds like the same 'searing' voice from Charles Fenby's poker sessions. But it makes good sense in relation to Mercutio: as an aging Peter Pan still hanging around with the boys.

At all events, the performance had the desired effect. It was seen by the people who mattered, and it brought the offer from Komisarjevsky of a part on the London stage.

Charles Fenby was as delighted as anyone by his friend's success, but it seemed to him that contacts were becoming more important to Devine than friendship. 'I remember a number of occasions when I felt either furious with him or terribly sad. During *Romeo* another great friend of mine came to Oxford and we were so thrilled with George's performance that we bought him a theatre book. When we went to see him he said, very curtly, "Thank you for the book. Here's another one I received." The other one was many times more expensive and it was from Gielgud.'

I said at the outset of this chapter that Devine substituted a theatrical family for his flesh and blood relatives: the OUDS was only the first of a series of magic circles he drew round himself; affectionate and loyal towards his fellow members, sometimes coldly forbidding towards intruders. To offset Fenby's picture of

Scatters Devine, the moody prankster and thrusting pachyderm, other people saw him as a straightforward drinking companion with a passion for shove-halfpenny. Down at Fonthill he and Peter Bayne gave a party, and 'although neither of us knew anything about cooking, we invented a six-course dinner out of tins, and George spent time concocting fantastic names for them and writing up the menu. I recall that sardines on toast ended the feast, appearing on the menu as "Toast à la Marie Elizabeth". This was typical. He was normally fun to be with in quite a simple and undemanding way.' In short, friendship for Devine meant what it often means for people who give themselves wholly to their profession. It did not happen out of thin air; it grew out of the context of work.

In the aftermath of *Romeo*, Devine must have felt a chill wind blowing down his neck. His presidential year was over and he was hard up. Final examinations were looming, and he had not done the work for them. Also Britain had struck the Depression and it was not a good time to be looking for a job in the theatre or anywhere else. However, Komisarjevsky had offered him a job. He had influential allies in Gielgud and Ashcroft (now married to Komisarjevsky). And his friendship with the Motleys had blossomed into a love affair with Sophia Harris, who would at least give him a roof over his head in London.

His choice lay between seizing these chances or grinding through his final term with the dim prospect of collecting a degree. It was a choice between the irresistible and the uninviting. Even if he passed his finals, a degree would have been no great use to him as an actor; and by then the London openings might well have snapped shut. At home with Peter Best, browsing through psychoanalytical texts instead of the official reading list, he did not try to hide his anxieties about the future. He even went back to Merton to ask the advice of the Grant family, who told him 'that if that's what he thought he ought to do, he ought to step out and get it while the chance was there'. That was the last time he visited the Grants, but he took their advice, and by the time the university reassembled in April for the Trinity term, he was already rehearsing for his first London show.

2

LONDON

'WHEN I came down from Oxford,' Devine recalled in later life, 'I was the most intolerable young man, I suppose, who ever walked the streets of London.' He still had his wide-brimmed hat and Lex's silver-topped cane. 'That', he said, 'was part of my actor effort. I wanted to be looked at. I wanted to be thought of as an important person in this get-up.'

As yet, he was not an important person. He was an ambitious amateur with powerful friends. So far as he was known at all, he was known as an actor; so it was in acting that he had first to prove himself. He was not a writer; and the day of the young professional director of the Guthrie type was only just dawning. It was clearly going to be a struggle. Theatrically it was the age of beautiful young men like Leslie Howard and Harold French. Devine was not conventionally good looking. Nor did he have a flair for wearing costume. Apart from his sheer bulk (conservatively estimated at fifteen stone), he had a harsh, constricted voice, and his eyes and mouth were too small. His face was not an actor's face.

Of course, even at that time, physical imperfections were common even among the finest actors. As a young man, Gielgud was very self-conscious about his legs and 'funny walk'. Some actors remain permanently handicapped by a mental image of themselves, like Michel Saint-Denis who felt incapable of playing tragedy because of 'mon drôle de derrière'. In Devine's case, though, it came down to a simple question of visibility. Pleasingly arranged or not, an actor's features should be large enough to be visible at a distance, and Devine's facial equipment was out of scale with his large unathletic body. It was only later that he learned to compensate for this by specializing in physical comedy so as to turn his whole figure into an expressive instrument.

On arriving in London he picked up two jobs straight away. The first of these was in *The Merchant of Venice*, which followed *Othello* in Ernest Milton's disastrous venture into commercial management at the St James's Theatre. *The Merchant* opened in April 1932 with a cast headed by Milton, Mary Newcomb and Athene Seyler. Devine played Salanio, one of the two Venetian playboys, and had to simulate gaiety while bulging out of an unbecoming pink costume and blonde wig. This was the first of several unhappy experiences with juvenile roles, and it left Athene Seyler feeling that he had no promise as an actor. His talk 'was not of an aspiring and ambitious actor but more of a general consuming interest in the theatre. It was a very tentative beginning that gave no hint on the stage of his later initiative and authority.' *The Times*, forgetting its compliments of two months before, got him in as 'John Devine'.

In May, he reaped another reward from the OUDS *Romeo*. Komisarjevsky had seen the show when it came to London and evidently been impressed by its Mercutio as he sent for Devine afterwards with the idea of offering him a part in his production of *Le Cocu magnifique*. According to Margaret Harris, Komisarjevsky was 'terribly surprised when he saw him and said, "Oh no I don't want you, you're not the man I'm looking for. I'm looking for the man who played Mercutio." And George said, "But that *was* me!"' Whereupon Komisarjevsky swallowed his disbelief and cast him.

It was another mistake. Crommelynck's tragi-farce tells the story of a husband so deranged with jealousy that he compels his wife to sleep with every man in the village as a means of unmasking her true lover. Ashcroft played the delectable Stella, and Devine queued up unhappily among the studs as the Herdsman, though palpably unsuited to impersonating a brawny sexual battering-ram. 'Komis', says Miss Harris, 'had completely misread him.'

The main benefit of that production was that it led to a friendship with Komisarjevsky and visits to the Komisarjevsky–Ashcroft flat in Berkeley Gardens. This was his first close contact with a major foreign director, and although far less important than his subsequent lifelong friendship with Michel Saint-Denis, it left a lasting mark. Komisarjevsky appreciated Devine's freedom from British insularity, and the fact that he spoke French and was better educated than most British actors. The two men shared a similar caustic sense of humour.

For idealistic young actors of Devine's generation, Komisarjevsky was an art theatre god. There were other crusaders around, launching Continental stagecraft and the new Continental repertory from unfireproofed garrets and converted skittle-alleys. But here was Feodor Komisarjevsky, brother of one of Russia's greatest actresses and former director of the Nezlobin Theatre and the Moscow Imperial Grand Opera, setting up as Mr Komis in a tiny cinema in Barnes and passing on the fruits of Russia's Great Experiment to a public brought up on the well-drilled spectacles of Basil Dean. Besides his innovations in dynamic lighting and psychologized décor, he gave his actors the key to an inner realist style which, according to numerous witnesses, was then quite new to the British stage.

The Barnes venture took place in the mid-twenties. By the time Devine arrived in London, Komisarjevsky was fifty and convinced that 'the work of a non-commercial producer is somewhat similar to the man who tries to break a wall with his head'. He was now in the course of striking a fresh compromise between satisfaction and survival; and it was here, in the long term, that his example meant most to Devine. Everyone has to make his own bargain with the system, but in Devine's case the bargaining process continued throughout his career. And it was from Komisarjevsky that he began to learn the art of operating within prevailing theatrical conditions without capitulating to them inside his own head. In the pre-war British theatre, the gulf between commercial and art theatre was far wider than it is now (the closing of that gulf is indeed the main subject of this book). For the middle-aged Russian, as for the ex-OUDS President, the West End presented a debased spectacle of profiteering middlemen, timid managements, and performances at the dead end of the du Maurier tradition. (For a young actor, Laurence Olivier says, 'there honestly wasn't anybody to admire; except one had to admire du Maurier as a technician.')

On the other hand, there was the art theatre, with its eternal slogan of purity and poverty. At the end of his book, Komisarjevsky quotes his father's sentiments:

> You are standing on the banks of a stagnant and stinking pond and you suffer because it is never drained. You are enthusiastistic about your work but you forget the simple truth that the theatrical pool

has existed for centuries and that only a few are chosen for the arduous task of draining the theatrical dyke ... You have a choice of two things: rich meals in the company of a pack of gluttons; or, as the result of sincere work ... a solitude in which you will often go hungry and a road through life which does not lead along the path of enjoyment but of unhappiness.

But Komisarjevsky saw a third choice. When the Barnes enterprise foundered he was left with no platform of his own, but with a highly marketable reputation; and he proceeded to sell himself on his own terms. He preserved an experimental lifeline in a series of Stage Society productions, of which the constructivist version of *Le Cocu magnifique* (based on Meyerhold's of ten years before) was one. At the same time, he waded into the stagnant waters of the British theatre, taking on not only Shakespeare but also C. B. Cochran.

It was Komisarjevsky's rule to have fun and never put up with boredom. If he disliked an actor in his company, he would ignore him (during rehearsals for the notorious 1936 *Antony and Cleopatra*, he decided that Eugénie Leontovich was going to be hopeless, and left her to her fate). When his 1932 production of *Musical Chairs* was being re-rehearsed for transfer, he was simultaneously directing another play called *The Heart Line* which, according to Gielgud, 'had a lift which went up and down on the stage; and he spent three days doing this. He wouldn't come to our rehearsals at all and I had to take over: it was chaos.' Two years later, directing Louis Golding's *Magnolia Street* (in which Devine played), he stopped a scene in which the young Anthony Quayle had to throw a brick through a plate-glass window. 'That's not right,' said Komisarjevsky. 'Bring a brick. Bring another plate-glass window. This is how you do it.' As Devine told the story, the rehearsal did not proceed until twelve bricks later.

The quality Komisarjevsky most frequently invokes in his book *Myself and the Theatre* is sincerity, but it hardly applies to these forays among the West End flesh-pots and his whirlwind descents on Stratford where he would turn a hallowed classic inside out after eight rehearsals. He had the brilliance to get away with it. Actors remember him as a Mephistophelean figure and count him among the few great directors to have worked in Britain this century. But in the 1930s, his reputation changed from that of a theatrical high priest to that of a dazzling chameleon who exploited the English reverence for a foreign genius; and who would sometimes take the money without doing the work.

These *enfant terrible* options were not open to Devine, either as a young man or later in life. But his reaction was anything but disapproving. He always admired people who were quick on their feet; and if he felt they had something to teach him, his attitude approached hero-worship. According to Marius Goring, he 'clung to' Komisarjevsky for several years, absorbing two beliefs which shaped his career. First, that good work can often be done by stealth inside a philistine system; second, that the theatre can only fully escape from bondage through the growth of like-minded companies with acting schools attached. If Komisarjevsky had had a company, no doubt Devine would have joined it: but the Russian had put that kind of idealistic slog behind him, and was living up to the hilt as a meteoric free-lance. What Devine took from him, technical expertise aside, was doctrine. For direct communal experience, his immediate sources were Gielgud and the Motleys.

Soon after coming down from Oxford he moved in with the Motleys and became one of the family; and, with various changes of address from Kensington to St Martin's Lane and Islington, the *ménage à quatre* stuck together until the outbreak of war. Sometimes they all moved down to the White House, the Harrises' home in Kent, and if country friends or relatives turned up and diverted the conversation into mundane non-theatrical channels, Devine would register his boredom by lying flat on the floor and putting a cushion over his head.

His relationship with Sophia Harris was now on a permanent footing, and although they did not marry until the war, Sophia completely assumed the role of loving wife. The Motleys are always referred to as a group: Gielgud's impressionistic phrase for them is 'Slade School charmers'. But as individuals, the trio were no more interchangeable than the Brontës, with whom they may be compared. Elizabeth Montgomery was the Emily of the partnership, possessing the boldest and most original imagination, expressed through a ravishing sense of colour. The independence of her talent also made it harder for her to submit to stage discipline. Margaret Harris, known to everyone as Percy, was the artist craftsman of the team. All three were skilful designers and makers of costumes and properties, but it was Margaret who learned how to translate their joint ideas into canvas and timber. In her Charlotte-like role, she specialized in set-design and held the family together with a tremendous sense of responsibility towards getting the show on. Sophia was a costume designer with a great facility for turning out quantities of small parts and walk-ons while her partners were battling with designs for the principals and the sets. She was also the most tactful of the three, and a practised confidante who acted as a mother to anyone with personal problems. More conventionally feminine than the others, and self-deprecating as an artist, she figures as the Anne Brontë of the trio. But, says Peter Bayne, 'all three had tremendous integrity: teeth and claws were out in a flash if a manager or a leading actor wanted a change which they felt went against their and the director's conception of what was right theatrically.'

Sophia was ten years Devine's senior, but this was not apparent at the time because he looked so much older than his age. Margaret Harris says that when they first met there was a powerful attraction followed by 'genuine love of a perfectly direct kind'. Which is not to deny a maternal element in the relationship. Sophia was somebody who liked to look after people, and she lavished attention on her man. Whatever the pressure of work, his meals were cooked, his shirts were ironed, his pipes were scraped, and her car was there to chauffeur him to appointments. She also assumed much of the responsibility for the one duty which Devine dreaded above everything else: the care of his own mother. Wearing the mask of Scatters and all the equipment of his 'actor effort', Devine had grown a tough carapace which, among other things, made him successful with girls. He was an exceptionally private person, and did not care for showing his old scars. But they were still there, and in Sophia he found someone who tried to restore his lost childhood: not merely by surrounding him with physical comforts, but by supplying the kind of unwavering affection on which a child builds a sense of self-esteem. For some years the relationship was what he needed.

After Oxford, London was a come-down, although the Motleys furnished him with another charmed circle in place of the OUDS. In London the flamboyant Oxford portrait dissolves into the picture of a much less confident man who was dissatisfied with the system and who seemed happier collaborating in a back room than competing in the limelight.

For a thrusting young actor, especially one with *avant-garde* tastes, it would surely have been possible to gain a foothold in the experimental clubs and play-producing societies, then no less numerous than the fringe theatres of the 1970s. Other OUDS actors, like Devlin and Frith Banbury, did so. But all Devine's early engagements came through his existing contacts: and, with the exception of the Stage Society's *Cocu magnifique*, this meant classical or West End shows where he was stuck with bit parts. Another one came up in June 1932 when he played a Spanish walk-on to Edith Evans's Melba in *Evensong* at the Queen's.

The week before it opened he had been engaged in a very different task. During the run of *Musical Chairs*, Gielgud had persuaded Bronson Albery to put on two special Arts Theatre performances of a new play by Gordon Daviot called *Richard of Bordeaux*. He showed the script to the Motleys who, as usual, were 'full of ingenious schemes for saving money over the décor', and the team went smartly into action. It was their first stage commission since the OUDS *Romeo*, and this time they insisted on designing sets as well as costumes. The play has a large cast, and as the Motleys – still operating from a little house in Duke's Lane, Kensington – had no space for extra staff, they made almost everything themselves. It was a rushed job. Devine, then camping in the basement, came up to help and sat sewing with them all night before the opening. In the morning they loaded the costumes into huge hampers which Devine and a friend dragged across London and delivered to the theatre.

On its first showing, *Bordeaux* did not create much of a stir, but the Motleys decided to move to a central address with more working space and room for assistants. They found a derelict third-floor studio at 67 St Martin's Lane. In the 1920s, Douglas Byng had run it as a night-club called the Kinde Dragon with waiters dressed as ostlers. But its real claim to fame was as the workshop of Thomas Chippendale whose lathe Byng had found still hanging from one of the beams. The studio backed on to the Garrick Club and its entrance was through the archway into Garrick Yard, the last kidney-cobbled yard in London. When the Motleys found it, it had been standing empty for years, and the rental was no great strain even for them. Outside, installed by Byng at the behest of the L.C.C., was an iron staircase leading up to the club. Before Chippendale's time it had been a coaching inn, and it had survived as a rural eighteenth-century oasis in the middle of the modern West End. 'It was,' says Elizabeth

Montgomery, 'a fabulous place. It was a barn with great oak beams, and a grain chute going down. All that had stayed through the night-club period. It was a last bit of old country London. It was very dingy, but we got a great army together and whitewashed it all. We'd go to the studio and stay all day; very often we stayed all night too. We found out that Chippendale used to entertain actors there. He used to have Garrick to tea.'

The Motleys followed Chippendale's lead, and their studio became not only a place of work but an unofficial club for the acting profession. Gielgud, whose flat was at 7 Upper St Martin's Lane (known to friends as Seven Upper), was one regular visitor; and for anyone working in Shaftesbury Avenue and St Martin's Lane, the studio was a handy place to drop into before or after the evening's show. One of the Motleys' main financial worries was over their soaring tea bill, rumoured to come to £100 a week. For meals they went over the road to Patmacks, a pub with an upstairs restaurant where they took a regular table which 'got longer and longer. Guinness and Ashcroft and Guthrie used to turn up, they knew they'd always find us there. We never ate at home. You could get a very good dinner for 1s. 6d., so what the hell?' They also received professional visitors, including emissaries from the established design houses. 'We were on the floor cutting out some enormous cloaks when someone from Nathans arrived and asked if they could buy us up. We said "No, thank you," and they went back and said "Do you know, the directors were crawling about on the floor!"'

'At the beginning,' says Gielgud, 'the *joie de vivre* was marvellous. We all used to go in there and have parties and giggle and laugh. Devine liked a good glass of wine and a rowdy party: he loved all that. He looked very Bohemian in that studio, like an artist from the Quartier Latin with his pipe and his corduroys: rather shock-headed, and twinkling and agreeable.'

Outside the studio, though, things were not so jolly. Shortly after the move to St Martin's Lane, Devine joined the Old Vic company for the 1932–3 season: again, as a protégé of Gielgud and friend of Peggy Ashcroft who joined the company at the same time. For Devine this was a particularly demoralizing episode about which he liked to tell funny stories in later life. There were, for instance, his encounters with Orlando Whitehead, the dreaded master of the Vic wardrobe. As the Vic budget did not run to designed productions, actors got their costumes by braving Mr Orlando in his lair and collecting a bundle. ''Ello, Mr Devine, *As You Like It* tonight? I suppose what you want is you'd like a nice red velvet cloak, wouldn't you, Mr Devine?' 'Yes please.' 'Well you can't bleedin' well 'ave it.'

As in Gielgud's time, the Vic director was Harcourt Williams, but after four years of grinding out a new show every three weeks on minimal budgets and coping with the managerial whims of Lilian Baylis, he was visibly sagging. 'It was', says Peggy Ashcroft, 'a very ropey season. Poor old Billee Williams was tired out, and it was agonizing because we never felt that we brought anything off. Our leading man was Malcolm Keen and he actually went on with his book as Leontes on the first night of *The Winter's Tale*. That shocked us terribly because we were all very serious.'

Devine joined at the beginning of the season at £3 a week, shortly followed by Quayle whose advantageously late arrival put him in the position to talk his way into £3 10s. The high spot of their week came after pay on Friday when they dropped in at the Café Royal and blew 4s. 6d. each on a lager and a canapé-royal (known in humbler circles as a Welsh rarebit). Devine was also a visitor at Quayle's home in Notting Hill Gate where Quayle's mother kept him supplied with home-made jam, often with a 10s. note smuggled under the cover. Although they were close friends it was years before Devine divulged this little secret. 'He was', says Quayle, 'a lone creature.'

The season opened in mid-September with Shaw's *Caesar and Cleopatra*, in which Devine made a capable début as the military tribune, Lucius Septimus, a small but commanding part in which he won some respect. Early in October the theatre returned to Shakespeare with results that were unhappy for the company and humiliating for Devine. The play was *Cymbeline*. 'My experience should have warned me', Williams wrote, 'that it was too complicated a problem for a second production. I bungled it.' Keen and Ashcroft were straightforward casting for Iachimo and Imogen; but there was no obvious choice for the cruelly high-minded Posthumus. Williams felt that none of his juveniles was subtle enough to play it. Whereupon Ashcroft and Goring persuaded him that it was time Devine got a break from character parts and played something of his own age. 'Oh God,' says Goring, 'if only I hadn't suggested it.'

Not long out of Oxford, Devine still had things to learn about elementary craftsmanship. Make-up was one of these. He remembered someone saying that yellow produces a glow of radiant youth, so he sat in front of his dressing-room mirror applying yellow in large quantities. Meanwhile the tears were trickling down his cheeks and washing it off again. What he produced, says Quayle, was the appearance of a jaundiced Arab; and, Goring adds, 'the curtain went up on an astonishing apparition of George, who was never actually a beauty, trying to be a juve. People started making rude remarks from the gallery.' Then, half way through the first scene, Ashcroft capped his waddling exit with Imogen's line, 'I chose an eagle', at which the house dissolved into derisive mirth. Somehow he struggled through the rest of the show and crept off, only to be waylaid by Lilian Baylis in the wings: 'Well dear,' she said, 'you've had your chance and they don't like you.'

Later on, the *Cymbeline* disaster became another of Devine's favourite stories. He shared a dressing room with William Fox (the elder) who was playing one of the lost boys. 'I got terrible notices, and Willie Fox used to get all these letters saying "Why aren't you playing Posthumus Leonatus?" And I say to myself, Where is William Fox now?' But at that time its effect was shattering. It would be painful enough for any actor, but excruciatingly so for the young Devine whom Quayle describes as 'a mixture of outer confidence and quivering jelly inside'.

For the rest of his time at the Vic he reverted to small character roles like Tubal in *The Merchant of Venice* and Moses in *The School for Scandal*. He must, at the same time, have been re-assessing his chances. Who, after all, was George Devine? He was an obscure young man with no money and a lot to learn. Any post-Oxford hopes of rapid success must by now have faded. He looked like something he was not, and if he was to succeed it would only be by slowly carving himself into shape. He had a flair for comedy, particularly for the mechanics of clowning; but so far this had only been seen at parties where he and Quayle would get into idiot arguments, strip for combat, and finish up dressed in each others' clothes. No one had yet found out how to cast him. The 'actor effort' was not paying off; and perhaps it was no longer what he really wanted. He knew he belonged somewhere in the theatre; he had energy and talent; and he wanted his life to have some influence. But how could he achieve that with the awkward cards he had been dealt?

His first solution was to attach himself even more firmly to the Motleys by becoming their business manager. They would have had to find someone for this job as, on their own admission, they were hopeless as businesswomen. 'Without him,' Margaret Harris says, 'we should have been down the drain.'

Initially it was a question of sorting out their business expenses from their personal expenses, and introducing a simple book-keeping system, though as the Motleys went out hunting for all the materials they used and invoices were apt to get buried in discarded wrapping paper, it was not such a simple matter. Petty cash entries such as 'Lost by the partners after dinner' sometimes had to be accepted. But by degrees Devine also analysed over-heads so as to relate them to a job on a time basis, and he devised methods of costing individual costumes and properties without badgering the girls for details.

As the Motleys were the owners of a private business, it was not a particularly complicated operation, and Devine's was not a full-time job. Things began to change from mid-1935 when Devine persuaded the Motleys to incorporate themselves as Motley Ltd. Financially this was a necessary move as they could barely live on one designer's fee split between three. As a limited liability company, they diversified the enterprise, allowing other designers to use their workrooms, which operated for that purpose under the name of Dix. Later they took over a green-grocers' shop in Garrick Street, had it adapted by Marcel Breuer, and launched Motley Couturier. Devine had faded out of the picture by then, but it was a continuation of his general strategy. 'From start to finish', says Peter Bayne, who inherited the job, 'he understood the basic problem, which was to commercialize the Motleys without jeopardizing their integrity or killing them with over-work. The Motleys always recognized the artist in George, and so trusted him not to harm the artist in them.'

Professionally there were two sides to Devine at this point. There was the struggling young actor, subject to the usual ups and downs of a personal career. There was also a disinterested reformer who was ambitious for the theatre rather than for him-self. But it is also clear that he needed someone else to give him a lead and turn his general dissatisfaction towards some specific purpose. By himself he was nobody: he became somebody by working in a group. From the start, he was attracted by the idea of artistic collectives (Bayne remembers his early enthusiasm for the Bauhaus). And in that sense, his double attachment to the Motleys and the Vic gave him a foot in the two camps from which change was to come. It also gave him a leader in the person of John Gielgud.

Gielgud is apt to shrug off high-sounding motives and belittle his past into personal careerism, but in the 1930s he had a cause. At the Vic he had emerged as a great classical actor; in the West End, he had blossomed as a matinée idol. The next step was to combine the two roles. He enjoyed being a star. But self-interest also involved raising the level of the commercial repertory and closing the gap between the West End and Waterloo Road. Someone had to do it as the perennial contrast between the classical stage and the boulevard had reached a particularly absurd pitch. In the West End it was the age of Cochran, who was recruiting even such artists as Komisarjevsky and Reinhardt into the glitter factory, while at the Vic a new tradition for staging British classics was being hammered out in conditions of Victorian pauperism. The time was ripe for attempting some marriage between presentation and content.

The first attempt came in December 1932 when Gielgud returned to the Vic to direct a guest production of *The Merchant of Venice*. This was a strategic move on Williams's part. Alone, he knew that he could never persuade Lilian Baylis to invest in the scenic reforms he was aiming at. But with Gielgud on his side even Baylis might be induced to part with a little money. Gielgud's terms were clear: he would take no fee for directing, but the whole production must be designed, an unheard-of thing at the Vic where the total budget for designing any show (including costumes) was then fixed at £50. Baylis, says Marius Goring, nearly had a fit at the proposal, but in the end she agreed to it.

Gielgud picked up the threads from his Oxford *Romeo* and brought in the Motleys, who supplied the play with a single set built on the false stage with fluted columns, curtains and a rope balcony, all carried out in unpainted hessian at a cost (costumes included) of £600. Again, Baylis nearly collapsed. But Williams had achieved his purpose: a brilliantly designed production which nowhere infringed his principle that 'no scenery or furniture ever devised are worth the price of slowing up a play.' And with the arrival of Guthrie and Laughton designed productions became the rule.

Guthrie said the production made Maugham and Coward seem like two Nonconformist parsons from the Midlands; and Ivor Brown wrote that it confirmed the overthrow of the Bensonian tradition. Somewhere in the midst of the fireworks, George Devine was to be observed in the role of Tubal.

Baylis may have regarded the Motleys' contribution as ruinously expensive, but looked at in the commercial perspective it was staggeringly cheap. Shylock's robe was made out of dishcloth at $3\frac{1}{4}d$. a yard, Morocco carried a cardboard scimitar, and other costumes were made of mosquito netting, painted linen and black tailor's canvas. Compare these materials with some that were on show in other London theatres at the time. At the Gaiety there was Jessie Matthews in *Hold My Hand* backed with a chorus clad in ostrich-plume capes, lace embroideries and satin evening dresses. At the Adelphi in the following month, Evelyn Laye opened in the Cochranized *opéra bouffe*, *Helen*. This Reinhardt-Messel collaboration dazzled the public with 'miles of dyed nets, vast quantitites of metal cloths, and many rich silks, taffetas, velvets, and plumes of ostrich feathers'. Even the Spartan chorus boys had appliquéd velvet skirts, and Miss Laye took leave of Troy wearing a tea-gown in ten shades of blue made from 160 yards of British net.

I owe these details to the 'London Fashion Notes' of *The Times*; stage costumes was then treated as a normal department of the fashion scene. The Motleys exploited this when they founded their own dress shop, but fashion did not overlap into their theatre work. Their designs were intended to make the right effect at the appropriate distance, and they made an aesthetic virtue of operating within a given budget.

Money apart, they were genuinely in revolt against what they saw as the clichés of their craft. 'We were determined to avoid the use of tinsel, bright gilt braid, and other elaborate ... trappings which had bedecked costumes for many years.' Instead of silks and velvets, they went in for upholstery cloth, huckaback towelling and unbleached calico. For leather, they used thick felt treated with kitchen soap and paint. For lace, they used pipe-cleaners. Gielgud's 1934 *Hamlet*, which they regard as their finest work, was carried out in the cheapest of all materials – scenery canvas, sprayed with metallic pigment in gold, silver and copper. Also, they did their own shopping: picking up an old bamboo window blind to create a necklace for Cleopatra, or a set of ironmonger's wire brushes to simulate silver shoulder ornaments in *Macbeth*.

Their second basic working principle was to go back to primary sources for costume research. As students, they had developed this technique through intensive visits to the National Gallery to examine where the seams were placed. The historical methods they learned in this way did not correspond to those of the existing London costume shops which were apt to distort the dress of any period to fit the modern view of the human figure. Nor did the shops like working in unconventional materials. The Motleys, therefore, set up a workroom where they did their own cutting, first with one old lady and a sewing machine and ultimately with a regular staff of sixty.

Shortly after the opening of Cochran's Trojan clothes-horse, the Motleys achieved their own breakthrough with the New Theatre run of *Richard of Bordeaux*, which brought Gielgud the biggest personal success of his career. It also confirmed the managerial alliance with Bronson Albery who went on to back Gielgud's classical seasons which were among the glories of the 1930s, and it laid the foundations for what almost amounted to a permanent company, drawn partly from young actors of the Devine–Ashcroft generation and partly from pre-war veterans like Frederick Lloyd and Ben Webster who anchored the company in the tradition of Forbes-Robertson and Tree.

Bordeaux was a history play for people who don't like history plays: it lifted a medieval power struggle into an airy region of colloquial lyricism, and the Motleys took their cue from this, flooding with light a period normally associated with darkness. Their sets evoked striped garden pavilions and cloisters through a strict range of three colours, indigo, cream and rust red, taken from tapestries in the South Kensington Museum. For costumes, they used nothing but wool, executed so as to create a dynamic relationship between costume design and character development. Although much elaborated from the original Arts Theatre version, the New Theatre designs were still produced on the cheap; which did not prevent audiences, so lately gorged on the toga and tea-gown splendours of the Adelphi, from responding as though to a second coming of the Ballets Russes.

After the opening, Gielgud celebrated the alliance by throwing a *Bordeaux* party in the Motleys' studio and inviting everyone he knew. Leslie Henson plunged the place into darkness by tampering with Devine's model theatre; which must have come as an annihilating blackout as the party was designed entirely in white. Montgomery: 'the wine was white, the food was white, we all wore white dresses. And we didn't know a soul in the theatre. People like Ernest Thesiger would arrive and Sophie said "Well, we don't know who you are but do come in."' They did, and it was not long before the Motleys knew everybody. Everybody, that is, whom they wanted to know. From being a friendly place to drop in for tea, the studio became the centre of the Gielgud circle: a power-house, a place where plans were hatched out and new recruits welcomed or cold-shouldered as the case might be.

For the members it was as jolly as ever. Margaret Harris remembers the group sitting up through the night 'talking terribly seriously about the theatre, as young people do. We didn't think that anything anybody else did was any good.' Residents apart, the core of the group consisted of Gielgud, Ashcroft, Jack Hawkins, Jessica Tandy, Glen Byam Shaw and Angela Baddeley. Sometimes there were parties, like the one the Motleys gave when they were designing the short-lived Hammerstein musical *Ball at the Savoy*, and Devine and Hawkins struggled into chorus girls' dresses and striped picture hats.

Such a group meeting today would spend much of its time discussing social and political issues; but it was not like that in the British 1930s. The Motleys' terribly serious conversations were devoted to strictly theatrical topics: gossip, career problems, specific production details, but rarely any theorizing. There was also a lot of telling of funny stories; particularly shaggy dog stories in which Devine specialized.

To all their guests the Motleys were a perfect audience because they were of the theatre, but not themselves performers. To outsiders, their studio was apt to appear an exclusive club: unavoidably so, as its members now represented the rising theatrical establishment, and being accepted there was likely to be professionally useful. Self-importance and complacency were unwelcome at the studio, likewise actors considered to be phoney. The difference was that where the Motleys were well mannered and kind to people they privately considered foolish or boring, Devine did not keep his blatant lack of interest to himself, and was sometimes rough with people who did not deserve it. Unlike the girls, he made enemies. And as the Motleys' fortunes rose, so did feelings of resentment against their business manager.

Who, once again, was George Devine? After the ignominy of *Cymbeline* he had found his level as a reliable supporting actor at the Vic, and when his contract ran out in March 1933 he was left minding the shop. Were these sufficient qualifications for sharing the inner councils of the Gielgud circle? That was the question that occurred to outsiders; and it was asked more insistently when Gielgud started favouring him with parts which – even in the opinion of a close friend like Anthony Quayle – many an out-of-work actor could have done better. 'George Devine', says Alec Guinness, 'was obviously a man of the theatre, but at that time people didn't think much of him as an actor.' So, with the ascent of Motley, another picture of Devine begins to take shape: that of a toad-like parasite, graced with no talent save that of winning the confidence of people on the way up, and seizing the rewards of influence, jobs and material security at the expense of better men who lacked his capacity for ingratiation. Although with every step he took Devine showed this picture to be false, it was one which dogged his career all through the 1930s.

As he was still under contract to the Vic when *Bordeaux* opened, Devine took no part in that show, and after his contract ran out it was almost a year before he got another London engagement. When work did start trickling through again it was the same old story: small parts in productions by old friends. In March 1934 he went into Komisarjevsky's window-smashing production of *Magnolia Street* at the Adelphi. In May, in the inconspicuous character of the Rev. Colpus, he moved on to Sadler's Wells for the Vic revival of Granville-Barker's *The Voysey Inheritance*. Although the production was credited to Harcourt Williams, it in fact gave Devine his one experience of being directed by Barker. According to Marius Goring, also in the company, Barker's descent from his Parisian Olympus into the vulgarities of theatrical trade was attended by much snobbish secrecy. 'He came in incognito in bowler hat and striped trousers, with a Rolls outside the door to rush him back to the Mayfair Hotel for lunch. But it was a fantastic experience. He demanded everything.'

Barker, typically, was now dissatisfied with his youthful masterpiece and had extensively revised it by bringing the action forward thirty years, and converting the bony dialogue into what *The Times* called 'rhetoric and over-elaborated sentiment' which also vastly prolonged the playing time. The show transferred for a brief run at the Shaftesbury, and Barker disdainfully quit the scene. 'There it is,' he said, 'another ploughing of the sands. Things have not changed in forty years.' But he left a message behind. 'For our sort of play', he wrote to Williams, 'and our sort of attitude to the theatre ... *real* repertory and a permanent company are the only solution.'

In fact, the second part of Barker's prescription was coming true. Gielgud had already built up one company and in June 1934 he reassembled them for another Gordon Daviot play which was intended to do for Gwen Ffrangcon-Davies what *Bordeaux* had done for him. This was *Queen of Scots*, and like its predecessor it opened under Albery's management at the New. During the run Frederick Lloyd fell ill and Devine took over the old codger role of the Earl of Morton: another obscure engagement, but it laid the foundation for his lifelong friendships with Laurence Olivier and Glen Byam Shaw, who were starring respectively as Bothwell and Darnley. To them, Devine was very much a new boy, still having make-up problems. Olivier: 'It was late in the run and not going well, so they couldn't afford a wig. He had to grease-paint his hair white and put on what he could for an old make-up over that fat face. I remember us all thinking, Well, he seems a nice sort of chap, but he's not very good, is he? And he wasn't yet.' The prospect of stepping into Lloyd's shoes had again reduced him to a jelly. Byam Shaw saw him waiting at the side of the stage before his first rehearsal with the principals. 'He was trembling with fear, and saying "I can't do it, I can't do it." I used to tease him about it afterwards.' Subsequently Devine took his revenge by sending out for some sandwiches and exploding the paper bag with gratifying effect at a crucial moment of Shaw's pre-performance *toilette*. Stage-fright was one thing they had in common, and in future productions when they dressed together they shared many a night sweating with terror. But thanks to Byam Shaw, we hear no more of Devine crying into the mirror. The son of an R.I. painter, Shaw was a master of make-up ('the only part of acting I ever liked'), and he passed a lot of his skill on to Devine who had the faculty, as Margaret Harris puts it, of 'learning through his paws'.

This was typical of the way in which he picked up his stage education *en route*, and of his growing love for the manual crafts of the theatre. His influential contacts were useless in this department. Gielgud may have been a good friend and a head-masterly director, but he was not a man a young actor could approach for advice on wig joins. Carpenters, lighting technicians, prop makers: these were Devine's teachers, and colleagues with whom he felt entirely at home.

In the Motley studio he built a model theatre, based on the New Theatre stage, which was used for testing the effect of light on different materials and for other experiments of his own. Margaret Harris worked designs out on this model before discussing them with stage managers and carpenters. Devine, she says, 'did endless experiments with it to reproduce the colour of candle-light. I remember hours when he'd have a candle on the stage, trying one thing after another to get it meticulously right.'

It is ironical that those who disliked Devine turned his all-round skills to his discredit. When he first arrived in London they dismissed him as an amateur; ten years later they were dismissing him as a mere stage manager. It is true that he never went out of his way to be polite, and people whom he found boring were left in no doubt as to his feelings. But the hostility, both now and later, had another source in sheer incomprehension. The theatre is supposed to be a self-seeking trade, and the spectacle of someone who appeared indifferent to money and star billing, and who chose as Devine did to immerse himself in teaching, aroused a good deal of suspicion. However unambitious he might seem, he must somehow be feathering his nest. To such observers it was inconceivable that he could be genuinely detached from ordinary careerist motives and pursuing rewards of a different kind.

Queen of Scots came off in the autumn of 1934. It had not been a success but, as Olivier says, 'it was marvellous because everybody in the company became friends. Lifelong friendships began then.' These started bearing fruit almost at once. Gielgud had already played *Hamlet* at the Vic and the Queen's Theatre, and when he mentioned his idea of presenting it as a sequel to *Bordeaux* Olivier told him he was mad. There was plenty of commercial Shakespeare around in the early 1930s, but the fate of Ernest Milton's *Othello* and Godfrey Tearle's *Julius Caesar* was not much encouragement to a star trying to follow up a thirteen-month smash hit. However, the production – designed by Motley on a £1,000 budget and cast from the Gielgud circle – duly opened at the New Theatre on November 14, 1934, and weathered some squirmingly evasive reviews to pass into legend.

Byam Shaw, who played Laertes, says, 'Nobody could believe his *Hamlet* could run five months in a West End theatre. Until then the London scene was a desert. There was no production as we understand it now at all. There were some good classical actors, but their costumes and scenery were unbelievably tatty and awful. The change really started from John's productions of *Bordeaux* and *Hamlet*. Directly after that, when other talented young actors saw that you could have that sort of success from doing interesting plays instead of little light comedies, they all followed suit. The standard went right up.'

Devine aroused some envy by landing the part of the Player King. The twenty-year-old Alec Guinness also received his first West End break in the role of Osric – though not before Gielgud had told him to 'Go away for a week and get someone to teach you how to act.' Guinness, in turn, remembers Devine being much bullied by Gielgud in rehearsal. '"Oh, you're so *stiff*!" Just the thing to stop an actor being stiff! George didn't have a good actor's voice; it was grating.' But they both survived until the opening and settled into the run.

The great party was under way. Thanks to the conjunction of an enlightened manager and an unselfish star, a generation of serious young actors were getting a chance to beat the system. Clustering around the invulnerable magician who was making it all happen, the group moved on from the New to the Queens, until it seemed that Barker's dream of a permanent company playing in repertory was coming true.

In time this proved to be a mirage which dissolved leaving the caravanserai still ploughing the sands. But for the time being there was nothing illusory about what Gielgud's actors were doing: they were picking up the threads of the Barker tradition, and bringing it to a vastly wider public than his pre-First World War Royal Court, at the audience. And not only the Barker tradition; a link was also being forged with Barker's French allies.

Hamlet finished its London run at the end of March 1935. In the first week of April it began its progress round the provinces: Manchester, Edinburgh, Leeds. One day in Glasgow, Devine had a phone call from the Motleys announcing that Michel Saint-Denis had arrived. 'Saint-Denis, who's that?' asked Glen Byam Shaw. So Devine told him.

3

SAINT-DENIS

As managing director of the New (now the Albery) Theatre, the Criterion and Wyndhams, Bronson Albery enjoyed an apparently commanding position in the pre-war West End. But nobody is water-tight; and in Albery's case the leak took the shape of two brothers who held shares in all three theatres but whose interest in the drama did not extend beyond the box office. Far from wielding absolute managerial control, Albery could not even get permission to keep his premises in good repair. So when an appeal for help arrived from the Arts Theatre, he was glad to respond to it. In running programmes at the Arts he would at least have a free hand.

Albery was not one to over-estimate the taste of the London playgoer. On one occasion, having the Criterion vacant for a dead fortnight around Holy Week, he plugged it despairingly with *The Doll's House* which, to his amazement, played to capacity for all thirteen performances. '*The Doll's House*,' he muttered afterwards to Charles Landstone, 'they must think it's an Easter children's play!' However, in his carefree role at the Arts he backed his fancy and brought over a lively new French troupe whom he had taken his family to see at the Vieux-Colombier on a night when the show went up late and the Paris audience smashed their way in through the glass doors. In London, too, La Compagnie des Quinze were a smash. They introduced two new plays, *Noé* and *Le Viol de Lucrèce*, both written for the company by André Obey; but it was not the texts that captivated British audiences so much as the playing style. The Quinze were acrobats, mimes and musicians whose work enlarged the whole definition of acting. 'It was', Tyrone Guthrie wrote, 'like a delightful ballet, only that it had fifty times more

content than any ballet ever had.' And although the individual
quality of artists like Suzanne Bing and Auguste Bovério – not
to mention Pierre Fresnay – was unmistakable, together they
functioned as a team in total opposition to the star hierarchy.
London, in short, was renewing contact with true ensemble and
the forgotten art of pantomime.

The Quinze were a touring company on the model of Molière's
pre-Parisian L'Illustre Théâtre. They travelled with a lightweight collapsible rostrum and a tent-like surround which did
away with the need for wings and which could be packed in a
single hamper. This was no mere economy but an expression of
their contempt for ordinary theatrical illusion. They could evoke
anything they wished without wading into what they called 'the
mud of naturalism'. For a village they used some miniature
roofs and a toy steeple set upon poles. When Lucrèce was seen
spinning with her maidens, they presented a picture composed
with the care of a Florentine painting, but they did not bother to
supply needle and thread. The style was not anti-realistic, but it
took off from where realism came to an end.

The response to the 1931 Arts tryout was such that Albery
was able to transfer the two productions to the Ambassadors and
the New, and to bring the Quinze back in 1932 and 1933. They
did not make money in Albery's larger theatres, but they acquired a tremendous following among the generation of artists
then heir-apparent to the British stage, and their long-term
influence ranks with that of the Berliner Ensemble's 1956
London season.

The Quinze had a new name but they were not a new company. They had already been working together since 1924 as Les
Copiaus – the young troupe whom Jacques Copeau had taken
down to Burgundy on his retirement from the Vieux Colombier.
Rehearsing in a disused *cuverie* in the village of Pernand-
Vergelesses, the troupe initially did much to prove Copeau's point
that a highly sophisticated return to the theatre's popular origins
would find its true audience at grass-roots level. But the success
of the enterprise was sabotaged by Copeau himself, who increasingly isolated himself from his actors. The greater their
appetite for an audience, the more rigidly the *patron* kept them
on a diet of studio exercises. In June 1929, expecting an appointment to the Comédie-Française, Copeau disbanded the company
who promptly regrouped themselves, with a few new recruits,

under the *patron*'s nephew, Michel Saint-Denis. All the pent-up energies they had accumulated as the Copiaus now went into their work as the Quinze.

Family attachments aside, Saint-Denis was Copeau's natural heir. General factotum to the Copiaus, he had taken a hand in every job from running their advance bookings to writing their open-air scenarios. He was one of the troupe's best actors; he had taught at the Vieux Colombier school. And he possessed a steely intellect and a monastic dedication to his theatrical ideals no less fanatical than his uncle's. At the same time, he was determined not to repeat what he saw as Copeau's mistakes. Where the Vieux Colombier repertory had always suffered from the lack of a house author, Saint-Denis lost no time in sealing a pact with André Obey and building the Quinze's specialized repertory from work Obey wrote with the personalities and playing style of the troupe in mind. Also, having witnessed the paralysing effect of Copeau's conversion, Saint-Denis proclaimed a defiant atheism to the end of his life. 'It is always the same,' he said to a friend after visiting the aging Granville-Barker, 'with sexual impotence they seek refuge in religion or theories.'

From the viewpoint of George Devine and the English stage, Saint-Denis first enters the story in 1928 when the Copiaus visited Britain with a touring production of Copeau's *L'Illusion*. One of their dates was at the Cambridge Festival Theatre, where they were seen by Marius Goring, then a sixteen-year-old schoolboy.

> I'd never seen anything like it; the entire movement of the company was wonderful. I remember Copeau sitting on the steps of the theatre inviting his children on to the stage. And there was a young man, running and waving the mask of an animal's head, shouting 'Jouons la comédie!' That was Michel. One day, I thought, I'll join that company.

Goring got his chance six years later, having by then made contact with Copeau while studying at the Sorbonne and played two seasons at the Old Vic. The same period had seen the rise and fall of the Quinze. *Noé* and *Lucrèce* had been followed by more Obey plays including *La Bataille de la Marne* of which Agate wrote, 'this is great, perhaps the greatest acting, since on a bare stage the actors re-create not the passion of one or two, but the agony of a nation.'

However, international acclaim was no protection against the dollar crisis, and in 1934 the bottom fell out of the Quinze. All but three of the original actors left the company, and Saint-Denis gathered the remnants together and embarked on a fresh plan. This centred on a large country house at Beaumanoir, near Aix-en-Provence, which would be the base for a new troupe whose members would also hold classes for summer school students. The attachment of a school to a producing company was a basic principle of the Copeau doctrine; given the reputation of the Quinze, it might also cover the bills. Among the newcomers Saint-Denis engaged were Goring and another British-based multilingual artist, Vera Lindsay (then Vera Poliakoff). 'You lucky devil,' Devine wrote to Goring from the *Queen of Scots* treadmill, 'theatre here is utterly depressing. How I envy you.' The adventure was rather less glamorous to the impoverished members of the new Quinze, who were rehearsing in a garage measuring five by six metres and trying to raise funds to light a barn.

The restructured Quinze duly went on the road in the autumn of 1934, but their financial plight grew increasingly desperate. In November Goring embarked on a fund-raising mission which began in a dream world of wild schemes and fantasy benefactors including a mad American millionaire and the King of Siam. More to the point was the approach Goring made to John Maynard Keynes, who replied that the task of supporting the company in Provence 'must be obviously primarily the responsibility of friends in France'; but if Saint-Denis chose to launch a troupe in Britain it might be a different matter. Armed with this letter, Goring returned to Beaumanoir, firing off a stack of Quinze Christmas cards. One of them brought an answer from Devine, now promoted to Gielgud's Player King but still as disgruntled as ever. 'We shall hope to see you in a show by your company which may, by the Grace of God or Bronson Albery, bring some light to the messy dirge of our theatrical life.' The campaign dragged on for a few more months, but life at Beaumanoir had come to a standstill, and at the end of February 1935, Saint-Denis took leave of his little community to direct Gielgud in an English version of *Noah*.

At the time, he had no thought of abandoning the Quinze. In any case, he was ill-equipped for a cosmopolitan career. He spoke virtually no English; and he had none of Komisarjevsky's

flair as an *enfant terrible*. He might temporarily fit in with
Gielgud's company or the Old Vic, but it would have been inconceivable for Saint-Denis to put on spectaculars for Cochran.
He took the New Theatre job for the money: but it led to his
changing both his country and his career.

Among his first meetings in London was one at the Motley
studio, and it was on that occasion that Devine met the man who
was to dominate his professional life for the next twenty years.
Vera Lindsay came with Saint-Denis, and recalls her first impression of Devine as 'this strange-looking man. We were all
young and rather designed; we hadn't taken on middle-aged fat.
But he was fat, and dark, and special. As a young person I found
it very difficult to accept him physically. But he got on well with
Michel right from the start; partly because the Motleys were
doing the décor for *Noah*, and Michel was attracted to the whole
ambiance of the studio. It was immediately a unit. Also they
were good in relation to each other, both square and big and
smoking their pipes; there was a real physical sympathy between
them.'

The fact that Devine spoke French supplied one immediate
link and there were other obvious points of contact. They both
combined acute intelligence with a peasant stolidity. They
shared a prodigious capacity for hard work and an artisan's sense
of craftsmanship. Their agreement over the kind of theatre they
wanted was probably the strongest bond between them. But, to
begin with, the best clue to their sympathy is that they made each
other laugh. They set about enlarging each others' vocabulary
with obscenity duels, swapping the filthiest words they knew in
French and English, and ringing each other up whenever they
thought of something to cap the latest taboo-breaker. They told
each other jokes, often missing the point until Devine had explained why mothers-in-law are funny in Britain and Saint-
Denis had shed similar light on French comic stereotypes. Not
that they needed words for this kind of exchange. Just as often it
consisted of Saint-Denis miming a Norman peasant driving his
cows, and Devine doing a London bobby making an arrest. And
before long their pantomime became a double act: they would
come back, for instance, from one of their money-raising expedi-
tions and build up a joint portrait of the patron as a pompous ass.
They also played together in French, and there are stories of
them corpsing through Molière and finally having to give up in

speechless hysteria. Given the seriousness of their future collaboration and the autocratic impression it made on some observers, it is worth preserving the image of these two large, pipe-smoking clowns.

Saint-Denis had a month to rehearse *Noah* and he did not so much produce the play as re-produce it, taking it move by move from the Quinze prompt book. The whole cast were locked in a rigid choreographic scheme. Alec Guinness, who trotted over the stage in the wordless role of the Wolf, says he was 'driven mad by Michel's meticulous little moves'. Gielgud says that, apart from humming 'The Sailor's Hornpipe' while he hammered the Ark, every detail in his performance was laid down by Saint-Denis. Devine came out of the show rather well: he had two small but decisive parts as the Wild Man who attacks Noah with an axe, and as the kindly Bear who turns savage after the voyage. Padded out as a Stone Age Michelin Man as the first and encased in a complete animal costume under a huge shaggy head as the second, he experienced professionally for the first time the release of working inside a mask. His lumbering movement and harsh voice, however limiting in other plays, were assets on this occasion. He was, as Gielgud says, obvious casting for a bear.

The production ran for ten weeks, and was received with interest and respect, though with nothing like the rapture that had greeted the Quinze version. 'The magic was gone,' wrote Tyrone Guthrie. Originally 'it was like a glamorous but rather *passée* woman in a big shady hat and heaps of tulle. The English production was the same lady in a cold, hard north-east light, a raincoat and no hat.'

What the venture had proved was that there was to be no grand alliance between the director and the star. For Saint-Denis it was a compromised excursion into alien boulevard territory. For Gielgud it was an instructive digression from his natural line of work. Temperamentally the two were as elementally opposed as earth and air. If Gielgud was a bird, Saint-Denis was a cage. So, although the two men were pushing for similar reforms, their paths were only once more to cross professionally. Otherwise, they retreated to their separate centres of power and viewed each other's work with respect from a distance.

Saint-Denis did not have the same inhibiting effect on other star actors. Olivier, for instance, was prepared to work for him in a spirit of blind obedience. Ashcroft, who went in fear of

Komisarjevsky the director, felt entirely confident with Saint-Denis. Upon Devine, his impact was akin to that of religious conversion, and the effect was apparent both on and off stage. 'He became', says Olivier, 'more important, and his opinions crystallized. His message was strictly bound up with Michel. But independently he was now somebody to be reckoned with in personality and opinion.' Meanwhile he had gone into Gielgud's New Theatre production of *Romeo and Juliet*. Ashcroft and Edith Evans returned to the parts they had played in the OUDS *Romeo*. Devine was cast as Peter, the same kind of marginal role that had come his way at the Vic, but he seized it as a chance to repay his debt to the Marx Brothers and Chaplin. He went on wearing a bowler hat and transformed this forgettable clown into a realist character study backed up with physical comedy tricks drawn from outside the classical theatre. Devine's Player King has vanished without trace, but there are plenty of people who remember his Peter. Ashcroft says he was 'wonderful' in the part, and Gielgud that he 'did marvels' with it. Olivier says, 'I was amazed how good he was. We were all surprised, because he hadn't shown that promise in his early appearances.'

But at the moment that the 'actor effort' was at last beginning to pay off, Devine turned his back on it. He continued to act when parts turned up, but henceforth his main energies were focused elsewhere. Saint-Denis had put solid ground under Devine's feet as a performer, and at the same time furnished him with an alternative ambition to the pursuit of good parts. Up in his New Theatre dressing room he took off Peter's hat and began drawing the next magic circle.

4

THE LONDON THEATRE STUDIO

In London, two things became clear to Saint-Denis. First, there was a keen interest in his own work and a market for it; second, there was absolutely no interest in supporting the Quinze in France. Together with Goring and Vera Lindsay, he had compiled exhaustive lists of possible subscribers; he visited university towns and invoked the aid of the Alliance Française; he went down to Devon and made an approach to Dartington Hall which had previously welcomed Michael Chekhov, the third great emigré director to take up residence in Britain. But no patrons materialized.

Meanwhile, Goring and Devine were jointly pushing him to launch a company in Britain. This was not exactly a new idea for them. 'There wasn't one of us in those days', Goring says, 'who didn't want to start a company. It was certainly what Devine wanted right from the beginning.' By themselves they stood no chance of raising the money for it: under the banner of Saint-Denis it became a feasible project. Saint-Denis was slow to surrender. For months, shuttling between the two countries and delivering whatever small sums he could muster for the Beaumanoir survivors, he clung to the idea of running a French and British operation simultaneously. But the situation was hopeless, and in the end he cut the last ties with Provence and settled for a new life in Britain.

As always, it was on his own terms. There was no question of starting a company from scratch. His work required a particular kind of actor, which meant starting a school from which actors of that kind would emerge. This article of the Copeau doctrine was not wholly unfamiliar in Britain. In ballet, the ideas of Diaghilev and Cecchetti had already filtered through, and it was no great leap to extend them to the training of actors. Although, according to Goring, no such idea had ever entered the head of George Devine, it quickly found sympathy inside the profession. Much of the support came from Bronson Albery's circle. Albery himself, after resisting the Beaumanoir appeal, first put money into the London scheme. Tyrone Guthrie backed it with an interest-free loan of £1,300, followed by Olivier, Gielgud and Charles Laughton.

Things were now moving. A supporting committee was set up consisting of Albery, Gielgud, Guthrie, and the banker Ian Black. At the end of July a first prospectus was issued for the so far nameless school, forecasting that 'the result of three years' work should be: the existence of a permanent company ready to leave the school; several new plays which have been performed and then form part of the repertory of the said company; and a school in full activity.' For the new productions, Saint-Denis planned to annex two of the Quinze's unrealized projects: a group version of *The Tempest*, and an adaptation of *The Odyssey* with music by his Provençal neighbour, Darius Milhaud. Devine, whom Saint-Denis had first encountered in the role of business manager to the Motleys, was now appointed business manager of the school. One of his first acts in that capacity was to prepare a breakdown of the studio's capital and running costs, producing an estimated total of £4,350; which seems startlingly low until you look back and notice that one item has not been costed: 'a house with a garden with a sufficient number of rooms and sufficiently large to enable classes to take place in them, and to provide for workshops, rehearsal rooms and management office'.

'Any news about the house?' Saint-Denis wrote anxiously to Goring from Beaumanoir at the end of August. He was also worried about how to pay his fare back to England. What news there was came from Goring's millionaire who bailed Saint-Denis out with a cheque for £50 and suggested that he might find suitable premises at the home of Maud Allan, a dancer then famed as Canada's answer to Isadora Duncan. Devine and Goring went round to Regent's Park to inspect her west wing, where it transpired that the school would have to hold classes in the basement. After further abortive searches they decided to start up at some temporary address before public interest cooled off.

So, when the London Theatre Studio first opened its doors in January 1936, its working space consisted of a single practice room in Beak Street. This had formerly been Diaghilev's studio. Saint-Denis contrived to find room there for sixty-four students who had enrolled for four separate courses. Beginners came in the morning; young professional actors in the afternoon; in the evening there were French classes; and production course students put up with one class a week and waited for better times to come. As administration devoured most of Devine's time and Saint-Denis's English was still erratic, much of the initial teaching was done by Goring. Part of the work consisted of standard gymnastics and speech training, but the beginners were also plunged into improvisation, mime, and mask exercises then unknown in English drama schools.

After its first twelve weeks, the L.T.S. quit Beak Street and reassembled for the next term – thanks to Guthrie – in a rehearsal room at the Vic during the company's summer holiday. This was no great improvement, but now the Studio had a goal in view. The scouts had found a disused Methodist chapel called Providence Hall in Upper Street, Islington. For their purposes its interior needed to be completely rebuilt; but it was just about close enough to central London, and it offered just about enough space. Early in April the L.T.S. incorporated itself as a limited liability company under a directorate of the old committee members with the addition of Laurence Olivier. The task of reconstruction was assigned to Gropius's disciple Marcel Breuer, who joined in L.T.S. planning parties at the Motleys' Thames-side cottage at Wraysbury. The hunt for money was on again, as Guthrie's loan did not take the company far towards increasing its authorized capital to the £6,250 which was Devine's estimate for the proposed installation. A fairy godmother then appeared in the person of Laura Dyas, an L.T.S. production course student and friend of Goring, who had lately come into a family inheritance. On the condition of absolute anonymity, she wrote Saint-Denis a cheque for £3,500, whereupon the dream of Providence Place became a reality.

At the end of April, the company signed a three-year lease on the building and gave Breuer the go-ahead to start work in July. In its interim term at the Vic, the Studio brought in the Motleys to run a course in décor. Devine, now billed as Assistant Director and Manager, issued a revised prospectus for Islington, listing six courses and plans for public shows. In May the enterprise received the blessing of Jacques Copeau who arrived in

London as guest of honour at an L.T.S. lunch at the Savoy. In the same month, Devine returned to the New Theatre as Shamraef in Komisarjevsky's production of *The Seagull*, which was the occasion of Edith Evans's celebrated four-minute pause after Konstantin's play by the lake. 'We sat there with tears streaming down our faces,' says Alec Guinness, 'until finally she moved her shoulders as if she was getting chilly, and said "Let's go in."' This was the first full-scale Chekhov production in the West End and it was a big success. It was also the end of Gielgud's four year attachment to the New Theatre; after drawing capacity audiences for six weeks he disappeared to play Hamlet on Broadway. Until this moment, the paths of Gielgud and Saint-Denis had run parallel. They now simultaneously diverged: Gielgud disbanded his family at the very time that Saint-Denis was setting up house for his followers. No one could serve both these masters, and Gielgud soon became conscious that he had lost George Devine: 'I was a bit jealous and slightly resented my flock being dispersed. He didn't leave me for good, but obviously he found Saint-Denis a new guiding light, as I'd found Komis in the past. I didn't realize he had this flair for organization; I just felt I'd lost him in my bailiwick.'

Reconstruction went ahead, and in the autumn of 1936 the L.T.S. reopened at Providence Place, where it was to remain until the outbreak of war. The school now had six rehearsal rooms, offices, a wardrobe and workroom, and its own theatre. Externally, the old chapel was unaltered. Inside, prompted equally by the demands of economy and Bauhaus aesthetics, the atmosphere was functional and austere. Besides his work on the building, Breuer had designed 'a lot of slippery furniture' including the first stacking chairs to reach Britain. When he proudly brought in a model, Saint-Denis eyed it with suspicion and asked Devine to sit down. Devine went straight through it on to the floor, after which he was credited with the additional title of official chair-breaker.

Architecturally, the unusual feature of the Providence Place school was its stage, which Breuer had designed in consultation with Motley. The available space for spectators and performers was only 42 ft by 32 ft; but within these limits, Breuer installed a 32 ft proscenium opening and a stage extending 22ft in depth to a movable screen wall. There was virtually no wing space; and the miniature auditorium (capacity 78) ran to within 2 ft of the adaptable forestage. In one sense, the L.T.S. theatre was an exposure machine: it demanded performances sufficiently large to fill the spatial volume, and also truthful enough to withstand scrutiny at point-blank range. More important, its dimensions were those of the average London stage opening so that any production could be transferred intact to the West End. The school, in short, was designed with a view to the company that was meant to emerge, and its babies had to make themselves comfortable in a full-sized bed.

Whatever company ambitions the students may have had, they all went through the exposure treatment. Besides the stage, there were the compulsory L.T.S. costumes. Designed by the Motleys, these were woollen outfits that could be roughly adapted to any period. The girls had skirts, cut in a full circle with draw-strings, which could be looped up into crinolines or panniers. The boys had bell-bottomed trousers which could be tightened or gathered up to suggest a Regency or Elizabethan figure. But for the physical classes that occupied most of the beginners' time, they stripped down to sleeveless tunics and bathing trunks. 'You were meant', says Yvonne Mitchell, 'to be as bare, as failing, as ugly as you didn't want to be. Anybody who had knock-knees or pimples had to face that the first day, and you all had to fail together. You had to forget about your body. You couldn't be self-conscious. That's what those costumes were about.'

Here is a hostile account of the same ordeal from Miss Mitchell's L.T.S. contemporary, Peter Ustinov. 'There was an element of cruelty. A Canadian girl turned up without her little outfit, and she had to go through the whole first day in her under-wear. We all pretended not to notice so as not to embarrass her, but she was terribly upset.'

The accusations of cruelty and insensitivity and of cultivating difficulty for its own sake – these recur throughout the career of the L.T.S. and its post-war successor, the Old Vic Theatre School. To put them in proportion, and to give a clearer picture of the doctrine that exerted such a spell on George Devine, a few words are due on Saint-Denis's long-term aims.

Both the L.T.S. and the Vic School began their lives in a cloud of manifestoes, and went on to inscribe themselves on British theatrical legend. But without any personal memory to draw on, it is no easy matter to separate their achievements from their intentions. How did they differ so much from other drama schools?

Marius Goring supplies one answer in a letter to Maud Allan:

> The general idea is to unify the various elements of the theatre in
> the school: that is to say, the intention is not to 'turn out' young
> actors and actresses, after the average model, to enable them to act
> in average plays in the West End; but to produce a homogeneous
> group of people working in the theatre – a troupe that can work by
> itself and for itself; with writers, musicians, mechanics trained to
> support it. As well as being a school, it will be a dramatic centre and
> will attract to itself many people who are already in the theatre.

This statement touches on three key ideas in the Saint-Denis
programme: the idea of an 'organic' approach to training in
which every aspect of the work would be sympathetically inter-
related; the idea of a self-sufficient creative cell, leading a life
independent of the theatre at large; and the idea of fostering
reciprocal links with leading members of the profession by whose
agency the message would infiltrate the conventional stage.
The first two ideas, if not the last, derive from Saint-Denis's
master, Copeau. One must beware of assuming an identity of
viewpoint between this formidable pair. But it is true that Saint-
Denis took his scenic vocabulary – *commedia*, the Noh – from
Copeau, and that he too was haunted by Copeau's theatrical
Mount Athos: a vision of such immaculate purity that no actual
piece of stage work could seem more than a gross shadow of the
ideal. For Copeau, as for Saint-Denis, nothing was ever quite
good enough, and they made their colleagues feel it. They also
exacted loyalty of the particularly intense kind that is reserved
for prophets. Here, for instance, is Roger Martin du Gard
writing about the *patron* in 1917:

> There is an indefinable but undeniable unity between all his con-
> ceptions – his stage, décor, choice of plays, *mis-en-scène*, acting,
> costume ... He is looking for *workers*: artists of the second rank who
> can carry out someone else's idea once they've grasped it. He's open
> to advice. But in future I doubt whether he will entrust the smallest
> decision to anyone else. There's nothing for us to say. We are in the
> presence of a creator of genius who has a clear vision of an ensemble
> which includes not only questions of performance but even the
> actors' moral lives: the creation of a simple and honest society of
> theatre workers, a troupe involving everything down to educating
> children at schools of rhythm and gymnastics. He's creating a kind
> of new city for the actors and their clientele. Little by little it will
> materialize.

Neither in Copeau's lifetime nor in Saint-Denis's did it materialize, but the idea goes marching on in the community and laboratory stages of the 1970s. It is a powerful myth, and when Saint-Denis invoked it in the London of 1936, he had the monopoly. Young actors and drama students then were no less idealistic than they are now, but when they looked around there was nowhere to make a living out of serious work. Gielgud had aroused hopes of change: but, as Ashcroft says, 'he gave us the opportunity to form what was really the first ensemble, and then just waved goodbye to it all.' No less than today, there was a hunger for gurus, and whether one views the L.T.S. as an oasis in the desert or a temple among the fleshpots, it commanded the field; as even the unsympathetic Ustinov acknowledges:

> It represented ideals to people who were embarking on a profession which in this country has always been linked to the fairground and show business. We were therefore very vulnerable to people who were trying to purify the theatre. 'I know I'm playing in *Happy Weekend* at the moment, but there are better things to do. I'll come back for a while and have my Sabbatical with the monks.' We were all apt to feel that sort of thing.

No one was more prone to that feeling than George Devine. He told me that well before the arrival of Saint-Denis, 'We used to have ten or fifteen *théâtres de poche*, all very esoteric and highbrow, but we poured in and I got my theatrical education from that.' There was Peter Godfrey's Gate, which introduced German expressionism to Britain; Rupert Doone's Group Theatre, which launched the Auden–Isherwood verse plays; and a number of other shoe-string outfits where spiritually starved young actors could briefly escape the insular fairground and enter a cosmopolitan world where the theatre was a serious matter. The arrival of the L.T.S. supplemented these spasmodic contacts with a regular London base, linked directly to the power-houses of Copeau and Stanislavsky. 'Subconsciously,' says Basil Langton, 'Saint-Denis gave focus to what we each sought as a way of life.' And when Langton says 'we' that goes for leading members of the profession as well as youngsters slogging through matinées of *Happy Weekend*. With his students, as Jocelyn Herbert says, he 'gave a lot of us a sense of direction not only in our work but in our lives'. He would not appeal to an artist like Ustinov whose work, however brilliant, rests more on flair than labour. But appeal is too mild a word for his hold over the marvellous generation of leading actors who emerged in the 1930s. Guinness and Redgrave speak with awe of how careers were transformed by his influence. Olivier placed an absolute trust in him and would follow his direction like a blind man. And, outside that group, a director-critic like Harold Clurman, who numbered Stanislavsky and Meyerhold among his acquaintances, lists Saint-Denis as 'the most cultivated, innately refined, spiritually pure person I had ever encountered in the theatre'. The problem of assessing his partly submerged and sometimes vilified career becomes easier once one accepts it as a simple fact that Saint-Denis cared for work and perfection and not for fame and money.

For Devine, Saint-Denis's Studio was yet another approach towards the ideal family. It was built to last, it fulfilled his love of France, and it embraced his existing friendship with the Motleys who had equally been drawn into Saint-Denis's orbit. More important, it also enabled him to tap the resources of his up-bringing. Inside the theatre he discovered his own variation on the Devine family pattern. Like Lex and his father, he expanded into the role of a reformer working with the young, and adopted the same mask – part pedagogue, part buffoon. And, as at Clayesmore, he emerges as Crown Prince inside a little absolute kingdom.

Initially, Marius Goring was a rival pretender to this title, and if the twin branches of the L.T.S. had grown side by side, the honours might have been shared with Goring as head of the acting company and Devine as head of the school. But they did not keep pace with each other. As before, Saint-Denis was riding only half a horse. With the Quinze he had a troupe but no school; now he had a school but no troupe. Goring was too am-bitious an actor to sacrifice his stage career to teaching, and once the Studio was installed at Providence Place he left Devine in the undisputed position of Saint-Denis's right-hand man.

So, returning to the question of 'Who was George Devine?' there is now a provisional answer. He was that rare theatrical bird, an all-rounder who chooses to put most of his energy into teaching. As a teacher, his stage practice saved him from staleness and empty theorizing; as an actor and director, his school work saved him from devaluing the theatre into a trade. Like Lex, he could appear to his students as a bit of comic relief, while to anyone he was professionally directing he could seem a head-masterly figure. But the confusions are easier to reconcile once you see him as a man with visionary aspirations who loved getting his hands dirty.

It was generally the case in Saint-Denis schools (the Old Vic School as well as the L.T.S.) that students learned about the stage from people who could do as well as teach: though the L.T.S. did employ some whole-time teachers, not to mention exotic figures like the future Mme Saint-Denis, Suria Magito, a choric dance artist who arrived from Paris with her personal collection of Asian gongs and Noh masks. It was a major point of policy that the staff should move around classes and learn from each other. Finally, unique then and non-existent among today's drama schools, the Studio incorporated its own design department, so that when it gave a public show everything that went into it had been produced by a group of students working under the same roof.

Like other theatre schools, the Studio held elementary voice and movement classes. Unlike them, it ran beginners' classes in pantomime and improvisation which aroused the same kind of controversy that Strasberg's New York Actors' Studio stirred up in the 1950s with its animated cash-registers. Providence Place was strategically situated between Collins' Music Hall and the Islington Agricultural Hall; right alongside the Studio was the Chapel Street Market, one of the liveliest street markets in London. All this had a bearing on the curriculum. At Collins', students could pick up physical comedy technique, which was Devine's department. At the Agricultural Hall, and at the zoo, they could do the ground-work for animal pantomime. In the market and in the streets of Islington they were expected to keep their eyes open and select living models for character improvisation, padding themselves out with bottoms, bellies and hunched shoulders designed by the Motleys. Side by side with the formal training, much of the work was based on direct observation of life.

Legends proliferate around this side of the work. Saint-Denis is said to have pounced on one silent girl and told her to be a lake. That kept her quiet for several weeks, until one day the class were stunned by a shrill cackle from the forgotten figure in the corner. 'Ah, my dear,' said Saint-Denis eagerly, 'what was that?' 'That', she said, 'was a gust of wind passing over the lake.' For his animal, Ustinov shrewdly chose a salamander and lay on his rock for a year, darting out his tongue from time to time, while the rest of the class were wearing themselves out as gazelles and tigers. 'Day after day', writes Peter Daubeny, 'we would improvise solemnly on what seemed to me extravagantly bizarre themes. "Now you're a dinosaur in labour" ... "Now you come home to find there's no tea and your mother has been raped." ' Daubeny hated his time at the Studio. Alec Guinness, who revered Saint-Denis as a director, quickly shied away from the Studio's professional actors' classes where the exercises struck him as 'pretty quaint; one was inclined to giggle through them.'

It appears from the *Log Book* of the Copiaus that the Islington street improvisations originated in observation of the Burgundian peasantry. But it is worth noting that Copeau's use of masks and non-human disguises relates to a single incident. This took place when he was rehearsing a Vieux-Colombier actress who was obsessed by her appearance. She worried about the audience; her movements became wooden, and her playing lacked concentration. In desperation, Copeau made her repeat the scene with a handkerchief over her face. She at once relaxed and her body became expressive, demonstrating the fact that by erasing his personality an actor may succeed in surpassing his normal limits. Subsequently a mystique grew up around the use of the mask; so it is important to remember that Copeau adopted it for practical reasons, as an aid to finished performance, to be discarded before the arrival of the public.

The actor we are talking about is the French *comédien*: a balletically neutral figure who can do anything, without necessarily being anything in himself. Hence Copeau's preference for those docile 'artists of the second rank'. Hence, too, the practice at his school and at the L.T.S. of putting students through a basic training in non-verbal exercises: miming animals and inanimate forces of nature, and improvising from behind the shelter of a mask, so as to detach the act of performance from the prison of self.

Within the Copiaus and the Quinze, each member sought to develop a personal mask which would define his own role in the troupe. Saint-Denis had such a mask which seems to have been strikingly unlike the face he showed the world. Based on a character called 'Knie' (which he had created in improvisation with Jean Dasté and Suzanne Bing), it represented a young face with an expression of pompous timidity. He wrote a play for it containing the line, 'Ai-je l'air d'un directeur?'

Devine had no personal mask. As he never worked in a *commedia* troupe he had no need to develop one. But that is not quite the end of the matter. A mask like that of Knie was plainly born out of something more than practical need. If it worked for Saint-Denis as a performance tool, that was because it gave him access to an otherwise submerged area of his personality, and turned his negative attributes to positive account.

Without speculating on the sources of this anti-self, one may fairly relate it to Yeats's saying, 'Give a man a mask if you want him to tell the truth.' But this saying does not apply to Devine. It is a critical reflex these days to associate comedy with pain: and when a man begins life unhappily, as Devine did, and grows up lacking in self-confidence until his identity takes shape through the act of comic display, there is a strong temptation to hang a therapeutic label round his neck. It would certainly be a bio-graphical convenience to do so. But there is no evidence that Devine used clowning as an anaesthetic; nor that he used his personal humiliations, his wretched childhood or any other private torment as material for comedy. Like his juvenile charac-ter part of Scatters, the role of the buffoon and the comic mask itself were means of keeping people out; not letting them in by a side door. And it is notable of the L.T.S. and Vic School training that Devine was apt to discourage any student improvisation that started moving into psychodrama, even if this meant stopping the work at the moment it was getting really interesting.

Returning to the question of why the L.T.S. held the exercises that made Alec Guinness giggle, the answer is that pantomime, mask work, group scenarios, together with the more conventional training in tumbling, acrobatics and singing, were there to assist in the formation of an omnicompetent ensemble who, when the time came for working on plays, would be able to support textual language with scenic language. As such, they incurred some ridicule from actors who were either too talented to need schools, or too intent on stardom to take an interest in ensembles.

Masks require a section to themselves. Devine first learned about them from Saint-Denis, and to some extent the two men exchanged classes at the Studio. But as a rule, Saint-Denis taught the neutral or 'tragic' mask and Devine the comedy or 'character' mask: two strictly separate disciplines. The tragic mask covers the whole of the actor's face and represents youth, middle age or old age. Otherwise it is expressionless until the actor brings it to life. As objects, Saint-Denis specified that the eight neutral masks should be supremely well made and surfaced in the Japanese style. Margaret Harris, who made many of them for the Studio, recalls experimental demonstrations in which the same mask, passing from Saint-Denis's face to Devine's, would appear to change into a totally different person. For students, the first exercise consisted simply of selecting a mask and putting it on; then raising the head and lowering it again without moving the body. The student would next repeat this exercise, having first thought of some reason for the movement, the important thing being that he should pick some situation likely to upset him. If the exercise was successful, the mask would now appear to be suffering.

Later, several masks could be brought together in wordless scenarios. Here, noted by Keith Johnstone, are three of Devine's exercises in the tragic mask.

1 A statue. A mourner comes with flowers, and on leaving kisses the statue's hand. It comes to life, descends from the pedestal, and crushes the mourner as if still of stone.

2 Two old people dream of themselves as young; he as a bird, she as a cat. They play. The cat finally kills the bird.

3 Two young people in love in the sunshine. A storm rises. She runs away in fright. He makes to go, but she returns with a very old face on her still young body.

The tragic mask was a development from the neutral mask; and, as those exercises suggest, it inhabited a region of dream and poetic archetype. Entering that region was not an instant process, and it was only by degrees that the tragic circumstance was introduced. The important thing (using Devine's term) was that the mask should be 'inhabited'. Other people have used the term 'possessed', which is no exaggeration, judging from the experience of students who succeeded in turning the mask on. Yvonne Mitchell recalls one of Saint-Denis's classes at the L.T.S. where she played a two-mask improvisation with a diminutive girl whom at first she easily dominated. But 'at the end of five minutes, I was an abject mask on the floor and this creature was the dominant one. I saw her as an aging man, sitting up there above me. Michel was in front; but when you're in masks it's the masks that direct, they're so powerful.'

Achieving this kind of experience was a gradual process, requiring a disciplined body. In later years, Devine said that learning to wear the tragic mask was like learning to sing. By contrast, the 'character mask' (Devine's term), was a means of instantaneous transformation. As objects, character masks did not require the same standard of workmanship. It was important that they should fit the face like a second skin, but instead of the long moment of preparation where the student holds and examines a tragic mask before putting it on, the half-mask technique was first to put it on and then glimpse the result in a mirror. If it worked, the shock image would catapult the wearer into character improvisation.

Devine taught the character mask at the L.T.S., at the Vic School, and at the classes that developed around the Royal Court Theatre; and it is the subject for which he is best remembered by ex-students from the 1930s to the 1950s. Over that period he introduced some modifications. In teaching broad comedy technique at the L.T.S. it was not his practice to approach new students, as he approached Helen Montagu at the Court, with the businesslike request: 'Bend over. Now fart.' In the main, though, the accounts of his classes are so similar that it makes more sense to group them together rather than in chronological sequence. I have already departed from chronology by quoting the exercises which Keith Johnstone transcribed in the 1950s. Here is another episode from the same source which illustrates the difference between Devine the lecturer and Devine the performer, and suggests the effect a mask can have when it is fully inhabited.

George gave a class to the Royal Court Writers' Group in 1958. He started with a standard forty-minute talk on the half-mask and the Copeau tradition. Then he retired to the end of the long shadowy room; he put a mask on, looked in a mirror, and turned to face us. Or rather 'It' turned to face us. What we saw was a sort of Balinese pig-god; a strange grey thing that laughed and laughed as if we were infinitely funny and despicable. It freaked us all out. We were appalled and very shaken. The whole thing probably lasted no more than two minutes, but it was timeless. Afterwards George took the mask off; perfectly normal. He had no idea of the effect he'd had on us, and he was a bit glum because he thought the class had been a failure. What he'd told us was not the same as what he'd shown us.

To Keith Johnstone, Devine seemed 'an anarchist who happened to be an English gentleman': which is one way of describing the gap between the mask and the intellect. Mask work begins with a startling regression. The conscious personality is put in abeyance, and in its place there appears a creature straight out of the egg; often ferociously energetic, ruled by primitive appetites and fears, and speechless until it finds its own voice and learns to put words together.

Devine's way of transforming a class of twelve bashful beginners into a wild nursery school was to let them loose on a pile of old clothes, half masks, funny noses, wigs and hats; and leave them alone with a mirror to 'find' a character. Once found, it had to learn how to walk, run, sit, and start relating to the other masks. At this stage the class was a free-for-all. Devine imposed nothing: but he was on hand to offer suggestions or help out those who were hopelessly stuck by teaching them comic tricks. Pratfalls, hiccoughs, trips, belching. Speaking with a cleft palate or whistling through the teeth. How to have your toe stamped on. How to fall over an imaginary carpet. Vocal imitations of bees and banjos. How to move the diaphragm so as to seem overcome by hysterical laughter.

Litz Pisk, the movement teacher, describes the difference between Saint-Denis's and Devine's approach as a contrast between unmasking and masking. As Devine was himself Saint-Denis's pupil, this can be no more than an approximation. But it is true in the sense that Devine recognized the need of immature performers to gain freedom by covering themselves up; and that he was ready to step outside the *commedia* discipline and enlist mechanical techniques from the English music-hall or anywhere else to save them from feeling helplessly exposed. 'He'd give you something to fall back on if you'd no idea yourself,' says Joan Plowright: 'a little armoury to prevent total despair.' Conversely, the best-remembered exercises of Saint-Denis are those that gave students nothing to fall back on. A goat climbing a rocky tor and becoming terrified when it reaches the peak; a trapeze artist scaling a rope ladder and swinging across to land on the other side of the stage: two little pantomimes, played in practice costume on a bare flat platform – both of which allegedly sent shivers up the audience's spine. And there are background stories of Saint-Denis making a student with bronchitis work through the night and give a performance the next morning; or getting a girl to play a statue and stand absolutely motionless for

1 Portrait of an only child

2 George Devine senior

3 Head boy and headmaster: (left) George Devine and
   (centre) Alex Devine

4 On holiday with the Grants

5 The OUDS Mercutio, 1932

6 Sophia Harris, at the time
   of the OUDS *Romeo and Juliet*

7 President of the OUDS:
   Devine and Peggy Ashcroft

twenty minutes with another girl on her back. 'Michel', Yvonne Mitchell says, 'did not admit pain.'

Devine achieved his results by the opposite process of acknowledging pain and turning it to positive use. James Cairncross speaks of his 'kindness to nervous beginners without which I doubt if I would ever have gone on to become an actor at all'. Plowright offers as typical the case of a beautiful ex-ballet dancer at the Vic School for whom the comedy clases were a torture. While the rest of the group were working up a sketch in a dentist's waiting room, she remained miserably on the outside with no ideas or character to contribute, totally closed in on herself. 'Finally George put her into a shapeless old mac and loaded her with parcels. She didn't have to act at all; just walk in, deadly serious, and cope with these parcels. All her despair was focused on doing that hopeless job. Where to put all those parcels down, where to move them when other people came in. That became the central thing in the scene, and it was hysterically funny. Tremendous for her, because it was the first time in her life she'd made anybody laugh.'

The dentist's waiting room was a characteristic setting; other sketches used fair grounds, dog tracks, markets, and always the setting was decided in the same way. Devine would watch the opening free-for-all until the masks began forming relationships, and would then start looking for a structure, either by taking ideas from the group or making his own suggestions. Here were three characters who would go well in a pub; or another three who could be having a day at the races. The trick was to devise a form to contain what the students gave him rather than impose any scheme of his own. This meant, among other things, that the setting was bound to be a public place that gave common ground to a great variety of character types. With that established, a simple plot was worked out and drafted as a scenario, with or without words according to the capacity of the masks. And on that foundation, the sketch was then formally rehearsed for performance.

Usually the performances were grotesque and vulgar, reminiscent of Brueghel in their view of humanity as comic monsters. In place of a central figure, there would be a central incident; and the scene would grow to a peak of noise and movement and then subside. Spectators who disliked them had to admit that they were well shaped. (Miro, with his strong comic shapes and colour contrasts, was another painterly influence.) The vulgarity, though he evidently relished it, was not imposed by Devine. As Yvonne Mitchell explains, 'At that age you don't want to be an ordinary girl, you want to be a dirty old woman; because you're covered. Nearly all our creations were vulgar and old.'

From Devine's point of view, it was a move from complete freedom to the most precise discipline. But anything was acceptable provided it came from the students' own imagination. One of his end-of-training shows was a fairground improvisation combining the comedy and movement classes. It had coconut shies and strongmen, side-shows, tight-rope walkers and jugglers: a mass of activity, all operating to a comic ground-plan involving an acrobat who carried his wife upside down while she played the violin, and a Harlequin figure (Pierre Lefevre) who dived through a window at the climax. In this kind of spectacle, the gymnastic side of *commedia* predominated over the funny noses.

If I seem to be making a lot of these little student shows it is because they played a big part in Devine's working life and later served as a bridge to his professional production. Ex-students who played in his post-war Young Vic shows remember them as an extension of his comedy classes. And post-war spectators who knew nothing of Devine the teacher describe the same scenes of tumultuous vitality created by crowds of minutely defined individuals. The young John Arden saw his 1950 production of Jonson's *Bartholomew Fair* at the Edinburgh Festival, and retained the main impression of 'having actually been at a fair, rather than having seen a play about some fictional people at a fair ... There was the whole of London, shuffling and prowling about on the Assembly Hall open stage – and all of them, in one way or another, absolutely barmy.' On the strength of this, Arden decided that 'If I were to write social comedy, Johnson was the man to follow.'

From this and other accounts, the point emerges that until the early 1950s Devine was regarded by many people as a potentially great comic director; a side of his talent that was subsequently suppressed during the years of his best known work at the Royal Court. To indicate what was lost by this exchange, perhaps the most revealing example comes from the early days of the Vic School, as it shows something of how Devine could theatricalize his experience. During a rehearsal on the Vic stage, one of the students changing the set was accidentally flown with the scenery, then a box of matches ignited in his pocket, and he went spinning up to the flies like the celebrated human torch. (Luckily the matches burnt out before doing him any damage.) During the term of this accident, Litz Pisk remembers having conversations with Devine about the Vienna Opera and its veteran stage hands who – unseen by the public – would do their changes in time to the music with the rhythmic precision of a *corps de ballet*. Devine then pulled these two strands together and produced a little entertainment called *The Quick Change*. Sandwiched between the formal items of a final-year show, this consisted of a scene change carried out in view of the audience.

Amid the applause for a cut version of *All's Well that Ends Well*, the curtain sailed up and got stuck, revealing the stage crew striking the set. Spotting the audience, they disappeared with a warning yell. Frantic off-stage dispute, and back they came to do a double-quick change for *The Clandestine Marriage* to a silent film piano accompaniment. The set then started fighting back. Maladroit stage hands were left clinging to the tops of flats; others got stranded on the stage bars which took off to the fly-tower and then went up and down like yo-yos with the terrified victims doing plank-walking feats *à la* Harold Lloyd. Two of them let go of a flat and then just caught it as it was falling out towards the audience. A clearing stick missed a fouled chandelier and knocked one of the crew off a step-ladder. Someone nailing down a piece of scenery nailed his trousers to the stage, ripping off one leg as he stood up. Enter numerous figures carrying flats over the stage; half way across, a figure walking down-stage vanished into the mobile maze and was fitfully glimpsed desperately signalling through gaps in the passing scenery. Meanwhile a personal feud had developed between the slow-witted flyman and the bossy head carpenter (Derek Godfrey, wearing spats), reaching its climax with the flyman's triumphant shout 'I've fixed the curtain;' whereupon the curtain fell, carrying his enraged adversary up to the flies by his belt.

The whole thing was over in ten minutes, leaving the stage set for the next item. Looking at Devine's scenario, like a slow-motion replay, enables you to see how much detail and structural care went into these bits of fun. To secure the long chain of co-ordinated calamities that made up *The Quick Change*, the action was split into five sections, every one of which bristles with incidental detail. The simplest of them, the opening striking of small properties, incorporates sofa vaults, about-turns with props, running somersaults, entrances over obstacles, trips and falls, rolls carrying a full glass, and 'lion's leaps' over furniture and through the window. 'It was', says Val May, 'the most brilliant piece of farcical business I've seen in many a day.' Years later, when the cares of the Royal Court were descending on him, Devine went along to see Robert Dhéry's masterpiece of organized disaster, *La Plume de ma tante*, and told a friend wistfully, 'I've wanted to do that all my life.'

The Quick Change summed up Devine's comic style. It depended more on skills and routines than on the display of personality; appropriating tricks from silent films and restoring them to the stage where they mingled with elements from the *commedia*, circus and music-hall. Everything was highly systematized, timing above all. There are no disagreements about his mastery in this department. By assiduous observation and practice, he had developed a cast-iron technique for telling funny stories. And the characteristic of his favourite stories, when repeated by other people or written down, is that they fall flat. There is one about a trembling young actor being taken out to dinner by George Grossmith after receiving stern instructions to ask only for hock: another about a Mr Presence-of-Mind Jones, an Oxford don who had the presence of mind to save himself by drowning his undergraduate companion when their punt capsized. With material like that and his armoury of shaggy dog stories, Devine was able to convulse people; likewise with his demonstrations of jug-smashing and the frustrations of trying to eat a tomato that keeps slipping down the fork. All this recalls his father's domestic clowning with threepenny bits and funny hats; the obvious difference being that in Devine's case it was the product of scrupulous analysis and that he taught as well as practised it.

Skills and routines alone do not add up to a style; the element that did define his work stylistically was the insistence on the physical properties of the stage. We are speaking here much more of work with students than of full public productions. But, as far as the school shows go, there is no doubt of his anti-illusionist bias; or, as he put it, a refusal to cheat: not to pretend that the stage is anything other than a stage, or the actors anything other than actors. When a show could incorporate the actual bricks and mortar of the building – as in the scene-setting sketch, or, years later, in Osborne's *The Entertainer* – so much the better. But, in any event, this acknowledgment of the material conditions was not a puritanical denial or ornament; rather it was an assertion of the latent power residing in doorways, traps, the division of the house, and all the basic anatomy of the stage. 'Mere technique is useless,' he told one class. 'There is a mysterious sense called a "sense of theatre" which is vital to the technician. With it, the curtain can be made to act as much as any actor, and lights can be made to talk as eloquently as any poetry ... From the man who works the tabs to the girl who designs the crown for King Lear, each of these people is an artist just as much as the producer or designer.'

With pronouncements of that kind, it is futile to try and separate Devine's viewpoint from the school's general policy. Saint-Denis was concerned at least as much as Devine with abolishing the idea of the stage manager as an unfeeling presser of buttons: and it was Saint-Denis who introduced the key term of 'artist-technician' into the training vocabulary. But however united their theoretical viewpoints, they differed markedly in performance. This was partly a question of their respective roles. Saint-Denis taught the craft of acting, but as the leader of the enterprise it was not his main business to impart particular skills. As a teacher, his domain was the pre-physical, and students who flinched under his devastating criticism also remember him as a great inspirer. Devine's domain was that of technique: he was there to translate Saint-Denis's dreams into fact.

The difference between them was also one of temperament. Saint-Denis's colleagues in the professional theatre who admired him hugely as an artist also remember his failures to work within a budget and get shows ready by the opening date. Devine never ran into that kind of miscalculation. He was good at budgeting and organizing time: so, as at the Motleys', administrative tasks were heaped on him.

At this point in the story – returning to chronological sequence – Devine took on his third role at the L.T.S., adding the duties of stage manager to his tasks as teacher and administrator. The studio did not initially hold lighting classes, but somebody had to light the shows and organize sound effects. Breuer had put in some lights. Devine added to the installation and supplied sound equipment which he paid for by scraping up £600 of his own. It was a far-sighted investment for himself as well as for the studio, as it enabled him to teach himself by experimenting with first-rate equipment. This was before the day of the independent lighting specialist. It was then the practice for stars or directors to light their own shows. Saint-Denis, according to his L.T.S. colleagues, did not even do that, despite the doctrine of the artist-technician. Goring: 'He'd say, "Light this for me; I know nothing about it." Devine completely took that over from him ... I'd say that from 1937 to 1939 there was nobody on the British stage to touch him as a lighter.'

To his students, Devine evidently had two faces; and for those who had first met him as the jovial maestro of the comedy classes, it could be disconcerting to encounter the forbiddingly perfectionist stage manager. But in neither capacity did he impress people, as Saint-Denis did, as an intellectual. His classroom manner was brusque and down-to-earth, never allowing students the dangerous luxury of detached speculation on what they were doing. According to Ustinov, he taught as well as learned through his paws. 'When he was trying to find something funny to do, he was apt to thump you. He'd make gruff noises and suck on his pipe. "How can we work this out?" He'd ruffle your hair or yank your tie down. More pummelling. "Would it be funny if ... ? No ... " But he did try to draw things out of you.' Saint-Denis, by contrast, had no inhibitions about mingling specific criticism with theoretical dicta, assuming a degree of maturity which some of his students did not possess. Their lectures differed in the same way. Where Saint-Denis would deliver sweeping dissertations on theatrical history and the psychology of acting, pinning his argument together with Gallic abstractions, Devine offered blunt information on practical matters, with no fear of banality as long as his meaning was clear. One could go on piling up the contrasts between the two men but they were in agreement about the work they had to do.

The L.T.S. came into existence with the aim of creating an alternative theatre, and in the straight material sense it did not achieve that aim. Why? One unsympathetic view is that it represented an artificial attempt to graft a French tradition on to British stage practice, and for that reason was bound to fail. Another is that this particular tradition was intrinsically self-defeating. Ustinov recalls a conversation with the Belgian playwright Herman Closson who at one time had been attached to the Quinze. 'French generals used to have a saying, "Nous vaincrerons parce que nous sommes les plus forts;" and I said the L.T.S. had put this motto into reverse, "Nous vaincrerons parce que nous sommes les plus faibles." Closson replied, "C'est pire que ça. Nous vaincrerons parce que nous sommes les plus *pauvres*."'

This may be a just comment on Copeau's Burgundian experiment, but it makes less sense when applied to Saint-Denis who did not swallow his uncle's monasticism along with his aesthetics. Their careers were both marked by returns to square one: but where it was Copeau's habit to walk out on any enterprise that threatened to become successful, with Saint-Denis it was more through bad luck that promising stages collapsed under his feet. As far as physical poverty was concerned, the Studio had no choice in the matter. It was poor. To keep it afloat in the beginning Saint-Denis took on a crippling workload of evening lectures and French readings. Devine's salary was £400 a year: Saint-Denis took only £600.

Precarious finances have an obvious bearing on selectivity of intake, though other factors were also involved. Like all drama schools, the L.T.S. was apt to embrace any candidate in trousers, and some of its boys were evidently duds. Less predictably, it also welcomed the kind of student who was least likely to gain admission to the establishment drama schools. 'Michel took one girl because her mother was a washer-up in the East End. He took another boy because his father was down the pits.' He also took in Singhalese, Chinese, Indian, French and Americans. The L.T.S. was ahead of its time in many ways; and one of those ways was that everybody could have a chance.

What does seem to have appealed to Saint-Denis was anything that marked out the applicant as an individual. He enrolled one American girl when she admitted to him that her hair was dyed. Yvonne Mitchell believes she was accepted because – out of sheer ignorance – she spoke her audition piece in an up-stage corner with her back to the house. Likewise the sixteen-year-old Ustinov – faithfully obeying instructions to prepare a page from Shaw's *St Joan* – turned up and played every part on the page including the heroine. Not that Ustinov got in easily in spite of the demand for boys:

> My mother took me to see Saint-Denis, and he said, 'He is too young to come to us; he is not yet formed,' tapping his face. So my mother made an appeal to him. 'You know,' she said, 'he's got eyes very similar to yours.' And he looked at me and said, 'Yes, he has got good eyes; for the theatre.' And then, 'You realize there will be divorce,

there will be scandal, but it *must* be like that!' he said, with a thin trickle of saliva going down the outside of his pipe with sheer excitement. It was really Japanese, all that. He had a Minotaur quality, even to look at.

Saint-Denis, in short, had a great variety of boys and girls wandering through his maze. So long as they were imitating penguins or miming fairground barkers, they knew where they were; but when it came to preparing a Coward scene or a few lines from Herrick, Ariadne's thread was cut. As the cause of regional speech did not figure on the L.T.S. agenda, a great deal of time had to go on drilling standard English into the polyglot student body. This meant employing standard English teachers and however much Saint-Denis might encourage his colleagues to drop in at each others' classes, it was too much to hope that hardened old elocutionists would undergo an instant conversion to the novelties he was trying to inculcate. Movement was another source of conflict. In one class, students would be improvising a group scenario while Suria Magito paced the floor clubbing a dumb-waiter festooned with Balinese gongs; in another, they would be limbering up under a conventional lady gymnast. For a school that set itself the goal of 'organic' training the L.T.S. had a long way to go.

What the L.T.S. stood for before it passed into legend was style: a now unfashionable word which has been turned against Saint-Denis as evidence of his indifference to dramatic content. It is true that his students rarely got the chance to measure themselves against great texts. The exception was Greek tragedy, and even that got in largely on formal grounds. Otherwise it was the modern French repertory and plays like Heywood's *A Woman Killed with Kindness* which he inherited from the Vieux Colombier. The modern British repertory, directed mostly by John Burrell and Oliver Reynolds, was represented by a curious selection of material (St John Hankin, Barker, Clemence Dane) equally remote from the experimental scene and the market place. There remained Devine's Restoration work with Wycherley, Farquhar and Vanbrugh, which enlisted comedy class techniques in the service of classic texts. His contribution, at least, had a connection with the outside world.

However, the choice of material looks rather less eccentric when you remember that reformist directors are apt to avoid plays that are already impregnated with an official style. Also, the Studio was there to create its own group work as well as staging existing texts. Besides Devine's improvised comedies, there were longer scenarios in which various aspects of the training converged in the expression of a given subject. The scenarios were scripted by L.T.S. associates like John Allen and Carl Wildman, and sometimes performed to commissioned music. One of them was taken from the Biblical story of Judith, recreated in the form of a Greek tragedy. Another was a dance drama based on Goya's 'Disasters of the War', with music by Stanley Bate. Preparation for this began with lectures and study of the Goya engravings, from which a six-scene piece was devised, partly through improvisation and partly through Magito's dance work. Mona Swann, one of the voice teachers, supplied the production with an invented, Spanish-sounding language. In terms of acting, it was a characteristic Saint-Denis exercise, requiring the total disappearance of the performer into the part. 'I chose, of course, to be in a madhouse,' says Yvonne Mitchell. 'That was all I did for half an hour. But I was convinced that I was mad, in Spain, at that date. It was a tiny thing, and I thought about it day and night for a term.'

Similarly on the design side, the show grew out of the collective work methods of the Compagnie des Quinze. Sets, costumes and props were made and designed by the students, and the first-year acting students did the sewing – it being a rule of the school that everyone had to act, to sew, and to paint scenery. The designer was Jocelyn Herbert, who was later to become a central figure in Devine's life. She was then a second-year student who had previously studied at André l'Hote's Paris studio and at the Slade School under the ballet designer Vladimir Palunin. Devine had already used her as his designer for the fairground improvisation, with £5 to spend on costumes. She had £10 to spend on the Goya piece: 'I trailed around the Caledonian Market, heavily pregnant, getting bits of lace. The day before the performance I realized I hadn't done anything about the madhouse. I'd watched the actors. One thought he was a king: another was struggling in a cobweb. I'd done the drawings, but I hadn't a clue how you conveyed madness through costume. I had to imagine why each person was mad. One thought she was a nun, and I thought, perhaps her husband's been killed and she's put his coat over her head to make it look like a cowl. That gave me the clue, and I got the costumes made, all very simple. At the costume parade next day, I remember Saint-Denis saying, "Well now, what about the madhouse?" because he suspected it hadn't been done. So when all these people came on he was very much surprised. He said, "Oh yes. Mmn. Not bad." What a relief!'

Episodes of that kind convey the flavour of the L.T.S. Not much praise. Not much money. No egoism. Total absorption in a collective act. A work process in which everyone became an industrious artisan, and everyone had the chance to respect himself as an artist. All that has to be set against the material evidence in weighing up whether or not the Studio achieved its intentions.

The hard facts are that it launched no permanent company of its own and was virtually unknown in the commercial theatre. Not many successful actors came out of the Studio. James Donald, Yvonne Mitchell, Marne Maitland, Noel Willman, James Cairncross and Peter Ustinov are really the ones who made the running; and Ustinov would clearly have done so if he had never set foot in Providence Place. Even if one adds the names of promising graduates who were killed in the war or disappeared into theatrical marriages, the total is still meagre. Yvonne Mitchell says: 'We were absolutely untrained for the theatre of the day. Nobody told us how to get a job. Nobody told us how to write to a rep and enclose a stamped addressed envelope. Nobody told us how to speak in drawing room plays. They developed us as inventors, improvisers, and we had no place.'

Saint-Denis, at least in the 1930s, would not have taken that as a criticism, as he did not view the existing English theatre as a fit place for any serious actor to be. If he was training students for a theatre that did not exist, it was because he meant, with their assistance, to create it. However, in spite of the plans that went into its construction, Breuer's little stage transferred no productions into the West End. The summer shows at Providence Place served to focus the school's energies, and they won admiration inside the profession; but in themselves they were not much of a goal for ambitious students, let alone for the two directors.

The L.T.S. was a tiny, heroic enterprise: it was in key with the mood of a young generation passionately attracted by the group idea, but at the same time it was working against the grain of the theatre as a whole. So, by definition, it was a long-term operation, and it did not have much time. With its precarious finances and its mere four years of life, it had barely long enough to root itself in British soil. The fruit came later: first with the wonderful crop of post-war students from the Vic School, and ultimately with the growth of ensemble companies in the main citadels of the English theatre.

With another two or three years, its own life might have been a more obvious success story. By the end of the 1930s it had developed a considerable impetus and was well on the way to establishing a parent company. The war stopped that, but – as we shall see – it took a lot of stopping.

Meanwhile, on a limited scale, the two directors were continuing outside careers. The limitations were markedly greater in Saint-Denis's case, partly through his total commitment to the studio, and partly because he was cut off by language from acting on the English stage. He began by disappointing his admirers with two inconclusive productions at the Old Vic: *The Witch of Edmonton* (1936), which Agate dismissed as 'a mixture of *Dr Faustus* and *Puss in Boots*'; and, more important, *Macbeth* (1937), the first postponed opening in the Vic's history. 'Everyone including me', says Olivier, who played Macbeth, 'thought that was really what killed Lilian Baylis.'

Over the same period, Devine resumed his connection with Gielgud and played in two productions of the 1937 season at the Queen's Theatre. In both, it was a return to the small parts of his Old Vic apprenticeship. He played Moses again in a slapdash production of *The School for Scandal* by Guthrie. Previously there was Gielgud's own production of *Richard II* in which Devine played the Gardener, incurring Agate's wrath for planting the bank of rue on a spot where the infant Duke of York was most likely to trip over it. Outside the L.T.S., 1937 was a fallow year for both its directors. However, 1938 was a different story.

While *The School for Scandal* was grinding through the last weeks of December the company's morale began picking up. They were rehearsing *Three Sisters*, a play Gielgud had longed to present ever since Komisarjevsky's Chekhov productions at Barnes. With characteristic unselfishness, he offered the production to Saint-Denis. In spite of his uneasy experience in *Noah* and although there was no obvious part for him, he felt that the play was right for his company and that Saint-Denis was right for the play. For Saint-Denis, this was a superb and unrepeatable opportunity. Uniquely in Britain at that time, it combined a star ensemble and ample rehearsal time (eight weeks, which was double the West End average) with the backing of a wealthy commercial management. Even in the heyday of the Quinze he had never had that set of advantages.

As with *Noah*, he prepared everything in advance, and when he finally began rehearsing the company, it was with every move written down. During *The School for Scandal*, Gielgud says, 'We were very miserable, having started with a certain *élan* in *Richard II*. Then Saint-Denis came with these sheets of paper, absolutely laid out. We had plenty of time and it all seemed to go like clockwork. Every week we said, "Isn't this wonderful, it's going to be splendid." And it was.'

Accounts of this famous production lay stress on its combination of exquisite visual composition with the sense of spontaneous life. Somehow what Saint-Denis imposed in rehearsal became nature in performance. Gielgud ascribes this to the fact that he already had a harmonious company. For the Queen's season he had reassembled the family – Ashcroft, Glen Byam Shaw, Quartermaine, Lloyd; they had played together often enough to develop the mutual sympathy of a permanent troupe who, for the first time, found themselves working with the security of 32-week contracts under Gielgud's personal management. Even so, there were initial discords with Gwen Ffrangcon-Davies, and it was Saint-Denis who coaxed her into accepting the role of Olga. For himself, Gielgud had settled on the part of Andrey, the sisters' brother. Saint-Denis cast him as Vershinin. Gielgud then offered Andrey to Michael Redgrave. Saint-Denis, who had an indifferent opinion of Redgrave after *The Witch of Edmonton*, cast him as the Baron instead, and gave the role of Andrey to Devine. So, whatever the company's family feeeling, the chemistry of their performance clearly derived also from Saint-Denis's blend of autocratic control and hypnotic charm.

Saint-Denis later described the production as 'my first experience of realism', by which he meant the realism of Stanislavsky. There were some English actors who doubted his competence to pick up the Stanislavskian torch from Komisarjevsky. Saint-Denis, however, had known and loved that style since the Moscow Art Theatre's 1922 Paris season. In *The Cherry Orchard* he had been caught up in the wild applause that greeted such wordless pieces of acting as Anya's return to the nursery, crouched on a sofa and 'caught up by a fit of that high-pitched laughter which is induced by a combination of tiredness and emotion'; and it was specific moments such as this which he subsequently passed on to his British casts. For Alec Guinness, the penny dropped when Saint-Denis was rehearsing another actor as Epihodov and held up the scene until the character was really listening to his squeaky boots. 'It was very funny and very moving; and it altered my whole attitude to acting, which until then had been would-be romantic ... ' 'Lots of people flowered in *Three Sisters*. So many people seemed to have capacities one hadn't previously credited them with. Devine had certainly got more to him than we thought. It was like going to some delightful and sad party: we couldn't wait to get back to the place every night.'

Ashcroft counts Andrey among the three best performances Devine ever gave (the others being Tesman in *Hedda Gabler* and Dorn in *The Seagull*). In it, she says, he used his whole personality; and one can believe this from the production photographs which transmit a powerful idea of who Andrey was and how he changes during the play. Act One shows him among the trim officers as an overweight figure in a baggy suit, partnering the Baron in a clownish dance while the rest of the company look on, laughing. At the end of the party scene, his embrace with Natasha is another focus for pointing fingers. As Angela Baddeley leaps up at him, making straight for her target, his arms go clumsily round her waist while he slumps into a half-sitting position with his bottom resting on the door-post. The contrast of the two figures already predicts how their marriage will work out. A pair of 'before and after' portraits vividly register the character's transformation. The first presents a moonfaced innocent, with the Prozorov gleam of hope in the eye. In the second, the gleam is extinguished and the still-youthful face stares out desolately like that of a life-sentence prisoner.

To some degree, his Andrey must have been autobiographical if only because of its reflection of his off-stage life with the Motleys. Like Andrey, Devine lived on fraternal terms with three girls who attracted the most brilliant local society under their roof; and in whose presence, when he first moved in, he had reason to feel a hanger-on. In a way, that *ménage* is like the story of *Three Sisters* gone right; for, unlike the Prozorovs, Devine and the Motleys did make it in the capital and did achieve their salvation through work.

The production also brought them together in a notable collaboration over sets and lighting. Motley regularly got their full due of attention from reviewers; but this time they shared it with Devine. Before commenting on his 'growing and deepening' performance of Andrey, *The Times* listed his 'control of lighting, particularly in the garden scene ... among the production's chief assets'. It was equally singled out by Ivor Brown in the *Observer*; and by Agate who wrote that Devine's 'imaginative lighting has given another part of the stage the indeterminate look of a Vuillard, while the right-hand window of the house in the last Act is like a bit of unusually gay Utrillo'. Margaret Harris says that he 'took immense trouble with exact colour; distinguishing between candle-light, lamp light, sunlight, misty light, and fire'. Perhaps these effects would not look so startling today; but good atmospheric lighting was a great rarity on the pre-war British stage.

The impact of *Three Sisters*, of course, was not due to any single factor, but to a combination of elements in which everything from the rages of Natasha to the slightly incorrect cut of the Baron's uniform contributed to the life of the play. 'Dear God,' wrote Agate, 'the very furniture seems to breathe!' As such, the main honours went to Saint-Denis who was at last accorded the maestro status which had eluded him since the dissolution of the Quinze. The production was the hit of the Queen's season: the most expensive of the four shows (it cost £2,200), it also made the most money. From this example it seemed that a crack troupe, working for prolonged rehearsal periods under a master director, could achieve financial as well as artistic success in the West End. Saint-Denis found himself in the unaccustomed role of a hot property, and in partnership with Albery he leased the Phoenix Theatre for an autumn season of his own, designed partly to continue his work with Gielgud's actors and partly to lay the foundations of an L.T.S. company.

In April the Queen's company embarked on their last lap with Gielgud's *Merchant of Venice*. Gielgud was also playing Shylock and the accumulated strain of the past six months was beginning to tell. Devine, adding another clown to his collection, went into the show as Lancelot Gobbo ('the best of Gobbos' according to Ivor Brown), and there are stories of the weary director standing at the back of the pit shouting 'For God's sake, make me laugh!' He was clearly going to wave goodbye again, leaving the family to look for a new home.

This was Saint-Denis's opportunity. He laid plans for a brilliant permanent company supplemented by the most promising Studio graduates, and announced an ambitious programme consisting provisionally of *The Cherry Orchard*, *Uncle Vanya*, *The Wild Duck*, *Twelfth Night*, and *Le Bourgeois Gentilhomme*. Building on what Gielgud had started, it seemed that Saint-Denis might at last be founding an English Vieux Colombier.

There are several explanations for the collapse of this enterprise, the simplest (advanced by the Albery family) being that Saint-Denis overspent his budget and the money ran out. But if Saint-Denis under-estimated the economic obstacles to establishing an art theatre in the West End, he also over-estimated the dedication of leading actors to that cause; and when the season opened in October it was with a much depleted company. Also, in the generally precarious times, his situation was particularly uncertain as a reserve officer in the French army liable to be called up at five days' notice.

Finally, if Saint-Denis was aiming to rescale the ivory tower of the Vieux Colombier he chose an odd way of doing it by opening the Phoenix season with Bulgakov's *The White Guard*, a Soviet piece dealing sympathetically with Tsarist Russia and reflecting the immediate turmoils of the Spanish Civil War.'The choice of this play was not accidental,' says Basil Langton who appeared in it. What was accidental was the fact that it opened exactly a week after the Munich Agreement. Reviewers welcomed it, but the public did not, and the production was soon withdrawn. As Agate remarked, 'Let a foreign producer attempt a new and strange work, and the critics eager to get in are trampled underfoot by a public anxious to get out.'

However, before it closed, it gave Devine another chance (like the Caliph in *Hassan*) to set gentlemanly British acting aside. Others in the company also tried to seize this chance but, as Agate wrote:

you may travel a long way from St Pancras without getting to St Petersburg! ... In the middle of all this entered Mr George Devine, whereupon the pretence that anybody else was Russian completely vanished. For this ingenious actor made us realize that, to a Russian, pouring out vodka into tumblers, mustard into a footbath, and his blood for his country are equally important manifestations of the poetic spirit. Also, he looked Russian.

The season was also to have included the British première of Giraudoux's *La Guerre de Troie n'aura pas lieu*, that stoically

neo-classic forecast of the coming German war. If it had come
off it would have stood as a terminal counterpart to the Saint-
Denis of *Bataille de la Marne*. It did not come off. *The White
Guard* was followed by *Twelfth Night* which was originally to
have featured Olivier, Ralph Richardson, Edith Evans and
Marius Goring. Olivier then departed for Hollywood to play in
Wuthering Heights, and the others also dispersed until, of the
originally proposed leads, only Ashcroft and Redgrave were left.
Efforts to find a replacement for Richardson's Sir Toby went on
until the last minute, but in vain, and the part finally went to
Devine who, Redgrave says, 'was not funny. His strength did
not lie in playing nobleness, and he didn't present Sir Toby as a
gentleman, which he should be. To use a word that critics like,
his performance was *voulu*. I don't think he was happy about it.'

The play was one which Saint-Denis knew from the French as
well as the British stage. As Copeau's *La Nuit des rois* it was a
great pre-1914 hit. This should have helped. But once again,
Saint-Denis was unlucky with the Elizabethans. Perhaps over-
familiarity with it addled the egg. Most uncharacteristically, he
told Redgrave at the very first reading that he had mastered the
role of Aguecheek; and then went on to 'ask me to do things I
knew Jouvet had done in the part'.

The production opened in December, and from their separate
standpoints, Gielgud, Bronson Albery and Ashcroft (who played
Viola) were all disappointed in it. They had expected something
extraordinary, and found something rather commonplace, under-
cast and over-decorated. Redgrave's assertive Aguecheek became
the play's comic centre: Devine's Sir Toby was dismissed by
Agate among a string of performances registering zero on his
critical thermometer. Ivor Brown roundly declared that Redgrave
acted Devine off the stage. Again, the show was soon withdrawn.

Saint-Denis had now failed with a good new play and with the
second most popular play of Shakespeare. A blight had descended
on the season. It was playing to half-empty houses, and it would
have been suicide to embark on a third production. Acknowledging defeat, Albery and his director withdrew from the Phoenix
and the company broke up without having found an audience.
It was a bitter decision. More had been at stake than a speculative
venture. The season had been intended to lay the basis for something permanent amid the perishable commodities of the West
End. It stood for the reforms in acting, repertory and mise-en-

8 The London Theatre Studio: Michel Saint-Denis and Devine

9 *The White Guard*, 1938: (left to right) Peggy Ashcroft,
Glen Byam Shaw, Michael Redgrave, Stephen Haggard, Basil
Langton; (extreme right) Devine as Viktor Myschlajevsky

10 *The Seagull*, 1936: (left to right, seated, front row) Martita Hunt,
Peggy Ashcroft; (second row) John Gielgud, Edith Evans, Frederick
Lloyd; (standing, centre) Stephen Haggard, George Devine as
Shamraev

11 *The Seagull*, 1964: (left to right, seated, front row) Ann Beach,
Vanessa Redgrave; (second row) Peter Finch, Peggy Ashcroft,
Paul Rogers; (third row) Philip Locke, Peter McEnery, Mark
Dignam, Rachel Kempson; (top) Devine as Dorn

scène of which so many of the brilliant generation of the 1950s felt deprived. It was the meeting point between the two main groups that had been moving in that direction; it offered the possibility of a home for Gielgud's actors, and it launched the second phase of the L.T.S. plan. It was the apex towards which all Saint-Denis's work in Britain had been leading. A lot of hope had been invested in it; and when it came, it foundered with a few weeks.

It was now 1939, and questions of long-term theatrical reform began to be overshadowed by other matters. The L.T.S. was still ticking over, but neither of its directors had any other coherent project to pursue. Some of the family (including Martita Hunt) regrouped under Saint-Denis for a Stage Society production of Lorca's *Blood Wedding*. In May, Devine joined forces with Glen Byam Shaw in a panoramic piece by the Welsh miner-author Jack Jones, called *Rhondda Roundabout*, staged by H. M. Tennent Ltd at the Globe. Devine lit the production and played a soap-box orator called Dai Hippo. The reviews went to gallant lengths in the show's defence, but there was no concealing the fact that this Welsh *Magnolia Street* was not West End material.

Tennents then made the obvious move of setting up a production of *The Cherry Orchard* with the aim of repeating their success with *Three Sisters*, and reassembling the same team: the Gielgud circle, Saint-Denis, and Motley. In the midst of the rehearsals, war was declared and the production was cancelled. 'I can see us now,' says Langton, 'sitting on the Queen's Theatre stage listening to a tiny radio that some stage-hand had brought in for the Chamberlain declaration. All the "stars" on stage: Michel, Hugh Beaumont, and Bronson Albery in the pit; and Gielgud suddenly there to listen out of nowhere. We retired to a restaurant to give Michel a farewell lunch before he marched off to the war. Gielgud joined us but left the table early; as he crossed the floor he turned to Saint-Denis and said, "Bonne chance". I thought this a very chic thing to say to a soldier; like a line from a well-made play. It was the end; it was the break-up of the family.'

Saint-Denis departed instantly for France; and the L.T.S., despite objections from some of its backers, was wound up and its assets sold off. But during the period of the phoney war there was a last attempt to hold the remnants of the family together. In his farewells, Saint-Denis had urged them to keep something going so that there would be some threads to pick up when the war was over.

Meeting after the collapse of *The Cherry Orchard*, Devine and Marius Goring resolved to open a theatre somewhere or other in whatever time they had left. They had both volunteered after Munich, Devine for Field Security and Goring for Intelligence; but as both had been turned down and told to wait for the routine call-up they still had a few months to carry out Saint-Denis's instructions. Goring then took up a BBC engagement to play Hitler in the three-month series, *The Shadow of the Swastika*, so it was left to Devine to get things moving. He found another ally in Michael Redgrave, and together they contacted everyone who had worked with Saint-Denis and set about drawing up a list of plays that might keep the family intact as a repertoire company. Redgrave then buoyantly presented the plan to his agent, and 'I shall never forget the awful disappointment: he clearly thought we hadn't a hope in hell.' Instead, he pounced on the first play on the list, Benn Levy's *Springtime for Henry*, and suggested taking it on tour. Redgrave, who had bills to pay, succumbed to this idea and faded out of the picture.

Devine still had other resolute allies, and with them he succeeded in forming a company with Alec Guinness, Martita Hunt and Vera Lindsay as his co-directors. This was the Actors' Company, a posthumous offshoot of the L.T.S., designed to preserve an oasis of intelligence in the desert of wartime entertainment. They also had tentative plans for productions of Molière and Shakespeare; but the immediate project was to stage Guinness's adaptation of *Great Expectations*.

Their collective morale was strong, as it needed to be at that moment of panic shut-downs and mass evacuation; added to which the company were penniless. Needing £700 to get started, their resources amounted to a £10 donation from the John Lewis Partnership. A deputation set out for Streatham to seek the advice of Edith Evans, and met her in her dressing room during a matinée of *The Importance of Being Earnest*. A fur coat was hanging over one of the chairs. They outlined the problem and then waited through a Lady Bracknell-like pause which Evans finally broke by turning to her dresser and asking, 'Where's my coat?' The dresser pointed to it. 'How much did I pay for it?' '£700,' said the dresser. 'I can't let actors be out of work when I spend £700 on a fur coat,' said Evans, and wrote them a cheque for the full amount.

Armed with this, the Actors' Company prepared to go into production at the Rudolf Steiner Hall, near Regent's Park. The choice of this obscure address in the Sherlock Holmes hinterland was another sign of the times. From the end of August, theatres in Central London had gone dark, and it was only possible to get a licence to perform at the Rudolf Steiner Hall because it lay outside the West End. It was not strictly a theatre at all; but, disguised as such for the première of *Great Expectations*, it ranks as one of the first to reopen in the winter of 1939.

The occasion also marked Devine's début as a professional director. This was a logical step. He was Saint-Denis's right-hand man, and had directed consistently at the L.T.S. As an actor, he had a reputation for giving the kind of explanatory reading known in the trade as 'a director's performance'. His own acting career made up only a small part of his interest in the theatre, and if there were any existing pigeon-hole for such an unclassifiable man it was in directing.

The Rudolf Steiner stage was small and ill-equipped. The play was elaborate; and besides its many scene changes, it required an area permanently reserved for narration. The battle with these physical obstacles put the group's comradeship to the test, and a rift developed between the author and his fellow directors. According to Guinness, this reached a climax with the discovery that there had been a mistake in the measurements for the set; whereupon he says he stormed at his colleagues as amateurs and resigned his directorship. Even so, *Great Expectations* went ahead with Guinness still in the cast, and opened on December 7.

No longer quite the same harmonious group they had been to begin with, the Actors' Company battled through to present a show that was received with delight. Its qualities can be partly guessed from the immensely successful 1947 film version which preserved some of the original casting (notably Guinness's Herbert Pockett and Martita Hunt's Miss Haversham), and the combination of uncluttered story-telling and copious Dickensian vigour which struck reviewers of Devine's production.

How much Devine contributed to it is impossible to disentangle, as he was working with a group of equals who threw in ideas of their own rather than submitting to directorial omniscience. It was Devine who cast Martita Hunt in the best-remembered role of her career (originally Edith Evans was to have played Miss Haversham). He also lit the show, and undertook the physical adaptation of the hall. The shape of the piece, with character narrators moving in and out of the action, was reminiscent of Obey, and Devine exploited this by means of a plan which changed the stage picture as though by the shakes of a kaleidoscope. The company, containing the highest proportion so far of ex-L.T.S. students, were a stimulus to his comic invention, and according to Goring the finished show worthily reflected the Quinze tradition. Reviewers admired the fluency it achieved on a tiny stage, and its modest attachment to story and character. *The Times* welcomed it as 'a remarkably successful attempt to achieve something that can never be achieved fully ... The Actors' Company will not fail for want of good acting and intelligent production.' Agate, who had lately been sniping at the Motleys for what he regarded as their fancy-dress ball style, was no less pleased:

> With Mr George Devine producing by the simple device of dropping a curtain when we were not intended to see and pulling it up again when we were, and Motley contenting themselves with the period and no fantastications, the stage was left to the players ... who proceeded to put the characters of this great novel on to the stage almost without exception as the mind's eye sees them in reading.

Great Expectations was a lucky show, in the sense that it ultimately led to something good for almost everyone in the cast. But it did not make the money to finance another production; and although the Actors' Company was not formally disbanded, it was put on ice from which it never thawed out. Its one immediate effect was to launch Devine as a free-lance director, and he enjoyed a busy period in this new role before disappearing into the war. First came a copper-bottomed West End hit in the shape of Daphne du Maurier's adaptation of *Rebecca* at the Queen's Theatre. Originally Glen Byam Shaw was to have directed this for Tennents: but, as a member of the Officers' Emergency Reserve, he resigned from the production and Devine took it over. Starring the urbane Owen Nares as the ominous master of Manderley and Celia Johnson as his panic-stricken spouse, this opened with marked *éclat* at the beginning of April. 'Brilliant directing by George Devine,' said Agate, scattering compliments like confetti. Nobody in *Rebecca* belonged to the family. They were a solid, number-one West End company appearing in a popular, middle-brow entertainment. With these actors there could be no question of a group-production safety net, and by delivering the goods in a fully commercial sense Devine proved himself as an independent director whom henceforth nobody could plausibly dismiss as a side-kick of Michel Saint-Denis.

There followed an invitation to direct at the Old Vic. This came from Guthrie, who was sympathetic towards the Actors' Company and impulsively engaged Devine and Marius Goring to co-direct Gielgud in *The Tempest* as a means of holding some of the group together until they could set up another project of their own. Rehearsals began in gloom during a particularly low ebb of the war; the show's opening coincided with Dunkirk and it closed on the day the French government capitulated. Also, Devine and Goring had to follow in the wake of Granville-Barker who had just staged one of his Olympian descents to direct Gielgud in the season's opening production of *King Lear*. After working for a revered master, Gielgud was now being directed by two of his own protégés. In this unenviable situation, they applied to Barker for advice on *The Tempest*, only to be told that it was not a play on which he had anything to offer.

In their favour they had a good company packed with old friends. With Devine out front and Goring on stage as Ariel, they held joint rehearsals in which co-direction consisted largely of clarifying each others statements. They were of one mind about the play, aiming to resist the then-fashionable masque approach and to restore Prospero from the frail old wizard of stage tradition to a vigorous middle-aged Duke with plenty to lose or gain in the real world. They were also in agreement about the importance of music, and insisted on what, in the circumstances, was the extraordinary luxury of eleven instrumentalists. The plan was to use music that was classical but not recognizable. This was selected and orchestrated for them by Berthold Goldschmidt, whom Goring knew from his work at the Berlin Staatstheater and whom Devine met as a Belsize Park refugee under threat of internment. Devine, Goldschmidt says, 'was not a musician at all, but he'd got understanding and knew what was right. Once he trusted somebody to do a job he gave that person *plein pouvoir*.'

Aiming at something at once familiar and strange, Goldschmidt made arrangements from Bach, Handel and Mozart which Devine had played under the stage with the players coming in on light cues. He also used optional amplification, so that at some moments the isle could be full of sweet sounds, and at others the auditorium could be flooded with musical tumult. The opening scene presented a ship based on a medieval painting which also pitched the characters about in the storm, while out front Goldschmidt's orchestration of Mozart's C minor Piano Fantasy was coming at the audience from all directions over loudspeakers. This kind of environmental treatment was ahead of its time, and when it reached the public there were those (like Harcourt Williams) who felt that poetry was being displaced by stage management.

Side by side with *The Tempest*, another drama, involving the future of the Old Vic, was unfolding off stage. It struck the two directors that there, assembled under the roof of the Vic, was the finest ensemble in Britain: they had worked together in *Lear* and *The Tempest* and they were still available. Why need they disband at all? Perhaps this was the chance to realize the dream of a permanent company and transform the Old Vic into Britain's National Theatre. The plan was to reconstitute the Vic ensemble as a National company, still under Guthrie's direction, and with the added funding appropriate to a State organization. With Guthrie's approval, approaches were made to Maynard Keynes and to C.E.M.A.: and there seemed a strong likelihood that the venture would get government recognition. The dream of a National Theatre was entering the sphere of reality, and the Vic directors hatched an immediate plan to celebrate its birth by taking *Lear* and *The Tempest* over to Paris.

In the midst of these developments came the collapse of France and the Italian declaration of war. And Guthrie, as impulsively as he had offered his stage to Goring and Devine, now decided to close it down. So, instead of gaining a National Theatre, London lost the Old Vic for the duration; and when the bomb fell on it a month later, it fell on an empty building.

The rise and fall of the National scheme took place within the three-and-a-half week run of *The Tempest*, and reflected directly on the production. The opening was not received with any great enthusiasm, and Gielgud felt it to be a come-down after *Lear*.

I remember thinking Devine not very helpful because I felt he was too much under my control. He'd been under me for so long that he couldn't treat me as if he hadn't known me before. I suppose he respected me for having started him in everything. He felt a bit embarrassed to direct me.

With the deteriorating war situation and news of the Vic's impending closure, a change overtook the show. Guthrie and his two directors were innocent of any topical premeditation in their choice and treatment of the play; and yet, through force of circumstances, it came exactly to express the feelings of the time. The production took on the atmosphere of a long goodbye; and on the last night, before the Vic went into its seven years of darkness, Prospero's dismissal of Ariel said it all: 'to the elements/ Be free, and fare thou well.'

In June, when *The Tempest* closed, Devine followed up *Rebecca* with the equally smart engagement of directing Edith Evans in Shaw's *The Millionairess*: but this show expired on tour before reaching the West End. So, as far as London was concerned, he went down with the Vic, which was a fitting place for the pre-war history of the family to come to an end. Its members now dispersed. Goring was in uniform by the end of the month. Vera Lindsay went into *Radio Newsreel*. Suria Magito settled down stoically to spend the war firewatching in a blanket and running the Glyndebourne Children's Theatre from Toynbee Hall. Two of the Motleys were already in America: having volunteered for camouflage work and been obtusely turned down, Margaret Harris and Elizabeth Montgomery sailed for New York to design *Romeo and Juliet* for Olivier. Once there, sickness, marriage and work detained them until after the war. Empty, like the Vic, their studio was also blitzed.

Ironically, the military disasters that accelerated the break-up had brought Saint-Denis himself back to England. On posting as an Infanterie Coloniale liaison officer to a British unit in France, he was swept up in the Dunkirk evacuation and finally landed at Weymouth. He even arrived in time for the *Tempest* rehearsals. ('Tell that German soldier to clear off the stage,' called Devine, not recognizing who it was.) But there was no question of his resuming theatre work until the war was over. He immediately accepted an appointment as Head of the BBC's French Section and, under the pseudonym of Jacques Duchesne, launched the resistance programme *Les Français parlent aux français*, which put out daily news and features to occupied Europe until D-Day.

Devine passed the last months of 1940 in waiting for his call-up. Shortly after Goring's marriage to Lucie Mannheim, he married Sophia Harris and moved to a flat in Mecklenburgh Square where the couple had their first spell of private domesticity. Elizabeth Montgomery and Margaret Harris were the only witnesses: then they departed for New York. In November Devine's papers arrived and he joined up as a Private in the Royal Regiment of Artillery. A bomb went through the Mecklenburgh Square flat. Sophie was alone, over forty, and pregnant with her first child. She went down to stay with the Albery family at their country house in Hertfordshire. To Lady Albery she seemed 'the most pessimistic person I've ever met'.

5

THE WAR

AFTER ten years of total immersion in the theatre, Devine spent most of the next five with an outfit known as the Nine-Mile Sharp-Shooters on whom conversation about English stage reform would have fallen flat. Temporary officers were not particularly welcome, let alone artist chappies. 'I'll be glad when this war's over,' one major was overheard to say; 'then we can get down to some real soldiering.'

As for countless other conscripts, the main feature of Devine's wartime career was its irrelevance. Other members of his circle achieved a measure of professional continuity: Goring supervising BBC broadcasts to Germany, Jack Hawkins running ENSA shows in India. But Devine simply vanished into a corner of South East Asia and did his bit as a Gunner Captain. It was an experience that brought him in contact with the 95 per cent of the British population who never go to the theatre.

Despite his hatred of the Army, Devine was recognized to be an extremely efficient soldier. On active service, he held the rank of adjutant, which meant running an office in the middle of a battle with a bearish C.O. breathing down his neck. He found his level in war, as in peace, in the sphere of administration. And converts to the 'character is destiny' theory may view the ogreish Colonel R. A. H. Soames, R.A., as Saint-Denis's successor in Devine's collection of masters.

He joined up at the Artillery Barracks, Shoeburyness, on November 14, 1940, as part of a mixed intake including a miner who wanted to escape the pits and a nineteen-year-old Mosleyite who wanted to join the Finns in defending the Karelian peninsula against the Russians. Thence, in March 1941 to a holding unit in Watford which ran a potential-officer training course.

On leave in June, he had a reunion with Glen Byam Shaw and poured out his observations on the life of His Majesty's under-dogs. 'He told one story about being issued with new spectacles to wear with a gas mask. There was a doctor slipping a lens in and saying "Better or worse?" and the chap next to George was a poor sad character who could hardly make himself coherent. The medico would roar, "That better or worse?" "Better, sir." "Better? What the hell do you mean? It can't be better." "Oh, sorry, sir; worse." "Oh. Well, try again. Now then. Better, or worse?" "Worse, sir." "You damned fool, it can't be worse. It must be better now!" In the end the chap was given a pair of glasses he couldn't see anything with at all. George told me this story, and the tears used to splash out of our eyes.' In autumn, he passed under the castellated gables of Alton Towers, a Pugin folly on the edge of the Potteries, as an officer cadet. Here he made one firm friendship with a Cambridge cadet, Graham Bell, which lasted through the war: and ran a Christmas concert party in which he mimed an elaborate toilette in silk dressing-gown at the head of a mutinous queue in the ablutions, and came on to sing 'Trees' as a Wagnerian soprano in horned helmet and breast-plate. Commissioned early in 1942, he and Graham Bell were posted in March to the First Medium Regiment, R.A., at Witton le Wear, Durham, where he struck up another friend-ship with one of the subalterns, Michael Chater. The rest of this chapter is drawn mainly from the memories of these two men.

At the end of May the regiment sailed for India, aboard an old P & O liner with officers travelling first class enjoying six-course dinners and tea in bed, while the other ranks dossed down in hammocks below decks. Devine shared a cabin with Chater and they broke up the luxurious monotony by staging a troop show including a renewed assault on 'Trees'. At the same time, bad news was on the way about Sophie, now living with Peter Bayne's family in Kingston-on-Thames, and enduring a trau-matic pregnancy. In the event she suffered a nervous breakdown after the birth of her daughter, Harriet, and went into a nursing home, leaving the baby in Kingston in the care of a nurse.

Devine had plenty of time to brood about these and other non-military affairs after the regiment's arrival in India in July. From Bangalore they moved on to a camp at Kolar Goldfield in Mysore where they remained stationed for a year and a half awaiting a Japanese invasion that never came. In preparation for this non-event, there were exercises in amphibious warfare: otherwise it was a matter of vegetating in the camp, beset by monsoon floods and the all-devouring kite-hawks, or savouring the pleasures of the nearby Kolar Goldfield Club with its bars, swimming pool and three dances a week.

If Kolar Goldfield was a cushy number, it soon bred a sense of deadly routine, and when gin-and-tonic hour descended on the bamboo walls of the mess, bringing the choice of another evening's cards or passing out on the coconut matting, Devine found his old mask of the buffoon wearing thin. He would disappear into his tent and read Shakespeare. He would subside into days of uncommunicative, surly depression, leaving his fellow officers in no doubt that he would have preferred other company. He was feared for his sharp tongue, and he showed no awe for superior rank. Bell remembers one stage-struck Brigadier asking, half in fun, if Devine could get him a job after the war. '"You come and see me," George said heartily, "and I can fix you up with a very good job," adding out of the corner of his mouth, "Make a splendid commissionaire in front of the theatre."'

Direct evidence of what he was thinking at the time comes in a battered diary consisting mainly of reflections on the theatre he had left behind. The entries begin in September 1943 with a sour note likening Noël Coward to a well-paid chorus girl. Magnitude, as appears from his notes on the epic and on William Morris's translation of *The Iliad*, was Devine's chief preoccupation just then: he wanted something to blow the roof off a theatre where nothing too big or too truthful was ever allowed to happen. '*The Iliad*', he concludes, 'could certainly not be presented on a West End stage unless it were larded with tasteful production by John Gielgud or Giraudouxized into an intellectual treat.'

After this, the entries break off until the following year, by which time Devine was on active service in Burma. His regiment pulled out of Kolar Goldfield in January 1944 as part of a general movement to halt a Japanese invasion of the Arakan peninsula. The campaign began with a trans-India journey from Mysore up to the Burmese border where the regiment first went into action in February. In May, the Japanese broke the road between the hill towns on Kohima and Imphal, and the British counter-attack was a last stand against an invasion of the plains of India. The fighting reached its turning point in September when the

Japanese, with their supply-lines over-extended, turned south to be pursued across the Irrawaddy, through the oil fields of North Burma, and down to Rangoon where the campaign ended in the following July.

For the British, whose casualties were light, there was less danger than discomfort. Much of the advance took place in the monsoon: a three-month downpour in an area with the highest rainfall in the world. If clothes and bedding got wet they stayed wet. As mud often stopped lorries getting through to the gun positions, the 100lb. shells had to be carried to them by hand. It was extremely cold in the mountainous Arakan where supplies were parachuted in through the clouds. Part of the route lay through the Kabaw Valley, a heavy malarious jungle supposedly completely untenable for European troops. Fatal diseases were held at bay with daily doses of Mecaprin, which turned the complexion bright yellow, but the slightest bite or scratch would quickly spread into an ugly festering sore. Sometimes, on the descent into the Kabaw, the monsoon would clear and reveal forests of mahogany stretching to the horizon. Also on the descent, the metalled road gave out and the guns were dragged along improvised tracks of chicken wire laid through the elephant grass. Meeting the Chindwin River, the British ferried their guns across and built a 600-yard boat bridge for the rest of the convoy. And it was here they began finding civilian cars with skeletons at the wheel: memorials of the British retreat from Burma.

With two spells of leave in the Himalayas, Devine went through the campaign from Imphal to Rangoon. On his first night in action, he and Bell were camping in a dried-up river bed when they noticed a huge spider crawling in their direction. They debated whether to shoot it, and decided not to risk the noise: which was lucky as the Japanese chose that night to come down the next valley and blow up two of the guns. Shortly after this incident, the regiment's colonel was succeeded by his second-in-command, the baleful figure of R. A. H. Soames, an extremely tough regular who took command after being kept too long as a subordinate, and who made friends with nobody.

More than the fighting and the pestilential climate, the relationship with Colonel Soames ranks as Devine's main wartime ordeal. As adjutant, Devine had to live in Soames's shadow: travelling, eating, and operating the command post with him.

In the command post, a unit of four packed into the back of a small truck, which was completely shut in at night. Here, in the itchy heat and tobacco smoke, Devine administered the fire-programmes, ammunition control, casualty contingencies and the rest of the elaborately timed combat schedule under the eye of his brooding superior, whose form of leadership Bell describes as 'kick people in the teeth as a means of showing them how insignificant they were.'

Soames respected Devine enough to have him twice mentioned in dispatches; but he was allegedly incapable of making ordinary human contact without the help of several gins. Along the road from the Chindwin to Mandalay, when the worst of the privations were over, the relationship boiled up into a crisis and Devine put in for a posting. Instead, Soames sent him on leave, from which he came back and stuck it out to the end. He remained Soames's adjutant in Rangoon. He was repatriated with Soames in September, and he shared a carriage with Soames on the Liverpool to London train. On arrival, Soames put out his hand. 'Well, goodbye, Devine,' he said: 'you didn't do a bad job,' and disappeared into the crowd.

However much Devine detested the Army, when he was working he could reduce warfare to problems of stage management. Off duty, he could not keep up the show of comradeship for very long. He lacked the herd instinct: and he was always the first to drop out of a drinking party and go off to read Sterne or Tolstoy; or to knit.

He sometimes discussed theatre with Bell and Chater, saying that he planned to pick up the threads as an actor before trying to launch any venture of his own, and insisting on the need to find writers capable of attracting more than the theatre's 5 per cent of the population. During the wait for repatriation he gave a solo reading of the whole of *Romeo and Juliet* for a troop audience and rounded up some helpers to convert a Rangoon factory into a theatre for ENSA shows.

Meanwhile, he had resumed the journal with a substantial essay on 'Theatre at War' written half way through the Burma campaign, and reflecting a marked change in attitude towards his profession. He begins:

It is now four years since I worked in the theatre: two and a half of those years have been spent in South East Asia. Such a separation has produced a lack of contact. It has also provided an experience, unique to most theatre workers, of viewing theatre activity at long range.

Wartime theatre first. An unprecedented chance of winning over a new public had been thrown away. In the services and in factories, the war had created large new communities with an appetite for entertainment. The fault lay with ENSA and the other authorities 'whose ideas date from the last war' and whose work 'has consistently insulted the forces' intelligence'. As a remedy, he suggests the formation of mobile service companies, operating under a central directorate and approaching their audience on equal terms. 'Difficulties have been dwelt on by a nation which has devised the floating invasion port!'

The essay then looks ahead to the post-war theatre with an announcement of Devine's credo: 'Anyone who is not planning is moribund.' Now was the time to start building new theatres to match Britain's new towns, and to start phasing out the picture-frame stage. The aim must be 'to broaden our scope artistically and to admit a larger and more popular audience'. And where were the new writers? Devine compares them to birds, easily scared away, and needing time and encouragement to overcome their mistrust of the theatrical cage. 'If the only criterion for a new playwright is his immediate success, there will be few new plays.' Mobility is his slogan for peace as well as for war. 'Let lightness be our aim. Nothing acceptable which cannot be carried in a transport plane.'

On the question of theatre workers, he starts with familiar prescriptions for gathering the best talents into companies with a common purpose and attaching them to drama schools as an investment for the future. But where, he asks, will graduate students act before they are ready to join the parent troupe? 'I consider the development of children's theatres to be one solution for this.'

Today, some of this sounds cliché-ridden and some of it sounds eccentric: because some of it happened and some of it didn't. At the time Devine wrote it, in December 1944, it must all have seemed equally remote. And yet the essay does not read like the impractical musings of a man a long way from home. It is a resolute plan of action, written to convince other people, and strengthened by his army experience as well as by his work with Saint-Denis. What Devine learned from the war was that, under the power of necessity, anything can be done. He had seen supply planes dropping food and ammunition on to impossibly small receiving areas; he had seen the engineers cutting roads through the jungle and flinging improvised bridges over monsoon-swollen rivers. Why should it take a war to release all that latent inventiveness and energy? Apathy and habit were the enemies. Henceforth, his standard answer to anyone who raised difficulties was the floating invasion port.

The essay represents a watershed in his thinking. So far as companies and schools are concerned, his opinions remain tied to Saint-Denis, and 'good theatre' is still accepted as an unquestioned benefit in itself. There is no thought of trying to develop a theatre with its own social attitude. Where he begins to split off from Saint-Denis is in the emphasis on writers, characterized not as house dramatists like Obey, but as talents to be helped to find their own direction. Also, there must be no repetition of the L.T.S.'s failure to reach an audience; and Devine's solution was to nominate a new public as well as a new breed of actor. If not an audience of munitions workers and servicemen, then an audience of children equally free from West End preconceptions.

All this reflects the general shake-up of social attitudes that took place during the war. On the voyage out to India, the classes were separated as on a luxury cruise. When the regiment re-embarked for the return trip in September 1945, it was bunks for all, with precious little distinction between officers and men.

6

⁂

THE OLD VIC CENTRE

WHILE Devine was laying plans to change things in London, London had its own plans in store for him. In 1944, the Old Vic directorate underwent another upheaval. At the request of the Governors, Olivier and Ralph Richardson were released from the Fleet Air Arm to operate the company jointly with Guthrie and John Burrell. There followed one of the most brilliant and lucrative chapters in the Vic's history, beginning with the 1944–5 season of Richardson's Peer Gynt and Olivier's Richard III. Armed with the bargaining power of these successes, the directors proposed that the Vic organization should be expanded to include a department run by the former heads of the L.T.S. and Glen Byam Shaw. Not yet realizing what was involved, the Governors gave this scheme their blessing.

It was now a question of gathering the scattered family together, devising a detailed plan, and getting it past the Governors. The groundwork was done by Saint-Denis who drafted the first outline of what was to become the Old Vic Theatre Centre and submitted it in June 1945. The idea of a comprehensive centre was in Saint-Denis's mind from the start, and to the end it never penetrated the heads of the Governors. The centre was to be a three-fold institution, consisting of a school, a children's theatre and an experimental stage; the last being the most important from Saint-Denis's point of view. It was intended as a spear-head in his crusade against the picture-frame, and as a 'laboratory of invention' for the acting company and for the development of new plays. New architecture, he believed, would give birth to new writing. This side of the project was always referred to as EXP: an unfinished word for a dream that was never realized.

Meanwhile, Saint-Denis's time had run out with the BBC, and his two co-directors were still off the scene. When Devine returned in November, a meeting took place at his Edwardes Square flat at which Saint-Denis outlined his plan. The opening of the centre was to be phased over the next two years, beginning with the children's theatre and completed with the building of a light architectural stage for EXP. Devine was to run the children's theatre; Byam Shaw, the school; and Saint-Denis was to act as general director of the centre with a special responsibility for EXP. The idea of a theatre for the young derived largely from Suria Magito, who quit the Glyndebourne Children's Theatre to join the Centre as Devine's Associate Director with the Young Vic.

Finance still had to be worked out, but John Burrell informed the meeting that the newly formed Arts Council had declared an emphatic interest in the project. With that, Saint-Denis handed over the negotiations to his colleagues and departed for Paris, stipulating that he needed an answer from the Governors by the following month.

Not yet demobilized, Devine spent the next two months shuttling between Salisbury Plain and the London flat where he was also having difficulties in adjusting to the role of parent to the three-year-old Harriet. His letters to Saint-Denis express a mounting exasperation with the officialdom that blocked his path more impenetrably than the Burmese elephant grass. The red-tape-snapping Guthrie had resigned. Now nothing could be done with the Board without the help of Burrell (unkindly characterized as the Lepidus of the Vic triumvirate) who was grossly overworked and apt to disappear on foreign business. Lord Lytton, the Chairman of the Governors, was an irregular attender at Board meetings. The plan had to be explained again and again for those who had not yet quite grasped the details and the particular purpose of EXP. After one diplomatic lunch where the Vic directors combined to get the scheme across to their Board, Devine commented: 'Why should *we* sell this idea to these people? If they are stupid enough not to see the value of the plan, then let them go to hell.'

This was the time of the Old Vic Expansion Scheme, a five-year plan conceived on the assumption of the company's continued prosperity. The Expansion Scheme shortly became identified with the Centre; but it was also connected with the promotion of the Vic into Britain's National Theatre. In January a Joint Council was set up between the Vic and the Shakespeare Memorial National Theatre Committee; and subsequently the council received official recognition together with a Treasury grant of £1 million towards the building. The two parties, had divergent ends in view. The Governors (among whom, following the quaint British custom, the theatrical profession had no representative) wanted to see their efforts crowned with the founding of a great national institution. Saint-Denis's group – known to the rest of the organization as the Three Boys – wanted to carry through their own plan of work irrespective of high-sounding titles and theatre politics. For the time being, and while money was flowing in from the Olivier–Richardson seasons, the two sides achieved some sort of common ground under the umbrella of the Vic Expansion Scheme. But it was a slow process.

December sped by with no decision from the Governors, and then January. Rather than abandon his hopes of the project, Saint-Denis – then grinding out weekly articles to support his dependents – turned down an offer to become Director General of French radio. Byam Shaw, likewise, refused a £10,000 film job which would have come between him and the Centre. Apart from declining to direct a thriller for Tennents, no such sacrifices were required of Devine, but as of old he found himself carrying the administrative burden. 'I want no meetings', said Byam Shaw, 'with hard-faced financial experts who treat one like a criminal if one is losing money or like a genius if one is making it.' It was this territory that Devine had to defend. 'The war of papers and figures goes on,' he wrote to Saint-Denis. 'I wanted least of all to use these weapons on my return. Perhaps it is the fate of the clown which I cannot elude.'

In January, the Governors yielded and offered three-year contracts to the three directors. Things were looking up. Margaret Harris had signalled her eagerness to return from America and join the team. Devine got himself placed on indefinite leave and began laying the ground for the children's theatre. Amid these brisk preparations, Suria Magito (shortly to become Mme Saint-Denis) reported from Grenoble that Saint-Denis had collapsed and was in the care of a heart specialist. This was the first sign of a malady that overshadows this story like a family curse: in the end, Copeau, Saint-Denis and Devine were all struck down in the same way. In Saint-Denis's case, the attack was first brought on by years of overwork and by the tensions of his complicated domestic life; also it coincided with the anniversary of his son Jerôme's death in the war. In the event, he made a quick recovery and resumed work early in March.

By now Margaret Harris was back in London and Devine was demobilized. They had been shaken by the news of the illness, but with the contractual question settled, preparation for the Centre went ahead with redoubled energy. Devine, still the tireless adjutant, combined meetings and property-viewing excursions with trips to Aix to debate strategy with Saint-Denis. Everything had to be tackled simultaneously. A base had to be chosen for the Centre. Plays, playwrights and touring circuits had to be found for the children's theatre, and the company set up. Then there was the question of staffing and advertising the school, and budgeting the whole venture.

The opening of the school was to be delayed until after Byam Shaw's September production of *Antony and Cleopatra*, and the venture was to be launched with the children's theatre. To that extent the work was phased. But the impression that comes over from Devine's methodical notes on this period is one of uniform urgency. Things had changed since the 1930s without yet reaching any destination: audience attitudes and financial structures were in a state of flux, and it was up to those with clear ideas to act before the system hardened into unalterable shape. Theatrical fashion of the time was bounded at one extreme by star-dominated classics and at the other by modern verse drama. From Devine's viewpoint, both represented a hangover from the 1930s. 'Stars hiding under the mask of art' was his ungrateful phrase for the Vic Company directorate. As for the new verse drama, here is a specimen comment on Ronald Duncan's *This Way to the Tomb*:

> I fear a disappointment from almost every point of view. A promising modern poet, I should say, once more completely out of gear with dramatic expression ... There is a frightful misunderstanding still going on about these 'little' theatres. In a magazine called the *New English Review* a gentleman writes that the answer to the finding of new dramatists lies in the 'little' theatres like the Mercury, which he goes so far as to describe as experimental. So we are really where we were before the war as far as experimentalism goes.

With the Centre, they were inserting a new piece into the theatrical game: it did not correspond to any other piece on the board, and they were not able fully to explain its function to the other players. The three directors had complete faith in each other, but they did not wholly trust anyone outside. The Arts Council, for one, was viewed as a doubtful ally, it being suspected that Lord Keynes, its Chairman, was no friend to the Old Vic's ambitions and greatly preferred the flair of H. M. Tennent Ltd. Inside the Vic organization, not only was the Governors' support in question; it was also assumed that in the event of any division of interests, the management of the Theatre Company would automatically prefer the company's claim to that of the Centre. Behind all these uncertainties there lay the question of who was to run the National Theatre. With that great prize waiting in the background, it was not surprising that factions developed inside the Vic hierarchy and would-be empire builders aroused mistrust.

However, in the Centre's honeymoon phase all this acted as a spur. The death of Lord Keynes at the end of March also removed an obstacle from the Vic's path; especially as his successor at the Arts Council, Sir Ernest Pooley, was a former Vice-Chairman of the Vic Governors and a friend to Saint-Denis's plans. Devine continued the 'heartbreaking' search for buildings, finally settling on the Froebel Institute at Colet Gardens, Baron's Court. Leased to Pickfords as a furniture depository, the building was unheated, infested with dry rot, noisy with passing trains, and stacked to the roof with furniture; but it seemed there was nothing better to be had, and the place was snatched from under the nose of Pickfords as a temporary home for the Centre. Even this was not the end. The Governors now asked them to consider the Old Vic itself as the Centre's premises: and after one term, the Centre surrendered Colet Gardens to Ninette de Valois as the home of the Royal Ballet School. From Belgravian mansions and stately country houses, the prospect narrowed to the abandoned shell on the corner of Waterloo Road, still lying untouched since the bomb had gone through its roof. There was no question of carrying out full structural repairs immediately, but certain time-consuming preparations had to be made before the building could become minimally habitable. For one thing, as Devine noted, the theatre too was 'full of stores of all kinds from the Vic and Wells, and could not be made usable without finding a store and workshop outside; which would be almost as hard as finding the school premises'.

Alongside the hunt for somewhere to work, there was the problem of raising money. Devine, who thought it essential that one of the Centre's directors should be present whenever its affairs were on the Governors' agenda, doggedly shouldered the task himself as the Centre's Chairman. It is beyond my competence to follow him through the 'war of papers and figures', but the picture that emerges is of a man trying to hack a path through a jungle of intertwined branches of finance. Charitable funding (going back to the Vic's origins and still vested in its Charity Commissioners) overlapped with straight theatrical backing and the new principle of State patronage. The Vic discussions took place at a cross-roads between these three. If Devine had any preference it was for private funding. At that time he was still all in favour of actor-managers, and suspected State subsidies as a cause of artistic complacency. But he was more than ready to snap up money for the Centre from any source.

Initially the Governors had planned to finance the Centre largely from the profits of the booming Theatre Company to the tune of £5,000 a year; which, as Devine pointed out, would have turned the Centre into a satellite organization wholly dependent on the company's fortunes. But there was no immediate alternative as the Arts Council at that time was empowered only to give guaranteees against loss, not to make capital grants. In May the situation changed: under its new constitution, the council became able to issue capital and interest-free loans. Devine was present at the Arts Council meeting when this was announced, and promptly took the floor 'to point out that it was not possible to consider the "losses" incurred in the launching of the plan as "losses" in the ordinary sense of the word – i.e. failure to cover expenses or to make profits. What was required was not a "guarantee against loss" but a subsidy. This remark was thought to be sensible by all concerned.' At the end of June, the Vic Sub-Committee resolved to ask the Arts Council for a foundation grant of £28,000 to launch the Centre over the next five years: but it was six months before the council committed itself to subsidizing the Centre, and then it was for two years, not five. The annual grant was £9,500, with £5000 going to the school and £4,500 to the Young Vic Company. These figures remained unchanged throughout the six years of the Centre's existence: which meant not only that it was always hard up, but that it was impossible to plan further than two years ahead (for instance, by extending the training to three years), as there was no telling whether the grant would be renewed.

Meanwhile there was the urgent question of the Young Vic (as the children's theatre had been renamed). This was Devine's personal concern. It was originally due to open in the autumn of 1946 as the first of the Centre's three phases, but Devine had been forced to combine it with other priorities, and what work he had done had met with discouragement. 'The real life blood of the new movement', he wrote, 'must be the dramatists who are stimulated by the possibilities offered.' And in his first burst of enthusiasm he drafted an open letter to writers, outlining his hopes for the Young Vic:

> Most of you have turned your backs on the theatre. We don't blame you. In the last thirty years we have offered you little; our means of expression have been thin, our willingness to co-operate non-existent. But here and now we are ready to do something new ... If you have any discarded ideas, rake them up again. If you have none, think about it. We'll play with anyone who is honest.

Ten years later, he delivered much the same invitation on behalf of the Royal Court; but for the time being it fell on deaf ears. As a writers' theatre, the Young Vic was a flop, though it was not alone in this failure. John Allen, who was conducting a similar enterprise with the Glyndebourne Children's Theatre, also drew a total blank with the writers he approached. Both directors had considerable authority, as their organizations then represented the summit of theatrical respectability. Writing on headed notepaper from the Old Vic and the Glyndebourne Opera, they could invite whoever they wanted, and they made strenuous efforts to attract both playwrights and specialist children's authors; but, Allen says, without arousing so much as a flicker of interest. Olivier urged Devine to approach J. B. Priestley on the 'vexed question of plays'. 'I fear this,' Devine noted, but a lunch duly took place at which he was invited to direct Priestley's new piece *Ever Since Paradise*:

> I told them I could not consider doing it because of the Theatre for Children ... This brought forth a storm of abuse from both of them [Priestley and Stephen Mitchell] against the Old Vic and me, on the grounds that people like us coming back fresh to the theatre should be given more important work to do, and not just asked to do children's theatre when the adult theatre is in such a bad state. This lasted nearly an hour and a half and was very embarrassing and difficult. I returned very shaken.

When a provisional programme was drawn up at the end of April, there was not a single new play on the list. There was also the problem of marketing the so far non-existent product. For all his mistrust of 'educational purists' Devine unavoidably had to work through local education authorities, as only they possessed the ready-made touring circuit and financial resources to support a youth theatre. The Children's Theatre arrived on the back of the new sixpenny rate and the 1944 Education Act, and could only survive through establishing that connection. Of the 146 L.E.A.s in England and Wales, Devine chose Lancashire, partly on the advice of Jo Hodgkinson, then Arts Council director for the region (Lancashire also had its wartime memories of the Vic). A twelve-week tour of Alexei Tolstoy's *The Golden Key* was planned from September, ending with a Christmas season in London; and an advance scout was dispatched north to pave the way. His report arrived in mid-June. Manchester, he said, had no suitable place for the company. The L.E.A. were prepared to offer neither school halls nor financial guarantees. Liverpool declared itself 'fed up' with these ventures: Salford, Warrington and St Helens likewise turned a cold shoulder.

From this 'shattering blow' Devine concluded that his plans were three months too late; that he should first have sounded out the regions by letter to find out who was interested; and that his scout was useless. His next move was to send out a Young Vic questionnaire to 100 Chief Education Officers from whom he hoped to learn where the company would be welcome and what stages were available. Of those who bothered to reply, most returned a flat 'No.' Other respondents said No politely, or declared themselves unable to raise the guarantee or find premises. There were no takers except the Lyric, Hammersmith, which was available for a Christmas show. A non-educational début in a London theatre was not the ideal either for Devine or for the Governors, who, above all, wanted to extend the Vic's operations into the provinces so as to strengthen their case for amalgamation with the National Theatre. But as there was nothing else in sight, a deal was concluded with the Lyric, and the Young Vic's opening was put off to the end of December.

Devine had now been at work for six months and the only tangible result was a solitary date for a children's play, and the prospect of installing a school at the Old Vic. Meanwhile, there was still no firm financial guarantee from the Arts Council, and the prospect of launching EXP was as remote as ever. It was not much to show for so much application to a task he detested.

> In July he wrote: The more we work in detail, the more snags crop up ... Because we have been obliged to visualize the five-year plan, we have tended to feel it was as good as realized. We must now come back to the beginning again.

And if six months had gone on building this house of cards, it was six years since he had worked professionally in the theatre. The artist in him was beginning to rebel.

It was at this moment that Olivier invited Devine to play opposite Vivien Leigh in his production of Thornton Wilder's *The Skin of our Teeth*. It was a difficult decision. The role of Mr Antrobus, the suburban Everyman in Wilder's cosmic comic-strip, amounted to a humdrum character part magnified to heroic size: as such it was cut out for Devine. On the other hand, he already had a crushing work-load for the Centre without burdening himself with tasks unrelated to his main concern, and in any case he was not even being called upon to create the part of Antrobus, merely to take over the role from Cecil Parker. Saint-Denis, still convalescing in France, made the further point that if he was going into the West End at all it would make more sense to go in as a director than as an actor.

Saint-Denis's continued absence was another factor that pushed Devine into a mood of 'exasperated depression'. 'I will not conceal from you', he wrote, 'that I am still anxious about the Young Vic. I am not giving it enough time ... As soon as you return to take the helm, I must devote myself very much to that.' In this mood he doubted his effectiveness as a committee man, and felt that by the time he struck, the iron had already begun to cool. 'The war-time scramble opened doors which peace and reconstruction have closed.' Everything moved so slowly: and he had still not carried out his wartime resolution of finding his feet as an actor before embarking on any institutional project. Now, at least, Olivier had offered him a piece of concrete theatrical work. He accepted the part, agreeing to go into the production with a two-thirds cut in his Vic salary for the duration of the run.

Early in July the Centre set up its first office at the Vic, and by the time Saint-Denis returned the spade-work had been finished. There was no rapid acceleration, but everything went

ahead as planned for the opening of the Young Vic in December
and the school a month later. From the preliminary publicity
there were already 120 applicants for places, and the number
swelled to 300 in the autumn as interviews and auditions got
under way. Permission from the Charity Commissioners to install
the Centre at the Old Vic came through in October, and Devine
was entrusted with supervising the interior decoration. Simultaneously, Saint-Denis was working with the French architect,
Pierre Sonrel, on plans to adapt the Vic stage into the experimental platform of his dreams ('l'idée d'une architecture nouvelle
m'exalte.') As for the Young Vic, Devine had discarded his first
choice of *The Golden Key* and settled on Gozzi's *King Stag* (a
great favourite with East European children's theatres), which
was booked into the Lyric for five-and-a-half weeks, to be
followed by a short tour of provincial theatres arranged by Cecil
Clarke, a doughty stage-managerial recruit who was to figure as
R.S.M. of basic training in the Vic School.

In September Devine went into *The Skin of our Teeth* on its
transfer from the Phoenix to the Piccadilly. This was a morale-
boosting experience in which he proved to himself and everyone
else that he had now turned his physical liabilities into expressive
assets. Olivier was delighted with the performance: so was an
eighteen-year-old Yorkshire boy, Tony Richardson, with whom
Devine launched the English Stage Company ten years later.
From friends who went round to his dressing room, the picture
emerges of a kindly, funny companion without a care in the
world. With the waning of personal ambition, there was nothing
Devine loved more than acting. In the years ahead, whenever he
could shed the weight of administration and escape into a part,
he gave the impression of being a happy man.

On Boxing Day, *King Stag* opened at the Lyric, Hammersmith,
directed by Devine with Motley décor and music by Francis
Chagrin. And on January 24, 1947, the school's opening ceremony took place on the stage of the Old Vic, with speeches from
Olivier, Lord Lytton and Ellen Wilkinson, the Minister of
Education. Nothing sums up the ideals of this rigorous institution
better than Olivier's address to the incoming students:

> An actor, above all, must be a great understander, either by intui-
> tion, observation or both, and that puts him on the level with a
> doctor, a priest or a philosopher. If I can get more from him than
> just belief, then I feel both fortunate and overjoyed ... There are

many dimensions in the art of acting, but NONE of them ... are good or interesting ... unless they are invested with the appearance, or complete illusions of truth. The difference between the actual truth and the illusion of the truth is what you are about to learn. You will not finish learning it until you are dead.

As for Ellen Wilkinson, this was her last public engagement. January 24 was a bitterly cold day, and the only source of heat was an oil stove in the prompt corner. On leaving the meeting she was taken ill and died shortly afterwards.

Olivier's speech came at the end of the third New Theatre season which, despite all the transatlantic glamour, had made a loss. Olivier, moreover, was on the point of taking leave from the Vic to make the film of *Hamlet*, and it was to be two and a half years before he reappeared as an actor with the company in London. A third factor was the expiry of the Vic's lease of the Liverpool Playhouse and the reversion of that theatre to its local directors. This represented another serious loss of income to the Vic organization. So, from the first moment of the Centre's life, there was a chill in the air.

7

THE SCHOOL

THE Vic Expansion Scheme, drafted by the Drama Directors in January 1946, listed five categories of development: a theatre school; a children's theatre; repertory centres for regional tours; an experimental theatre; and two large number one companies alternating between London and either the provinces or abroad. A year later, the Vic's days of prosperity had run out and the scheme had developed as far as it ever went. There was a school and a theatre for the young. Regionally, the organization had lost Liverpool and gained Bristol. There was no experimental theatre. A secondary company was indeed installed at the New Theatre when Olivier led off his crack troupe to the Antipodes, but whether both counted as 'number one' companies was another matter. Other Olympian factors governing the career of the Centre were the deaths first of Lord Lytton in 1947 and then of his successor, Lord Hambledon, in March of the following year. The Chairman of the Vic Governors in the Centre's decisive years was Lord Esher, who allegedly dreaded the prospect of Britain's National Theatre falling into the hands of a Frenchman and who confessed that he could never understand a word Saint-Denis said.

Descending from the boardroom to the workshop, there were more immediate problems than theatre politics. First, the building which was to house the school and Young Vic offices for the next two years. 'Perishing cold' is how Byam Shaw remembers it. There was a gaping hole in the roof and rainwater was apt to overflow buckets in the void and drip through into the auditorium. Most of the running repairs were carried out by junior staff members, working with an ex-naval chiefie who had been taken on as a general handy-man. There were no house seats. The most conspicuous items were an eccentrically Thespian safety curtain dating back to the Baylis era, and a set of hanging wicker cages left over from the madhouse scene of Guthrie's *Peer Gynt*. The stage had hardly any equipment or usable scenery, and the auditorium was full of rubble, consisting partly of fallen plaster and partly of scenic débris including some property thrones on which the directors were wont to sit watching student rehearsals. Classes also took place in the big rehearsal room at the top of the building, and in the dressing rooms, bars and foyer. In the words of Val May, who was among the early students,

> the whole place had the most extraordinary smell. It had been wounded in the war and had none of the creature comforts, but you could still sense that it had masses of tradition behind it. As wide-eyed students, we drank in that atmosphere. The discomfort didn't matter.

To match the atmosphere, professional discipline was likewise laid on the line. 'You are now actors,' Byam Shaw told them on the first day. 'You will be prompt for rehearsals and for all your classes, because actors don't keep their fellow artists waiting.' That winter there was a power breakdown and all tube trains had stopped. On a day when their class work was being assessed, several students failed to arrive. Devine cast a cold eye over those who had struggled in, and remarked, 'There you are, it always shows. The good people are all here.' And when the late-comers did appear, he summoned them together for a tongue-lashing on 'rude, anti-social, inefficient, and unprofessional' conduct.

The school and Young Vic formed part of what was then fashionably known as a 'ladder system', the theory being that outgoing students would have the chance of moving up to professional work with the children's troupe or in the main company, thus supplying the parent stage with a regular flow of new talent. From the start, therefore, students were enmeshed in a living theatrical context. This was the greatest single advantage the Vic School had over the L.T.S. It also had more scholarships to offer, and two years' guaranteed existence.

It was still a small school. The average annual intake was of forty acting and thirty technical students; and a high proportion of these were weeded out at the end of the first year. For technical students this was not necessarily the end of the world, as their first year (run by Cecil Clarke and Margaret Harris) consisted of a thorough grounding in the practical crafts of the theatre, so that even if they fell by the wayside, they were equipped to make a living as stage managers. Those who survived, usually no more than twelve, went on to the advanced technical course, which was the only seriously organized course in directing ever run by a British theatre school, either before or since.

Although no outsider can fully disentangle the separate contribution of the three directors, the broad division was as it had been at the L.T.S. Saint-Denis's field was the pre- and post-physical, and did not include instructing novices in how to canvas a flat or prepare ground-plans. Devine was in his element on the technical side and, as before, he countered Saint-Denis's theoretical pronouncements with unashamed statements of the obvious. Taking a lighting class, he would whip out an electric fire with a dramatic flourish and begin: 'THIS. Is an electric fire!' Or, delivering a paper on finance, he would lead off: 'There are fifty-two weeks in the year.' 'Holland is a FLAT country,' he informed an astounded Young Vic company during their Benelux tour briefing.

In the acting course, the presence of Saint-Denis was all-pervasive, from his opening address on the privilege of working at the Vic and the notorious first exercise into which unsuspecting students were plunged. This consisted of rehearsing and performing scenes from a big Shakespeare text in three weeks; and then hearing Saint-Denis's comments on the result. *Antony and Cleopatra* was the chosen text in the opening term, and the exercise was staged at the Piccadilly Theatre where Byam Shaw's production of the play was then running. Peter Dugid, who went through this ordeal in the role of Antony, says:

> the criticism was about as brutal as one could take: it was out of all proportion. You were led by the hand along a little garden path, and then dropped. The idea was to show you just what you had to face: the long road ahead. And that this was absolutely no bloody good at all; and with proper humility on your part, we can now start to show you. It was really hell. It broke down whatever confidence I had when I arrived, and some people never recovered.

This was the beginning of the famous Vic School 'tunnel' into which the students descended to blunder helplessly through the dark for an unspecified length of time before (with luck) emerging transformed at the other end.

Motley's adaptable costumes were resurrected from the L.T.S. together with navy blue swimsuits; and, as before, much of the basic training was performed in these garments which revealed every physical defect. Aside from the cold, another source of discomfort was the age-gap between the men and the girls; and there were cases of acute embarrassment in Litz Pisk's movement class when grant-aided ex-servicemen were required to melt into heaps with convent school virgins. In these classes, too, each student in turn would parade before the others and be subjected to comments on stiff shoulders, poor leg co-ordination, or whatever fault caught the eye.

As time went by, this kind of mutual criticism gradually replaced the style of the brutal initiation. But Saint-Denis continued to hold regular critical sessions attended by everyone on the course, at which he would follow up comments by other staff members with blistering *ex cathedra* judgments on individual work. Again, this mercilessly prolonged exposure was useful to people with stamina and intelligence, and who were not turned off by the atmosphere of a public trial. There were also cases of students crying and fainting, either from shock or from the sheer exhaustion of sitting around until midnight waiting for their turn to come. George Hall says, 'There really was a feeling of people who had commanded battleships being reduced to tears.'

In some quarters, the treatment was likened to brain-washing; but for the survivors it simply meant an uncomfortable transition period between the 'gifted and un-self-conscious amateur and the gifted and apparently un-self-conscious professional'. That phrase is Joan Plowright's, whose own sympathies are clear from the story of how she emerged from the tunnel while playing the Courtesan in Devine's production of *The Comedy of Errors*. 'As I came off the stage after the performance I met Michel Saint-Denis and George a little further along. Michel said, "You are out of the tunnel. Do you know what you did? Can you remember how you did it? Can you do it again?" This nearly sent me back in again. George slapped me on the bottom and roared, "There you are, you see!" and strolled on smoking his pipe.'

There is no rule on whether talent develops better in a warm or a cold climate. But once you grant the Vic School's premiss – that it was better to lop off premature blossoms and cultivate the roots – everything else follows logically from that. The school went much further than the L.T.S. towards the ideal of 'organic' training. As at the L.T.S., the staff constantly watched each others' classes during the first year; but this time there was no lingering trace of specalist rivalries. This was partly thanks to the fact that voice classes were now based on singing technique; and Jani Strasser, who took them, was not an English elocutionist but a Hungarian operatic coach from Glyndebourne. Teachers like Strasser and the Viennese Litz Pisk, says Peter Duguid, 'thought alike, so that when a problem arose they were able to help each other. It was unlikely that someone would be a beautiful mover and yet be vocally tense.' All kinds of detailed links grew up between separate classes. A movement exercise for the foot would lead on to an improvisation exercise of walking over rough or slippery ground. Spine or hip exercises would change into animal pantomime. Then there were transformation exercises: having learned how to be a balloon, you would go on to play a drunken man swelling up and bursting. It was a process of developing physical skills and then incorporating them in expressive work.

Embarrassment was seen as irrelevant because the training took no account of ugliness or beauty. All bodies were instruments, each with its proper range. And whether the student was in possession of a flute or a double-bass, what had to be done was to correct its faults and put it in tune. Hence the initial stripping-down process in which the personality was dismantled and the physique returned to the cradle.

'Sincerity' and 'truth' were key words in the school vocabulary. Stanislavsky was their obvious source, but it was Stanislavsky filtered through a French sensibility and then applied to students working mainly on English texts. You might describe it as an attempt to marry the inheritance of French formal theatre with the Russian inheritance of psychological acting, but there was no such thing as a Saint-Denis System and the course changed considerably during the school's six years. From its spartan beginnings, it started acknowledging the market value of good looks; talented students were given a chance to shine in the annual public shows, instead of being submerged in the ensemble; and there were crash productions where, instead of endlessly perfecting a few scenes of Chekhov, the class would get a taste of weekly rep conditions. And there were innovations like the monthly 'Style Day' where everyone turned up for a party wearing immense crinolines, huge floppy hats, and other period costumes whose difficulties had been intentionally exaggerated.

As Devine's work makes sense only in relation to the whole pattern, here is an outline of what the school was aiming at. The whole training was divided between improvisation and interpretation: improvisation being 'the creative part of an actor's work' and interpretation 'the line of submission to a good text'. Acting talent was recognized to be a mysterious and unteachable power, but it could only express itself through a well-tuned instrument. Hence the study of technique as a way of removing blockages. The ideal was the 'balanced actor': one who achieved natural behaviour within the given convention of the play. Acting was the point of balance between technique and inspiration. It was like a hand holding a bird, Saint-Denis said. 'If you clench your fist you will kill it. If you loosen your hand too much it will fly away.'

The Centre saw itself as a classical school, but naturalism was not excluded from the training. For acting and technical students alike, theatre history was divided into three main phases. First was the 'big style' which hopefully embraced everything from the Greeks to Shakespeare, and implied a drama dealing with cosmic events; this also had to do with the return from the proscenium to open staging. Second, there was a style they were forced to label 'Restoration', as Saint-Denis felt there must be some English equivalent to Molière: this inclined to improvisation and the *commedia*, acknowledging the presence of the public and treating theatre as a game. Third came the 'modern' or 'realist' style, which meant everything from Chekhov onwards: the determining convention here was the invisibility of the audience. (Devine's term for this style was 'aquarium theatre'.)

On the technical course, the same categories were expressed in three basic design precepts: that Shakespeare moves in curves; Restoration comedy, being set in front of cloths, presents a flat picture; and that modern plays reflect the random complexity of the real world. Design students were required to consider space architecturally, always starting with a ground-plan; and the criterion of a successful design was whether it faithfully translated a dramatic style into spatial form and assisted actors in articulating the play's rhythm.

The test of this approach came with the annual show, at which point the acting and technical courses converged. Unlike other schools, which generally booked a West End matinée to exhibit their wares to agents, the Vic presented a week's run of two programmes on its own premises. The drawing power of the three directors and the results they achieved guaranteed an extraordinary public for this event. The annual show formed the grand exercise towards which all the training led. It involved everyone in the school, and during the three weeks of rehearsal the place changed into a production unit. The show was performed and usually designed by second-year students, while all the back room and front-of-house work was done by first-year juniors. Every costume, every prop, every piece of scenery was made inside the school. The first-year acting course was roped in for scene painting and prop-making. The printed programme for the first show, in 1948, credits juniors like Geoffrey Bayldon and Maurice Kaufmann with preparing the auditorium, while Derek Godfrey figures as an assistant to the head carpenter. Other names that first reached the public through these shows include actors like Alan Dobie, Denis Quilley, Clive Revill, Edgar Wreford, James Maxwell, Prunella Scales, Joan Plowright, Dilys Hamlett, Rosalind Knight and Sheila Ballantine: and designers like Richard Negri, Alan Tagg, Voytek, Malcolm Pride, Stephen Doncaster and Carl Toms. Directors who trained at the Vic School include Frank Dunlop, Eric Thompson, Christopher Morahan, Val May, Casper Wrede, not to mention those who built their future careers in other countries, like Michael Cacoyannis and Peter Zadek. That list omits the group of actors who moved from the school to the Young Vic and thence to the open stages of North America (notably Powys Thomas, Tony van Bridge and Mervyn Blake). But it includes the nucleus (Maxwell, Hamlett, Negri and Wrede) who went on to found the Manchester Royal Exchange Company. Saint-Denis always said that he was training students not for instant success but for long-term careers, and time has confirmed that claim.

Devine had three roles inside the school. As at the L.T.S., students encountered him as a teacher of comic improvisation, as a director, and as a despotically perfectionist stage manager. There were some differences. The experience of the war had particularly affected him in the third capacity, and increased his dissatisfaction with the English theatre's readiness to soldier on with wood and canvas flats. He wrote:

> In the 'domestic' period, if managers could have been sure of a long run, they would surely have built their scenes of brick and mortar, and had the plumbers in to fit the wash-basins and lavatories off-stage. This nonsensical era is passing, but the timber and canvas, the ponderous tools of the trade, do not.

George Hall (subsequently Head of Drama at the Central School) says that 'long before anyone else I knew' he was searching for new lightweight flexible materials and for flying systems that need not operate in parallel with the proscenium. '"If we applied the Bailey Bridge approach to theatrical invention," he said, "we'd find a way of flying things diagonally."'

Allied to this was his feeling that drama students were damagingly cut off from life outside, as he himself had been during the twelve pre-war years before 'I came out of my theatrical shell'. L.T.S. students had been encouraged to base improvised character on local street observation; and Devine now took this a stage further by shepherding his class round areas of London they might not have come across in their ordinary lives. One tour sampled a collection of dockland pubs from which they developed a scenario (scripted by James Forsyth) for one of the public shows. Another went round the greyhound tracks and produced a betting sketch called *Going to the Dogs*. Aligned with this was a corresponding change in the mask work. Margaret Harris designed a new set of character masks for use in modernized *commedia* exercises. Made to Devine's specifications to fit the actor's face like a second skin, these resembled Donald McGill grotesques – a fat blowsy character with a red blob for a nose, a thin mean character with a long rat-like nose. This was another move towards the old Vieux-Colombier idea of a fully socialized *commedia*, but it remained based on personality and did not yet include work types.

In all essentials, the Vic School improvisations continued on the same lines as the those of the L.T.S., with the same opening dive into a jumble-sale wardrobe, and the same emphasis on animal pantomime. Again, some students responded to one approach and some to another. Plowright, who felt at home with the animals, went through the classes as a boxer puppy. Lee Montague, who did not, sat motionless among the snakes and bears until he was asked to identify himself. 'I'm a chameleon,' he said. 'I have changed colour ten times while I've been here, and if you can't see it, I'm sorry.' But the virtue of the system, as Montague agrees, was that it gave students the chance of sampling a wide range of exercises until they found one that switched on the imagination; it being a basic doctrine of the school that it was through improvisation that you first discover the sensation of acting.

For the annual shows, 'big style' and modern texts were generally carved up between Saint-Denis and Byam Shaw, leaving Devine in charge of the comedy, which meant three student productions a year in addition to his work with the Young Vic. Plays he directed at the school consisted not only of eighteenth-century pieces and character improvisations, but comedy from other periods, such as *The Comedy of Errors*, Pinero's *The Gay Lord Quex*, and Chekhov and Labiche farces. On Devine the Vic Centre director, there are two diametrically opposed views. For Peter Duguid (among others) he was 'the best comedy director I've ever worked with'. For Frank Dunlop, he was 'rather a bumbler who led people to the water very nicely, but lacked the final drive to bring the thing off; he hadn't got a final cutting edge'.

Memory of his work from the late 1950s is of little help in deciding between these two opinions, as by then Devine was no longer much involved in comic production. But in filtering through the second-hand evidence one is left with some points of agreement. First, that he was a shy man who had developed an extremely life-like mask of authority; second, that he was theatrically the most down-to-earth of the Vic trio; third, that off-the-cuff directing was a rarer phenomenon in the theatre of Devine's generation than it became among the generation he fostered at the Royal Court. From that, one may deduce a gap between what Devine was and how he had learned to function, that he could work with spontaneity, but was apt to retreat into the rules whenever he felt threatened. In professional rehearsal he would prepare an annotated prompt copy, but without Saint-Denis's capacity for getting actors to follow it. Duguid recalls such a moment with Roger Livesey when 'George said, "Move over here," and Livesey said, "I think I'd prefer to go over there." There was an almighty pause, and George was completely thrown.' Set against that Joan Plowright's memory that

'George was the only one at the Vic School who did not place you in a scene. Saint-Denis would say, "You are five inches off your position for that speech." George would let it go and then shape it: you could try anything.'

His comedy-class exercises were aimed to produce an impersonal result. Music-hall tricks were safe because they could be used by anyone who learned the drill; improvisation likewise was an escape from the self. (One of the most absurd allegations against the Vic School was that it 'psychoanalysed' the students.) When it came to public performance, some people were liberated by this training, and others found it restrictive and alien to the spirit of English comedy which so often arises from personal fear. 'There was a feeling,' says George Hall, 'that acting could be made funny if you did it with a hop, skip and a jump; and that the moment you can walk on a stage and fart you become a free comic creature.'

The pedantry of popular theatre is one of Saint-Denis's negative bequests to the English speaking stage. Dunlop, for one, thought Devine fundamentally a pedant. 'He used to *act* a relationship with his casts. He couldn't convince them that *they'd* thought of what he wanted them to do.' But Dunlop is speaking as a director of the young, off-the-cuff generation, to whom painstaking preparation appears a strait-jacket.

'Imposing' was not then the crime it has now become. It was a common practice for directors to prefix rehearsals with model character sketches of a kind that modern directors would dismiss with a shudder. Byam Shaw would sum up a Shakespeare heroine as 'a provocative nun': Devine would label a Chekhov seductress 'a sweating bird of paradise'. Vay May recalls his opening comment to a girl playing a Restoration *belle*: 'When you enter, you've got to feel as if you've just had a hot bath and drunk a glass of champagne.' That may be phrase-making, but it is not a set of handcuffs such as May says Saint-Denis applied on similar occasions ('Ten years ago you probably had a very difficult love affair ... ') Whatever partial liberties Devine did introduce into his rehearsals have to be measured against the authoritarian norm.

In every case, objections to Devine's work as a director fasten on to his personality rather than to his technique. With that obstacle removed, even a non-enthusiast like Dunlop comes round in his favour. 'The best thing he ever did was the Young

Vic's *Knight of the Burning Pestle*. All the business was fresh and joyful. It didn't appear calculated. And I'm sure this was because it was such an extraordinarily difficult play that he couldn't work it out in advance.' Another such case was his school production of *The Comedy of Errors*, which developed from comedy-class improvisations. The cast came on in the drabbest or most garish costumes according to character rather than social rank. Plowright, who escaped from the tunnel in this show, played the Courtesan as a Midas-like gypsy transforming everything she touched into a sex object. New focal points and major speeches emerged in place of the expected climaxes, and in this sense Plowright compares the production to Zeffirelli's *Much Ado About Nothing*: 'it was Devine freeing himself and saying "To hell with everything we've been taught about the classical tradition."' Another glimpse of Devine in this mood comes from Litz Pisk who assisted him on the Young Vic production of *The Servant of Two Masters*. 'He was the one director who incorporated acrobatic training in performance. We had a chorus of waiters who linked the scenes with folding table-cloths and carrying chairs, all done to music with a lot of physical invention. George would take what was given him and carry it further: he had a terrific facility for making comic links, they literally poured out of him.'

Outside the sphere of direction, but in the same mood, were his school show burlesques when (as in the Motley studio days) he would drag up and take a comic holiday from the rules of the *commedia*. In one of these he appeared as Lorca's Bernarda Alba; in another, following a highly perfumed piece on Penthesilea by James Forsyth, he appeared as the Queen of the Amazons, tantalizing Pierre Lefevre's Achilles with one breast hanging out. One senses just as much fun from this description by Val May of his work at its most disciplined. 'He was directing Elvi Hale and Keith Michell in a scene from *The Gay Lord Quex*: just one page, but it took him an hour and a half and about seventeen repetitions to get the laugh as he wanted it. This taught one the craftsmanship of directing: the sheer practicality of going back and back until every detail of movement, timing, gesture, and interpretation is exactly right. I've never forgotten that.'

The evidence points towards two conclusions. First, that with the right text and company, Devine was a director with an extremely effective cutting edge. Second, that he possessed a natural comic talent that was as much hampered as strengthened by his attachment to an academic comic tradition. He was a physical but unathletic person: stolid in himself, but fascinated by grace and mobility. At this stage of his career one gets the impression of a bird perfectly capable of natural flight but preferring the safety of artificial wings.

Speculation aside, here – taken from his notes for the technical course – are Devine's own basic views on the art of the theatre.

1 A theatrical performance is transitory. Therefore the impact of the art must be immediate, clear, and forceful.

2 Perfection can only be attained when the audience is participating in the great sum total of activity which is called a Performance. There is, therefore, an unknown element which has always to be taken into account.

3 The element of chance is very great because one is dealing in human beings as one's currency. It is therefore necessary to plan. The attitude of keeping a thing 'in' because something happens in a way no one had thought of at the rehearsal and seems quite good at the time, ought to be regarded with suspicion.

4 The basis of everything in the theatre is the dramatist.

5 Drama is a collective art. Each person, from the man who works the tabs to the girl who designs the crown for King Lear, is an artist just as much as the producer or designer.

6 Mere technique is useless. There is a mysterious sense called a 'sense of theatre' which is vital to the technician. With it, the curtain can be made to act as much as any actor, and lights can be made to talk as eloquently as any poetry.

8

THE YOUNG VIC

DEVINE chose *The King Stag* to launch the Young Vic as 'a play most likely to be understood and enjoyed by children between the ages of eight and fourteen.' It was also claimed as the first professional production of Gozzi in English, and had obvious links both with the L.T.S. (where Gozzi's scenarios were one source of the *commedia* work) and with the Soviet children's theatre which the Young Vic hoped to emulate. The piece has magic, clowning, group spectacle, animal transformation – in short, all the key elements of the Vic School's improvisation classes.

However, the piece went into rehearsal during the school's first term, and it was two years before students started joining the company. So the cast for this most stylized of the Young Vic's plays consisted mainly of incoming professionals (Rupert Davies, Hattie Jacques, John Byron) who were newcomers to the world of Motley stomachs and noses. One old hand reappeared in the person of Stuart Burge, who had played in Saint-Denis's pre-war *Witch of Edmonton* and was now desperate to rejoin the team. Knowing that Devine wanted actors who could sing, dance and perform gymnastics, he auditioned by reciting 'You Are Old, Father William' standing on his head, which earned him the reputation of an expert on 'le mouvement'. More to the point, he was engaged on the spot and cast in the Harlequin role of the Birdcatcher. The part involved some intricate pantomime, which he worked out with Devine, and a good deal of direct address; which, in this case, meant learning to play to children – an art which the company had to pick up through trial and error. Unlike some of their future shows, *The King Stag* appealed directly to its chosen public: it was the rare case of a piece that bypassed the age barrier and was equally apt as a classic revival and as a holiday entertainment. The play was afterwards rated the one most successful in pleasing all age groups.

It did not, however, do good business. Opening on Boxing Day, it clashed with other Christmas shows, so that while the reviews were mainly favourable they gave it little space. As advance publicity had been minimal the company were playing to thin houses. Nor did matters improve when they went on the road in the bitter February of 1947. Ironically, their best week was in Cardiff, where fewer children saw the play than in any other town. By March, the deficit was such that Devine was being pressed to cancel the tour, but the company volunteered to take a salary cut and played on until May 10 as planned. Except in Leamington, the season played entirely in commercial houses on the standard sharing arrangement of 60 per cent of the gross to the producing management and 40 per cent to the theatre owner. The Young Vic's running cost was £450 a week; and the average gross was only £580. So between December and May the season lost something in the region of £850. To offset this, four education authorities had made block bookings, and in every one of the twelve towns they visited the authorities and teachers had asked the troupe to come back.

Summing up the lesson of the pilot season, Devine concluded that it was impossible for the Young Vic to thrive under normal theatre conditions: it could only do so by sacrificing the young audience which constituted its *raison d'être*. How was it possible for the company to pay its way, and to offer seats at a price children could afford? There was no scope for cuts on the artistic side. A company of fifteen actors and three staff was a minimum requirement for classical production. Nor, for this kind of work, could there be any question of playing in school halls instead of properly equipped theatres. Short of a vastly increased central grant, the only solution lay in securing guarantees of local support. This, in turn, meant contacting youth organizations, rotary clubs, public libraries, and every civic institution they could lay hands on, the most important, of course, being the local education office.

Typically, Devine set about putting the Young Vic on the map by drawing up a tactical chart (visitors to his various offices were often impressed by the acres of colourful graph paper on the walls). He had one, entitled 'THE LEACYCLE: Puzzle –

How to Get On It?', which came in four colours with blocks of cross-hatching and lines of contrasted squiggles, the whole being designed to reconcile theatrical and educational seasons over a five-year period. (The educational year, of course, also affected the company directly through its annual intake of Vic School students, and the fact that its scenery was built in the Vic workshops during the school's summer holiday.) The Leacycle consisted of four segments: a planning period when the next season's programme was chosen; an approach period, when these plans were laid before selected L.E.A.s for allocation in their estimates; a financial period, covered by these estimates; and a final 'buttoning up' period when all the touring dates were confirmed.

In the scramble to get *The King Stag* on stage, all preparation had been crammed into the last months of 1946. Under the Leacycle each season was phased a full year in advance. Each year was broken down into ten-month seasons with August and September out for rehearsals. On this basis, and with the aid of two indefatigable advance managers, Devine constructed a machine which was shortly chugging away under its own steam.

That makes the enterprise sound rather humdrum, which it was not. Setting aside the question of the Young Vic's artistic achievement, there is no disputing its triumph in practical organization. Before its time Britain was not wholly without children's theatre, but it was only with the arrival of the Young Vic that it began operating on a national scale. Its only companion in the field was the Glyndebourne Children's Theatre which, as its director John Allen says, had the hopelessly divided task of fitting shows into school halls and maintaining the production standards demanded by John Christie and Rudolph Bing.

The success of the Young Vic was its creation of a new performance circuit, distinct from school tours and number one commercial dates. With a few exceptions like the Cambridge Arts Theatre and the Birmingham Alexandra, the company were out in the wilds, playing in sea-side pavilions, community centres, and obscure Theatre Royals, taking all their lighting as well as scenery with them on the road. This is what Devine wanted. From his time in the Army, he had been fired with the impulse to reach the vast potential audience that lay outside the normal touring channels, but which might pick up a taste for drama if the theatre came to them. The fact that no new public took root is no criticism of the Young Vic, as it did not have enough time to effect any lasting change in playgoing habits. But it did create the instrument that might have promoted such a change. When the company commenced operations it had no precedent to build on. It had to familiarize local authorities with a new system of cultural patronage and to define a new relationship between education and the theatre. One of its successes was to earn the trust of the teaching profession while remaining free from educational associations in the material it presented. (There was never any question of mounting a School Cert. play.) 'I find it significant', Devine told an educationists' conference in 1947, 'that we are sitting here today, you the experts in education and myself the expert of a one-time condemned profession ... For me, this meeting and others like it marks the end of the banishment of the theatre from the category of serious pursuits, started in Puritan times.'

In that sense, his hopes were fulfilled. It did become normal for education directors to view the Young Vic as an ally and for schools to make block bookings. Cinema-bred children did start latching on to theatrical convention, and with repeated returns even the most apathetic places began to respond. A track was carved through the wilderness, and when the Young Vic was finally taken off the road it was within sight of paying its way. Sadder, perhaps, than the death of the company was the vacuum it left behind. Caryl Jenner's Mobile Theatre was by then taking children's shows round the country; but concerted seasons, run on subsidy, became a thing of the past, and many of the dates fell by the wayside.

It is not so easy to make definite statements about the troupe's artistic contribution. So far as the actors were concerned, the operation had powerful attractions and forbidding drawbacks. They had the excitement of working in a pioneer venture and discovering that even poverty could pay imaginative dividends (a discovery made long before by the Motleys who, typically, furnished the Young Vic with brilliantly unconventional costumes for *A Midsummer Night's Dream* at a cost of around £70, including such items as a fairy-tale crown made from Woolworth pot-scourers).

There was all the unplanned farce that goes with fit-up production. Stuart Burge, doubling his part in *Noah* with the role of business manager, startled the staff in Huddersfield by paying

out in his monkey costume; and when *Noah* moved on to a
Barnsley music-hall, the local pit band stretched a two-minute
scene change to a twenty-minute interval while they rehearsed
for the following week's *Belle of New York*. Not so funny was the
appearance of *King Stag* in Cardiff, minus scenery, in the midst
of a blizzard: the sets arrived half an hour after the show went
up, and were only hammered into place by the last act. After the
Stag season there was also an interesting mixture of ex-L.T.S.
people, inexperienced newcomers, and wild incoming professionals
like Harold Lang who joined at short notice to play Hammon in
The Shoemakers' Holiday and convulsed the prudish leading
lady by ceremoniously handing her a Durex on the line, 'Here's
a letter sent from France.'

For actors, short of joining one of the Old Vic Theatre companies, there was nothing better to be had than the Young Vic
in terms of direction, repertory, décor and artistic purpose.
Against this there were two major disadvantages. First, like
every enterprise associated with Saint-Denis, the Young Vic
gave small scope for personal ambitions. Its work was mainly
done in obscure places which neither attracted national attention
nor allowed anyone to pick up part-time radio or film engagements. More important, perhaps, was the fact that a tour with
the Young Vic meant playing only two parts a year. This was a
particularly fustrating restriction for young actors who would
have stood a better chance of developing their range in a weekly
rep.

Hence the turnover of actors and the generally shared opinion
that although the performances were of a high ensemble standard
no recognizable Young Vic style emerged. Devine's own preference was for clarity and boldness bordering on the grotesque.
But when Saint-Denis, Magito and Byam Shaw came in to
direct, other priorities came to the surface. The main question,
of course, was how successful they were in approaching children;
and it was a question which Devine took very seriously, at least
in theory. During the *Stag* season, a questionnaire went out to
grammar school spectators, and the process was repeated in the
succeeding tour of *Noah* and *The Shoemakers' Holiday*.

This, of course, was before market research had been promoted
into a branch of psychiatry, and the questions consisted of flat
inquiries about the most and least liked characters, and the
choice of plays. If they had been framed to yield answers starting

with 'because' the results might have been more illuminating. As it was, the answers that did come in contained so many identical statements that they seemed to have been filtered through class discussion. The main, unstartling conclusions were that the company had two distinct audiences: those of nine to fifteen, and those of fifteen and over. And that where the younger children preferred fantasy, the teenagers were sticklers for realism. Slightly less predictable was the discovery that the bulk of the audience (thirteen- to fifteen-year-olds) were also the most critical, and loved seeing how things worked.

Whatever weight the questionnaires carried, it was on the stage that the company learned most about children; and to begin with they evidently had a lot to learn. 'No need', wrote Stuart Burge, 'to enlarge upon the disastrous results of playing *Noah* to huge houses of screaming little savages.' This comes from a report Burge sent to Devine at the end of the 1947–8 tour. In it he puts forward what became the golden rule for Young Vic actors: the need to bend a performance to accommodate audience response. As Devine later put it to John Allen, acting for children differed from adult playing in the required degree of resilience and flexibility; it was necessary first to create a tight structure, within which the actor should then be capable of improvising.

As this amounts to a definition of the *commedia dell'arte* it is odd that it took the Young Vic experience to drive it home; and equally strange that the company's comic playing is so often described as heavy and plodding – terms which nobody applies to Devine's student productions. One possible explanation is that even though the Young Vic was set up as a youth crusade, Devine was more interested in his company than in his audience. His assistant Yolande Bird remembers him watching public performances from the house, 'and if there was anything he didn't like he'd pad out leaving the doors wildly flapping while he went round the back to see the cast. We used to have complaints from local managers, asking if we couldn't stop that man from disturbing everybody by going in and out. It always seemed that the production was very much a thing between him and the actors. He can't have been listening to the audience reaction or he couldn't have done what he did.'

This, again, was partly a sign of the times. The Young Vic came up before the Drama in Education movement and the professional theatre's attempts to enlist children's imagination in creating a show. Beyond the idea that children might acquire a taste for theatre if they were given the chance, the company's work did not stem from any theory about the young – their contribution was simply to fill the seats.

This brings us back to the vexed question of repertory, and the conditions in which children attended Young Vic shows. At the time, the comparison was between the Young Vic and the Glyndebourne troupe. Glyndebourne played in matinées for school parties who crocodiled in with their teachers: this at once put a damper on the fun, but at least it meant that the troupe were playing to children of all kinds. The Young Vic, on the other hand, generally booked a commercial house and played late afternoon and evening performances at a gruelling average of ten a week. This meant that although the school atmosphere was dispelled, audiences were drawn mainly from L.E.A. groups or children with theatregoing (middle-class) parents. Neither Glyndebourne nor Devine's company was a youth theatre in the specific sense of Frank Dunlop's latter-day Young Vic which uses plays to reflect teenage attitudes and to give its members the sense of being on their own territory. In Devine's case there was no question of mirroring children's preoccupations or allowing their tastes to determine the performance style. How little the work did depend on children appears from the fact that the Young Vic's *As You Like It* and *A Midsummer Night's Dream* were subsequently reproduced for the regular public at Stratford-on-Avon.

The main impasse was the repertory. There was no existing body of work which Devine and his colleagues could respect, and none that they could summon into existence. So, in the end, the only Young Vic plays specifically addressed to children were Magito's adaptation of *The Snow Queen* and John Blatchley's adaptation of Stevenson's *The Black Arrow*. Otherwise, all the work was taken from the adult repertory. And in that sense, it is straining the point to call the Young Vic a youth theatre at all. Its own reports acknowledge that children were baffled by the intellectual content of *Noah* and by the language of *The Shoemakers' Holiday* in which, according to Stuart Burge, the cast were obliged to 'use the words as a sort of musical accompaniment to actions we invent to convey the meaning'.

John Allen says that stylistically the Young Vic remained

hung up on the poetic realism of Saint-Denis and the Motleys, which prevented the company from originating any line of its own. He puts down the whole venture as 'good clean fun with a great deal of sensibility; but artistically, a mildly distinguished failure'. This leaves several things unaccounted for. First, although Devine disclaimed any didactic aims, it is clear from the plays themselves that a moral purpose was involved. Dekker, Shakespeare, Goldoni, Beaumont and Fletcher, Obey: they may often have been over their audience's heads, but they all belong to the category of wise comedy, showing life as a tough, on-going process in which the good have a fair chance of winning if they push hard enough. It was not an exercise in empty theatricalism, uncoloured by any point of view. 'Any theatre run by artists', Devine wrote in 1951, 'is bound to be the expression of a point of view.'

Second, whatever its artistic limitations, the Young Vic ranks indisputably as a success story. No sooner had the first defences started crumbling and the main touring circuit taken shape than Devine launched a second troupe, the Young Vic Players, to operate in totally theatreless zones. Consisting of ten performers, travelling by truck together with their costumes, lamps and telescopic aluminium set, this outfit at last fulfilled Devine's wartime idea of an entirely self-sufficient mobile unit. Derek Godfrey, Duncan Ross, Sheila Ballantine and Ann Morrish were among the members of this all-purpose song, dance and acting team who took to the road in September 1949 with a triple bill of Chekhov farce, a carve-up of the *Henry* plays, and *Round the World in Twenty Minutes*, a Victorian 'musical journey' devised by Magito.

While the Young Vic Players were prospecting in the Scottish hinterland, their parent company had struck it rich in mainland Europe. The previous season (1948–9) had seen the first intake of Vic School students into the company, for a tour of *The Snow Queen* and *As You Like It*. This was also the Young Vic's first excursion into Shakespeare, and it drew an invitation from Jan de Blieck of the Nederlandsch Impresariaat for a three-week Benelux engagement. Backed by the British Council, Byam Shaw's production went out in November for a 700-mile tour covering fourteen towns. This gruelling trek turned into a royal progress. In Brussels, at the Palais des Beaux Arts, the production broke audience records, and at The Hague and Amsterdam theatres sold out in three hours for an evening performance. At the end of the tour, the troupe were invited to return to Holland the following July and give six more performances to launch the new Bloemendaal Theatre, then the largest open-air theatre in Europe.

The response, says Yolande Bird, 'was tumultuous. All the houses were full. We were up night after night with party after party. We were about the first British company to come across since the war, and we were the people who'd stood up to Hitler. But apart from that, there was the response to Shakespeare which was better than anything we'd had at home.'

In November 1949, the company made its second European tour with Devine's production of *A Midsummer Night's Dream*, this time taking in Denmark, Norway and Sweden as well as Holland, and returning to Bloemendaal for the Holland Festival in the following June. So far, the Continental theatres had only been interested in booking Shakespeare. But on the third tour (the last of the company's existence) the Young Vic had sufficiently proved its own market value to come over with a repertory programme and fill houses as effectively with Devine's production of *The Knight of the Burning Pestle* as with Byam Shaw's *The Merchant of Venice*.

Neither Devine nor the other Vic Centre directors did anything to collect their personal share of the kudos. They did not even go over with the company for the triumphant Benelux début. Yolande Bird again: 'Money was not slung around. Never has there been a more responsible approach to budgeting and the weighing up of every penny. There just wasn't the money for the big boys to come over and see what was happening.'

Such was the career of the Young Vic. It was evidently not a troupe of the first rank, but the Continental experience alone is enough to establish its artistic credentials. Whatever the post-war atmosphere, unsupported mediocrity could never have won such acclaim. As to its achievement in Britain, conceding all the alleged stylistic limitations, it remains a fact that within five years the Young Vic changed official thinking about the stage across the face of the country, pioneered a nationwide playing circuit, and built up a substantial new audience who began to accept serious theatregoing as a normal part of life. In its last season it was playing to over 100 towns and covering 15,000 miles a year. Considering the number of Young Vic actors who went on to occupy leading positions on the open stages of North America, I am not even so sure about the artistic limitations. The North American movement is usually credited to Tyrone Guthrie, but it was actors such as Powys Thomas and Tony van Bridge, coming to Stratford, Ontario, already knowing what it was like to play Cockney Elizabethans to a Belfast audience, who initially defined the boldness and gallantry of the mid-Atlantic style.

Nothing in the theatre starts from zero. And over the past quarter-century, the Young Vic has repeatedly served as a foundation on which others could build. In their separate ways, the North American companies, Frank Dunlop's Young Vic, Michael Croft's Youth Theatre, and the post-1968 civic playhouse network all owe it ground-rent. Like the rest of the Vic Centre organization, it was conducted by a team working all the year round on ridiculous salaries. It is true that, with the exception of Keith Michell, it produced good actors rather than stars. But that was deliberate. Perhaps the training and the group ideal were fatal to certain essential kinds of egoism. The most damaging thing I have heard said of the Young Vic casts is that they were too nice to upstage each other. A generation of stars would never have attempted what the Vic Centre achieved; namely, to inject the British stage with a new ethic celebrating the community in place of the heroic individual, preferring hard-won skills to instant genius, and paying as much respect to the man on the lighting-board as to the girl playing Electra. 'It was all one,' says Yolande Bird. 'It wasn't them and us. It was all of us together. It was a theatrical Garden of Eden the like of which one has not found again.'

9

THE BREAK-UP

IF the Vic Centre received scant recognition in its lifetime, its death abundantly redressed the balance. The break-up of the enterprise created a far bigger stir than anyone (least of all the Governors) can have expected, and has lingered in the public memory ever since like an unsolved crime. It remains a skeleton in the Old Vic cupboard, and is unlikely to be brought fully into the light until all the principals in the case are dead.

Charles Landstone in his book *Off-stage* likens the episode to a Greek tragedy. On that analogy, you could say that its action was overshadowed by a primal curse in the shape of the National Theatre. Considering the money, friendships and organizations that were sacrificed in pursuit of this fatally alluring vision, it is remarkable that the survivors then had the stomach to go on and turn the National Theatre into a reality. At the beginning of the post-war period, the Vic Governors, the Olivier triumvirate, and Saint-Denis's group were all allies in the same cause. By 1952 they had split into separate factions, while the objective of their alliance remained as unattainable as ever.

Picking up the thread of the story, we have seen that from its birth the Vic Centre was living under a cloud. In June 1946, Devine estimated that the Arts Council grant would leave an annual deficit of £4,000, and it was hoped that this would be made up from the profits of the Theatre Company whose directors, he noted, 'have grandiose plans for touring the world which are as yet undisclosed'. As it turned out, those plans dealt the Centre a body blow. In February 1948, Olivier led out his company on the Old Vic's Australia / New Zealand tour. By the time they returned in November it was two and a half years since Olivier had set foot on a London stage.

In the meantime, the Theatre Company in London had gone into a steep decline. With Richardson away filming in Hollywood, the luckless John Burrell was left alone to mind the shop. He was criticized for failing to supply any substitute for the two missing stars, or any sense of artistic continuity, and at the end of 1948 the Governors were contemplating a bank overdraft of £8,000.

It was a bad situation, but what most alarmed the Governors was that it undermined the Old Vic's status in relation to the National Theatre. Olivier recalls a meeting at the time the Joint Committee was set up when 'Ralph Richardson said to me, "You know, old fellow, this will be the end of us. These boys are not going to stand for two actors having this power." But under Lord Lytton we'd had our wicked way with the Board. It was lovely, everybody did whatever we said. Then Lord Esher came on the scene.' Esher, who succeeded Lord Hambledon in March 1948, was the man who talked the Stafford Cripps Treasury into authorizing the National Theatre's £1 million building grant: and to some of his associates he seemed unduly interested in getting the National Theatre built and launched no matter what happened to the Old Vic. If that sounds harsh, it is no harsher than his own actions as Chairman. In their two London seasons, Olivier, Richardson and Burrell had immensely advanced the fortunes of the Old Vic; and now Olivier's company were performing the same service to a deliriously enthusiastic Australian public. Setting these contributions aside, Esher, half way through the tour, wrote to Olivier informing him that the five-year contracts of the three directors would not be renewed when they expired in 1949. Olivier, then playing in *Richard III*, telephoned Burrell in London and expressed his feelings in one line: 'Ah me, I see the ruin of our house.'

Esher and his Board were set on forming a stable production unit which could smoothly assume the mantle of the National troupe when the time came. Continuity of direction was essential, and directors who failed to supply it – no matter how great as artists – were expendable. However, as the Board recognized, there was no easy equation between stability and quality. Not only Olivier and Richardson had other professional lives to lead. Increasingly after the war, film studios were reducing stage acting to a part-time activity. The Board, accordingly, envisaged a rota system whereby leading performers would periodically return for a season with the Vic, but the man mainly responsible for making the whole thing work would be an administrator, engaged on a longer contract and higher salary than any of the artistic staff. In short, the artistic continuity of the organization was to be under the control of an official whose sphere of activity lay outside artistic practice.

At this point, two new key figures appear on the scene. The first was Llewellyn Rees, Drama Director of the Arts Council and a former Governor of the Vic, who was appointed to take over as Administrator after the wind-up of the Olivier régime. The second was Devine's old OUDS ally Hugh Hunt, who had made his career outside London as director of the Dublin Abbey Theatre and the Bristol Old Vic, and who was now promoted as artistic director of the London company with effect from the autumn season of 1949.

Being a pawn in the larger game, the Vic Centre for the time being remained undisturbed by these board room upheavals. But a first crack in its structure had already appeared by January 1948 when the Board announced that it would no longer be possible to house the school at the theatre after its reopening to the public. Devine renewed his weary round of vacant properties, and settled on a girls' high school in West Dulwich. The Vic School moved there in December 1949.

By that time, another blow had befallen the parent organization. Repairs to the Old Vic Theatre had been costed at about £40,000, an expense the Governors expected to take in their stride with a £50,000 building grant from the Festival of Britain. In July, to the consternation of the Arts Council no less than the Vic, the Treasury announced that this money would not be available. Devine and his colleagues thus found themselves marooned in Dulwich with no prospect of fulfilling their original plan. It was Byam Shaw who then suggested that the only way of raising funds for the building would be to reinstate the Theatre Company in Waterloo Road on sharing terms with the Centre.

Hugh Hunt was more than ready to oblige. He was already thoroughly dissatisfied with the New Theatre, where the annual tenancy was too short to allow more than seasonal contracts. As a substitute for the two star actor-managers, Hunt believed the company needed to develop its own identity in its own home. From the start, he disputed the Centre's prior claim to the building, arguing that whatever promises the Governors had made, the natural home for the Old Vic Company was the Old Vic Theatre. He put this view to Devine who, of course, did not accept it. Nevertheless, the Three Boys agreed to amalgamate with Hunt in a quadruple directorship, with joint responsibility to the Company and the Centre, under Rees's administration. Rees rightly suspected that the scheme would prove unwieldy. Hunt also says 'there was some apprehension that the Company might fall under the influence of Michel Saint-Denis if amalgamation of the directorate took place.' It would be surprising if Hunt, too, had not shared this apprehension, for in his eyes the Saint-Denis operation was a mistaken attempt to impose French theory on English practice; also, if it came to any internal power struggle, Saint-Denis ranked as his main rival. Someone, after all, had to take over the National Theatre at its expected opening in 1955.

From all the evidence of their past careers it is transparently clear that the Three Boys were fighting for their own project; they were not gunning for top jobs. But, in the atmosphere then prevailing at the Vic, they were as much open to suspicion as anyone else. Devine, for one, recognized this in a set of notes on the amalgamation addressed to his three co-directors. The fusion, he said, 'should not be too idealistically planned, but should be so constructed that the necessary opportunities occur for both sides to get to know each other with the ultimate object of their not wanting to be separated'. They had already had their fill of 'jealousies and suspicions'.

With amalgamation agreed, the Vic steamed off on its new course. By running up a £50,000 overdraft, the Governors raised the money for repairing the theatre and installing Sonrel's forestage with a view to reopening in autumn 1950. Splitting the work between them, the Centre group and Margaret Harris took charge of the structural changes, leaving Hunt with responsibility for front-of-house decoration. Meanwhile, Hunt's first season at the New had begun auspiciously with his now legendary production of *Love's Labour's Lost*, continued less happily with Saint-Denis's remorselessly uncut version of *A Month in the Country*, and concluded with another success for Hunt in the Redgrave *Hamlet* in the spring of 1950.

By now, the strain of enforced co-operation was beginning to tell. The four directors had not improved the atmosphere by making it plain that they did not wish Rees to attend their meetings. Not that Rees was over-anxious to attend anyway, as the exhaustive Centre discussions were not to his brisk taste. Hunt, too, grew weary of the Centre meetings. 'The three of them were closely associated and it seemed to be very difficult to get decisions as to practicalities without a lengthy discussion period in which Saint-Denis dominated. It didn't help, arguing all night about style when one had to decide on an opening date and who would play the lead.'

At the same time, the Centre trio found themselves cut off from the Governors. Previously they had had direct access to the Old Vic Trust (who controlled the Company). Now a barrier descended, and they had to negotiate through Hunt and Rees, without any assurance that their views were being sympathetically stated. The situation was particularly infuriating for Devine, who had formerly spoken as the Centre's Chairman in meetings with Esher.

Meanwhile, the first whispers of disapproval began to affect the atmosphere of the school. This was a department in which the Governors had never interfered, but now the visits began. 'I went into a class of Saint-Denis', says Rees, 'and these boys and girls were all being animals; it was like going into a lunatic asylum.' Here come the stock objections: 'It seemed to me that they were practising a sort of amateur psychoanalysis. I felt they were preparing the students for a theatre that didn't exist.' According to Rees there was nothing sinister about these tours of inspection. 'Perhaps Lord Pool went round rather like a C.O. visiting the barracks. But they couldn't in fairness expect him to appreciate what they were up to.' (Why not, if it lay within his responsibilities as a Governor?) Plowright remembers another occasion when 'a group of Vic Governors visited classes and found them unwholesome'. In Saint-Denis's version: 'When the authorities cut our grant some high official was sent to the school for an inspection. He was a very nice man. He smoked a cigar. And the first thing he said was that he didn't know why, but the girls at the school didn't seem to be as pretty as they were at the Royal Academy of Dramatic Art ... More serious, he went into a class and saw that we were improvising animals of all types. And he wrote in his report that he had been the witness of some exercises by which we were debasing human nature to the level of animals. And that he did not think that this was necessary to learn the interpretation of our great national poet Shakespeare.'

Rees declares that he never interfered with the directors in any way beyond telling them when they were overspending. But it is hard to square Rees the modest financial adviser with the Rees who wrote to Lord Esher: 'The Administrator's position must be equivalent to that of Miss Baylis at the Old Vic or Mr Hugh Beaumont in H. M. Tennent Ltd.' However disinterested his role, no one could claim more power than that.

On November 14 the Old Vic Theatre reopened with the first production of the jointly planned season, Hugh Hunt's *Twelfth Night*. According to Devine, it was from this moment, with all the contending parties occupying the same building, that official policy changed and Rees openly assumed the role of 'boss'.

He was sceptical about the second production, Saint-Denis's *Electra*, designed by Barbara Hepworth and intended as a revelation of the new forestage. He complained that there were nervous breakdowns in rehearsal, and that when Hepworth's statue of Apollo arrived, 'Saint-Denis said "Don't put it on the stage yet because I don't know which way round it goes."' Rees says he warned the trio that *Electra* would lose money, which it did. Peter Duguid recalls 'Stephen Arlen coming into the dressing room one night and saying, "Look at this bloody *Electra*. Empty houses. Who the hell wants to do this?" It had good notices and was obviously a major event. And for a company manager to say that to the actors! Not good.' On the first night there were three separate first-night parties in three separate offices.

The third production, Devine's *Bartholomew Fair*, was another exercise in bringing the action forward into the house by virtue of the Sonrel forestage. Perhaps through financial compromise, the new stage did not succeed in delivering the intended knockout blow to the proscenium. It consisted of three bulging hemispheres approached by forestage doors and steps down to the pit. The hemispheres could be linked up, but the idea was to provide acting areas that could be used remotely from the central platform. This carving up of the space greatly restricted the actors' movement, especially as the stage was built on two levels. Anyone making a sweeping entrance through a forestage door was liable to plunge over the edge and straight down into the pit. Val May says, 'the real flaw in the design was that it pushed the audience back from the action because of the moat. Everybody working on it felt that it didn't really help to promote the feeling of contact with the house, which was its main purpose.'

For Rees, not surprisingly, the forestage was a plain case of the Emperor's New Clothes. 'I remember standing in the stalls with Saint-Denis during the dress rehearsal of *Electra*, and he said: "You see, we could not have done this without the forestage." Then the company went on tour to the Alexandra Theatre, Birmingham, which has no forestage. He looked at it and said, "It's very strange, it seems to work better." '

So far, the only open division was between the Administrator and the directorate. This broke into a three-way split when, early in December, Hunt gave the Centre trio to understand that he was to be appointed senior director over the other three. A week later, to Hunt's humiliation, Lord Esher denied that the offer had ever been made. After that, any lingering hopes of a stable *ménage à quatre* were finally extinguished. It was Rees who broke the deadlock by persuading the Governors to dissolve the amalgamation and revert to the former separation of the Centre from the Company. The Governors not only agreed to this: they went on to say that because of the grave financial position of the Old Vic it would be impossible to maintain more than three directors. From this point, the situation swiftly accelerated to its climax. In February Devine wrote to Esher proposing a rota system, under which Byam Shaw would retire for a year and return at the expiry of Hunt's three-year contract. To this, the Governors replied with a nine-point memorandum stating it as their intention that 'sooner or later' the trio should be given a term of office with Shaw running the company, Devine the Young Vic and Saint-Denis the school. But they gave no assurance of this because 'unlike the Theatre Company, both these institutions may lose Arts Council and Treasury support'.

This disclaimer, Devine remarked in a letter to Esher, gave them little confidence, as in the past, 'You, Sir, as Chairman, even in the most difficult times, have declared that the Governors would not be dictated to by the Arts Council.'

However, on the basis of a verbal hearing, the trio assented to the nine-points paper. A fortnight later, on April 12, the paper reached them in its official form, now embellished with an addendum extending Hunt's appointment until June 1953 and leaving Saint-Denis's future a blank. It was to be two more years before anything would change. If four directors were too many now, no doubt three would be too many next year. It was pretty clear who the next sacrifice would be. Shaw had the school and Devine had the Young Vic. What, precisely, did Saint-Denis do? As the Governors had chopped off the head of the scheme by doing away with EXP, it was only logical to axe its creator as well.

Devine replied with an embittered letter to Esher, restating the circumstances that had infected the organization with 'an atmosphere of petty squabbling and jockeying for position ... which has turned the Vic into a miserable place in which everyone feels lost and many feel disgusted'. Voicing the suspicion that the Governors were only maintaining the Centre 'out of a sort of half conviction', he concludes, 'We feel strongly enough about what we have written to bring ourselves to offer, with the greatest regret and difficulty, that we should resign if these matters cannot be resolved.' On May 7, without further consultation, Esher replied, accepting the resignations; and two days later, they were announced to the press. 'The Governors of the Old Vic', says Byam Shaw, 'had quite a good record for getting rid of directors. Tyrone Guthrie, Richardson, Olivier, Saint-Denis, Devine, and myself. All sacked. But not Hugh Hunt: he kept on.'

The resignations were reported in the morning papers of May 10. The evening papers of the same day announced that all but one of the school's teaching staff were also walking out. In a letter to Rees, pledging their support for the directors, the fifteen signatories asked to be released at the end of the term. Their spokesman, Peter Streuli (Shaw's assistant on the acting course), described this decision as an act of 'blind loyalty'. Their superiors, who knew why they had resigned, were likewise giving nothing away. All the *Daily Mail* succeeded in extracting from Devine was: 'We have agreed with the Governors not to reveal our reasons.' 'The chief inference', observed a *Times* leader, 'is that each party to the dispute believes itself to have a strong, if inarticulate, case.' The trio later came to recognize that their silence at this point had been their greatest tactical error.

The official silence had its guaranteed effect of exciting the press into a fever of curiosity. Life back at the Edwardes Square flat was enlivened with incessant phone calls and unannounced visits by reporters from whom Devine would take refuge in the garden. It all seemed very silly to his nine-year-old daughter

Harriet: 'Some fuss about a little theatre school; and yet he seemed to be this big celebrity with everybody trying to see him. I couldn't imagine why.'

The Governors could not have put it better themselves. Why should anyone care about a school with a mere 120 students and a troupe for children, when the fate of the Old Vic Theatre Company and the National Theatre itself was at stake? Unfortunately for the Governors, a lot of people did care. Follow-up stories kept the subject alive on news pages, and letters started pouring in, many of them contrasting the Governors' blood-stained track-record with the achievements of the Centre trio. One of the first, signed by James Maxwell and eighty-nine other students, appeared in *The Times* after their direct plea to the Governors had met with a chilly silence. Motley announced that in future they would not design for the Vic. Letters came not only from theatre workers, but from politicians, writers, artists, publishers and musicians: in short, a substantial cross-section of the intellectual community who awoke with outrage to the sight of one of its limbs being amputated by the philistines.

J. B. Priestley put the case diplomatically in a letter to the *Listener* praising *Bartholomew Fair* as

> a superb evening's entertainment, crammed with colour, bustle, clowning and Johnson's tangy prose, and some astonishingly good character acting from the younger members of the Old Vic Company. The producer of the uproarious piece – and I cannot imagine a harder job – is Mr George Devine, and it will be a great pity if he, together with his two brilliant colleagues, is allowed to resign from the Old Vic.

If other correspondents had opted likewise for a mollifying approach they might have had a positive effect. But in the face of such an onslaught, retraction would have cost the Governors what shreds of credibility they still retained. Meanwhile, time was fast ticking away to the date of July 13 when the Queen was due to lay the foundation stone of the National Theatre on the South Bank. By then perhaps the Old Vic would have injured itself beyond repair. The old chance was to find a leader from outside with enough authority to halt the collapse.

Hunt and his general manager, Stephen Arlen, both had the same idea and appealed to Tyrone Guthrie to come to the rescue. Guthrie agreed, but on his own terms: not as co-equal with Hunt, but as a general manager with sweeping powers who would come in, do a decisive salvage job, and then get out. Glad to have found their strongman, all parties agreed to this, including the Centre trio even though they had not been consulted over the appointment. Guthrie, after all, was an old comrade who had supported Saint-Denis's work since the beginning of the L.T.S. On June 3 the papers reported that Guthrie had been released by the Liverpool Festival Society to join the Old Vic as manager with 'undefined powers'. He then invited his three old friends out to dinner in Soho for a scene here recalled by Byam Shaw.

> He started off by saying, 'I think I'd better tell you that I've advised the Governors to close the school.' Michel said, 'But why, Tony?' He said, 'Because I don't believe in training for actors.' Michel said, 'But are you mad? Do you remember that you gave me £1,000 of your own money to help start the L.T.S.? Why have you changed?' Tony said, 'I don't know, but I have changed and that's it.' Michel said, 'And what about the Young Vic?' He said, 'I've told them that in my opinion it's not worth the money being spent on it.' Michel said, 'But have you ever seen a performance of the Young Vic?' Tony went red and said, 'No, I haven't.' And that was the end of the party. It was to us inexplicable. One can only assume there was a feeling of resentment towards Michel because of his nationality and his possible influence on the English theatre.

To Marius Goring, who was equally stunned by this move, Guthrie gave another explanation for it. 'Pity. Two sports masters in love with the head. Very unhealthy. Got to be stopped.'

The disbanding of the Young Vic 'for the present' was reported within a fortnight of Guthrie's appointment; but the future of the school was still unresolved. Evidently the Governors had qualms about turning students adrift in mid-course; and they invited the trio to stay on for three more terms, by which time the school might have found another patron.

To the three beneficiaries, the reprieve appeared a blatant face-saving manoeuvre. 'We will not exonerate the Governors', Devine wrote, 'for their abominable treatment of us; nor Tony for his careless attitude to ... our side of the organization.' However, they agreed to the three-term extension. Saving the school was more important than prosecuting a vendetta against the Old Vic, and the scheme did offer some chance of survival. There were various possibilities. Devine listed the ideas of a link with Hugh Beaumont and the Tennent management, and of reassembling under the banner of the Olivier–Richardson group who had first brought them into the Vic. Likeliest of all was the hope of transferring the school from the Vic to the Shakespeare Memorial Theatre, now under the control of another old friend from Waterloo Road, Anthony Quayle.

One by one, however, the lifelines snapped. This time there was no King of Siam to wave his wand over the scene, as there had been at the birth of the L.T.S. After the war, eccentric millionaire patrons were thin on the ground, and any help the school might hope for was liable to come too late. In September we find Devine noting that the Director of the Arts Council 'in the guarded fashion that is the privilege of wretches in his position' had indicated that the council might be interested in lending a hand. Otherwise 'the future for the trio and their plans is, at present, a blank.' He wrote:

> It is my firm conviction that we will never forgive ourselves as long as we live if we do not make a desperate effort to continue and to crown our work of the past five years. We should announce our plans as soon as possible so that everyone knows what we want to do, and if we fail to find the necessary money, it will not be our fault.

Devine penned this challenge while holidaying on the Côte d'Azur where he had described the situation to Gordon Craig. The story made Craig 'roar with laughter and suddenly go black with rage', and finally advise Devine to 're-attack more strongly than ever. You're bound to win in the end. The others are nothing.' But, like Devine's previous outburst over the three-term compromise, this battle-cry died on his lips. No defiant announcements appeared. No bold new plans emerged. Still hoping something would turn up, the three directors returned for the winter term. The Governors' position now was that while they declared themselves anxious to save the school, they also felt obliged to sell it, offering the trio a first refusal on the Dulwich premises. The trio, needless to relate, were unable to embrace this magnanimous offer, and in May they informed the staff that their engagements would be concluded at the end of term. They were also starting to cut themselves adrift. One tangible product of the Stratford negotiations was Byam Shaw's appointment as co-director with Quayle. Saint-Denis had re-opened the lines for a return to France. Devine had picked up his West End connections and directed Samuel Taylor's Broadway comedy *The Happy Time*. They were making themselves professionally available again for the first time in five years.

Within the school, former tensions between staff and students dissolved. It was one of the most rebellious of the students, Frank Dunlop, who set the wheels turning to bring the matter up in Parliament. Saint-Denis was amazed and touched by the loyalty that now bound his family together. Ustinov's Minotaur mellowed to a much gentler beast in the final year. And Michael Redgrave recalls that when Saint-Denis took him round the school for the last time, he was in tears.

Devine and Dunlop's co-production of *The Provok'd Wife* appeared in the June end-of-term programme, bringing the Dulwich curtain down for the last time. The *News Chronicle* reported that it cost £40 to stage, and 'could be shifted lock, stock and barrel to any West End theatre tomorrow and more than hold its own'.

The matter finally reached the House of Commons on July 17 when two Opposition members took it up with the Financial Secretary, John Boyd-Carpenter. Wedgwood Benn opened up by asking the Chancellor of the Exchequer to make future grants to the Arts Council conditional on their providing funds to maintain the school. Philip Noel-Baker followed with a question summarizing the events of the year:

> In view of the fact that the Governors of the Old Vic have received very large sums of public money, and since, instead of making the theatre into a national theatre – as we had all hoped they would – they have lost money, lost the best directors and producers, lost the best artists, closed the Young Vic and now have closed the school, can the Government do nothing to secure a better system of administration for this great national institution? (Cheers)

To this, Boyd-Carpenter replied that he would prefer not to comment. No one spoke up for the Governors. There were the makings here of a promising row which the trio might well have turned to their advantage. Dunlop believes that 'if they had chosen to fight at that moment, the school would have gone on. But Saint-Denis was too tired. Everything had been taken away from him, and he'd had such a battering that he didn't want to fight any more.' On July 31 he returned to France to start again from scratch as founding director of the Centre Nationale Dramatique de l'Est at Strasbourg. Devine and Saint-Denis remained friends to the end of their lives; but this was the end of their twenty-year working alliance. Saint-Denis, the elder man, outlived Devine. But it was from the collapse of the Vic Centre that his own decline – the long sequence of minor strokes and almost-perfect recoveries – began.

In recounting the rise and fall of the Vic Centre I am aware that I have not kept Devine in the foreground. Although it dominated his life for six years, he played only a supporting role in the events, and it would be falsifying the drama to magnify him into its hero. But the Vic story cannot be glossed over. Second only to the Royal Court, it was the most important episode in Devine's career, and it cast a shadow over his future path.

Twenty-five years later, most of the key issues determining how the British theatre works can be traced back to their origin in the post-war Old Vic. The hazards of centralized funding and the arbitrary power of Governing Boards; the relationship between directors and administrators; the official preference for institutions rather than men, and the question of how far smaller ventures should be sacrificed on the altar of the National Theatre.

These and other issues were dramatized in the career of the Vic Centre; and, as a drama, it is there for everyone to interpret in his own way. The story leaves a lot of 'ifs' behind. What would have happened if EXP had been built; if Saint-Denis had gained control of the National Theatre; if there had been money to build it in 1955 and if the Queen had not laid the foundation stone in the wrong place? And, more to the immediate point, what direction would Devine have taken if he had been in the position to spend his remaining years with the old team?

Weighing the facts against the possibilities, one would not exchange the career Devine went on to make for the career he might have had as Saint-Denis's second-in-command. He had seen the Centre discarded as an unnecessary luxury and the 'principle of the organized development of young talent at various levels' destroyed. He had observed that no one else came to the Centre's rescue when the Vic Governors abandoned it, and that the combined work of the L.T.S. and the Vic School had not appreciably dinted the existing system. From this he had good reason to conclude that there was no further point in attempting a reform of the English theatre through the training

of actors. His loyalty to Saint-Denis was total, but he also wanted
to make things happen. The lesson he most took to heart from
the whole embittering experience, once the air had cleared and
he had time to lick his wounds, can be summed up in two words:
'Never resign.'

10

FREE-LANCE

FOR the first time in his career, Devine was now a free man. Unlike his two co-directors, who had gone straight from the Vic Centre into other institutions, he dropped out of organizational life. This, if he had wanted it, was his chance to build up a personal reputation. All the options were open again. Having made his 'actor-effort' in the early 1930s, it was logical for him to go on to his director-effort, especially as he now had public respect, long experience and ready-made contacts on his side.

For anyone with conventional ambitions, this situation would have come as a relief. It was not so for Devine, who began laying plans for another long-term project while the débris of the last was still subsiding. If there had been another family like the Vic Centre, he would have joined it immediately. But there was no such family, and it was not until 1956 that his new scheme finally emerged as the English Stage Company. In the meantime he settled for working as well as he could inside the existing system, and the director-effort duly took place, yielding four busy free-lance years. Never was Devine's name, as an artist, more often before the public than between 1952 and 1955. But his heart was not fully in the work, and these are the years in which he left the least impression behind.

Most of his work was divided between two addresses. When Byam Shaw joined Quayle at the Stratford Memorial Theatre, he retained Devine as a regular free-lance director contributing at least one show a season. A year before that, when Stephen Arlen moved from the Old Vic to become General Manager of Sadler's Wells in 1951, he enlisted Devine as a director of opera. The first attachment was a straight continuation of his previous work, with old friends and a repertory he knew inside out. The second was new territory, not only for Devine but for the English operatic stage.

Some cross-fertilization had already taken place in the post-war years between the operatic and dramatic theatres, notably with Guthrie's lightning descents on the Wells and Peter Brook's *enfant terrible* operations at Covent Garden. But there was no continuity: and, with the exception of the actor-producer-composer Dennis Arundell, the figure of the professional operatic director had not yet emerged in Britain. When Arlen joined the Wells it was with the intention of remedying this state of affairs. A small house with a nucleus of regular principals and two manageable choruses, the Wells was more suited to his purpose than any great operatic battleship would have been. And, with the approval of his Director Norman Tucker, Arlen embarked on a long-range plan to transplant the work of the Old Vic Centre into the world of opera. Engaging Devine was only the first move. Later he secured Saint-Denis for the 1960 production of Stravinsky's *Oedipus Rex* (which remained in the repertory for some fifteen years); and after that, the appointment of Byam Shaw as a staff director and the formation of Margaret Harris's design school.

Unlike the young generation of theatrical musicians (Colin Graham, John Cox) who started emerging at the turn of the 1960s, none of the Centre directors could read music. Arlen's priority was dramatic. He wanted to correct a lop-sided tradition and demonstrate that Verdi and Mozart could speak as truthfully as Shakespeare. So when Devine went to the Wells he was again involving himself in a theatrical cause as well as learning a new skill. His first production, in January 1951, was *Don Carlos* with Amy Shuard and Joan Hammond. As this was in an adapted version of the score, he had to learn it from a taped piano performance; a most unsatisfactory compromise which denies the director the dramatic clues of orchestration. But *Carlos*, according to Lord Harewood and others, was a robust début, in which he had already mastered the problem of reconciling natural movement with trio and quartet groupings. People found it to be Schiller plus Verdi; not a ridiculous old melodrama clothed in marvellous music.

In all, he directed five operas for the Wells: following *Carlos* with *Eugene Onegin* (1952), Heinrich Sutermeister's *Romeo and Juliet* (1953), Lennox Berkeley's *Nelson* (1954) and *The Magic Flute* (1955). Within the company he became a byword for reliability. If you were in a Devine production, you knew that nothing would be left to chance, that everything would be prepared without rows or last-minute panics, and that nobody's time would be wasted. As one veteran Wells singer puts it: 'He knew his business and he knew his composer: he was musician enough for that.' Another ranks him as 'top on dialogue and recitative of all the straight theatre directors I've worked with'.

Although he was striving to advance the cause of realism on the operatic stage, he did not go out of his way to shake things up. There were occasional clashes with the musical establishment, as where he directed Shuard to sing one of Eboli's big arias lying flat on her stomach. In *Onegin*, he and Margaret Harris set the house on a truck that turned round showing the interior of Tatiana's bedroom, logically upstairs. This meant that the Letter Scene was sung up in the air; at which point musical authority intervened and brought the heroine back to earth. But such collisons were few, partly because Devine preferred working outside the traditional repertory. In *Romeo and Juliet* (a British première) he made his first attempt to apply the principle of Shakespearian continuity to an episodic score. In *Nelson*, a world première, Alan Pryce-Jones's libretto gave him a straight invitation to historical realism, which he seized as much in the drawing-room hostilities between Lady Hamilton and Lady Nelson (Anna Pollak in curl-papers) as in the documentary reconstruction of the death scene in the cockpit of the *Victory*.

Tom Hammond, a repetiteur at the Wells, says that Devine's work there had an 'earnest, almost Russian feeling'. There was not much trace of Devine the comic specialist, with the possible exception of his final production, *The Magic Flute*. This was another Shakespearian exercise with Margaret Harris who looks back on it with a shudder. In *Onegin*, Devine and Harris compressed the staging into four sets, memorably linking the two dance scenes with a pillar motif: simple and rustic for the local hop, ornately classical for the ballroom. Here, as in *The Magic Flute*, they were working for a kind of theatrical unity which had not yet reached the operatic stage, but their achievement remained inconclusive.

Before the *Flute*, Devine's operatic career had already hit its peak in the one production he directed outside the Wells: the world première, at Covent Garden, of William Walton's *Troilus and Cressida*. This was one of a series of large-scale pieces (like *Nelson*

and the Bliss–Priestley *The Olympians*) in which English composers were trying to keep alive the public appetite for new opera
awakened by Britten's *Peter Grimes*. It was by far the biggest
thing Devine had tackled, and in place of his two well-behaved
choruses at the Wells he met the seventy-strong Garden mob,
who talked incessantly through rehearsals and were apt to come
on with handbags and umbrellas in the last act.

The invitation came through Christopher Hassall, Walton's
librettist and Devine's former protégé in the OUDS *Romeo*. In
the summer of 1954 Hassall was collaborating with Walton in
Italy. Over the same period Devine was working at Stratford,
rehearsing to tour in *Hedda Gabler*, preparing *Nelson* for the
Wells, and visiting Greece and Turkey for the British Council.
To these labours he added the vetting of the *Troilus* libretto.
Walton and Hassall had bypassed Shakespeare and gone back to
the non-dramatic sources of Boccaccio and Chaucer. This meant
that they had acquired a heroic story in place of a misanthropic
parable. It also meant that they had to construct the drama themselves, which was where Devine came in as a consultant on plot
mechanics. 'Hassall really had no idea,' says Walton, 'nor had I,
what would go on the stage.'

It had been assumed at Covent Garden that the opera would
be designed by Isabel Lambert, to whom approaches had already
been made on the strength of her *Tiresias*. Devine saw *Tiresias*
and declined to work with her, much to the embarrassment of
the authors and the General Administrator, David Webster.
Devine dug his heels in, and proposed the unexpected name of
Hugh Casson. The piece, he felt, needed 'a certain architectural
strength and stillness that one is much likelier to get from an
architect'. Webster, fearing to lumber a popular touring hit with
monumental sets, grudgingly complied. The conductor, Walton's
nomination, was Malcolm Sargent. It thus came about that the
three artistic arbiters of the production were all newcomers to the
Royal Opera House.

The Casson collaboration yielded a workable set of the required grandeur containing only one serious miscalculation.
Casson had placed the first act temple upstage, with the result
that when the chorus were appealing for the high priest to show
himself, they were facing away from the conductor and singing
into the back wall. Devine solved this by splitting the moment in
half; with the chorus focusing first on the temple doorway, then

turning to focus on a point out front. By this time he had won his battle with the Royal Opera House choristers. 'Listen', he said to them, 'I like to talk to you like this in my normal voice. I can't talk to the principals if I've got to shout. But if you want me to shout, I can.' Ande Anderson, the stage manager, says, 'I suddenly heard this immense voice behind me. QUIET! A roar of sound.' After that, Anderson says, he had them eating out of his hand; the proof of this being that, notwithstanding pub closing times and last buses, the kilted Greeks and Trojans consented without demur to brown up from the big toe to the crotch.

Devine had two reliable colleagues in Casson and Hassall, but where, at the Wells, he was used to going through piano rehearsals with his musical director, this time the musical director was otherwise engaged. Sargent did not arrive until he had an orchestra to conduct; with the result that staging problems that could have been foreseen much earlier (such as the temple scene) had to be solved at the last minute. Devine was as much shocked by this as by Sargent's breezy demand for a personal spotlight. Covent Garden itself was taken aback to discover that the Lion of the Proms was in the habit of marking up time changes in red and then conducting from the time signatures. This was put to the test when one of the staff surreptitiously removed Sargent's own score and substituted an unmarked copy, with gratifyingly apoplectic effect when Sargent came to face the orchestra.

At its opening, the opera achieved popular success without arousing much critical fervour. Devine's contribution was admired for its clear-cut craftsmanship, but hardly as a glittering personal triumph. Harewood, by then working at the Garden, recalls the production as a 'pretty good, solid piece of work' but not in the same class as Devine's *Onegin*. As at the Wells, he had an almost all-British cast (excepting Magda Laszlo's Cressida); among them, such exemplary actor-singers as Richard Lewis and Peter Pears, and newcomers like Geraint Evans. Looking back on that time, Anderson remembers it as normal for a visiting soprano to come in and sing Salome, Musetta and the Queen of Night without changing her hair-style. But in Devine's production, 'you were looking at Troilus and Cressida, not Lewis and Laszlo. When we presented work in English, we brought in English directors, who brought with them their feeling for the straight theatre. I think this is why the standard of English operatic acting is probably the best in the world today, because of those early days when we began to create an acting singer.'

The struggle then going on within the operatic world had already been won on the classical stage. Barker's reforms had passed into standard practice at the Vic and Stratford, and those two stages represented the summit of theatrical art in Britain. There was not a great deal of money about (a director's fee at Stratford was £400, and the top salary for actors was £60 a week), but stars came all the same, confident of basking in an atmosphere of public and critical esteem.

It made obvious sense for Devine to go to Stratford. He was claiming the inheritance of his generation, the reformers of the 1930s who had become the establishment of the 1950s. And for that very reason, the prospect bored him to death. He had done twenty years' spadework on the reform of classical acting, and it could now look after itself. Where was the challenge in working a successful treadmill? He went, all the same, and had his misgivings confirmed. He was soon telling Litz Pisk that he wanted to start again, using none of the people with whom he had worked in the past. Looking back on the Stratford experience, he wrote: 'I found that the reliance of actors on the director was much too great ... They expected you to tell them absolutely everything about the characters they were playing.'

One thing that lured him to Stratford was Quayle's plan of setting up a London base, so as to create a two-stroke engine and save Stratford actors from being cut off from the West End. But although Quayle devoted the whole of 1953 to an Australian fund-raising tour for this scheme, it came to nothing until Peter Hall took over the Aldwych in 1960. It remained business as usual at Stratford in Devine's time. He did not attend planning meetings and was in no position to influence the theatre's policy except through unofficial suggestions. He simply accepted the plays as they came up without any long-term end in view. Scanning the list of his productions, you are left with the impression of a man looking for areas of legitimate novelty within the old routines: bringing in new scenic artists, and composers like John Gardener and Roberto Gerhard.

Volpone, his first Stratford show, seems to have been his own choice. Jonson was certainly a writer after his own heart, and it was a long time since Stratford had presented anything except

Shakespeare. For this production, Devine mobilized the long-neglected machinery installed during the Bridges–Adams régime. This included a sliding stage split in the middle with a 22-foot wing clearance on each side. Under the sliding stage there were two massive lifts which between them could fill the entire space left vacant by the sliding stage. Additionally there were two revolves in the Prompt and O.P. corners. Devine used the lot. Volpone's bed-chamber with its vast four-poster slid out of view to make room for the arrival of the Senate, arising from the deep like a mighty Venetian Wurlitzer. Houses stood or spun round in the corners. The sets were by Malcolm Pride who framed them within a Venetian surround complete with gondolas. 'The stage', commented the *Evening Standard*, 'ascended, dived, capered sideways – did everything, in fact, except sit up and beg.' Inevitably there came the night of a power failure, but the stage management were equal to that. They took up the curtain and gave the audience the added spectacle of the stage staff cranking sets into position with huge windlasses.

Quayle played Mosca to Ralph Richardson's Volpone. This was at a time when British reviewers had stumbled on the discovery that Richardson was a 'mannered actor' and had been telling the readers so all through the 1952 season. As the July opening approached, Devine worked hard to stop this happening again, insistently requesting Richardson to speed up his delivery. Richardson listened with grave courtesy and invariably acquiesced. 'Absolutely,' he would agree: 'of course. I do see;' only to revert to his old tempo when the scene came round again. 'In the end,' says Quayle, 'Richardson did it his way. In performance the actor always wins.'

This generally applies to Devine's relationships with leading actors. He had authority, but not the hypnotic dominance of directors like Guthrie or Brook. Actors enjoyed working with him because they knew they were in safe hands: the homework would always have been done, and rehearsal etiquette strictly observed. Quayle says he was 'like a cabinet-maker, making a beautiful box. You felt in the presence of a man who'd been through something. There was nothing lop-sided about him.' But, as the Richardson story illustrates, he could be overshadowed by outsize personalities. When he directed his first *King Lear* in 1953, there was no question of its being Devine's *Lear*: it was Redgrave's. Also, in the 1953 *Taming of the Shrew*, when the wife-taming scenes started turning ugly and sadistic, Yvonne Mitchell says he was unable to get them back on the originally planned lines as a love game.

What he did supply was a structural reworking of the text. By going back to the pre-Shakespearian comedy, *The Taming of a Shrew*, he kept Sly on stage throughout so as to present the Kate and Petruchio scenes from first to last as a play within a play. To reviewers in the 1950s this came as a delightful shock, especially when coupled with Vivienne Kernot's sumptuously inlaid Jacobean hall which melted away to afford a distant view of Padua with the shadowy figures of the travelling players finally trudging off into the dawn.

For *Lear*, Devine wanted to enlist Henry Moore as designer. When Moore declined, he turned instead to Robert Colquhoun of the famed Hibernian partnership of Colquhoun and MacBryde. Frank Dunlop, as assistant director on this show, was delegated to extract the designs from them which he did by going to their mill in Great Dunmow and sitting out some stupendous binges until the work was finished. Devine, he says, wanted something simple and austere, but failed to get the message across to Colquhoun who produced a set resembling a monolithic bunch of bananas. Drenched in personal symbolism, it was not so much a set as an independent artwork which said everything it had to say without the help of actors. To some reviewers the stage suggested a Stonehenge-like haunt of pagan gods 'with ominous shapes and treeless bogs, lapped round by a green waste of water'. To Kenneth Tynan it simply lacked variety. 'To feel the cold of the heath we must first feel the warmth of the hearth. The present décor dumps us out of doors at curtain-rise and leaves us there.' Thanks to Redgrave, the production was saluted as the finest of Stratford's Coronation season, but not much attention went to its director. However, considering the stage evolution of *King Lear* over the next ten years (including Devine's second attempt), it is worth noting that one feature that did draw comment was its lucidity and restraint, particularly in the mad scenes with Edgar and the Fool: this isolates one of his main disagreements with the post-war classical theatre and his point of exit from it.

A Midsummer Night's Dream, his last contribution to the regular seasons, followed in 1954 – the year of his two operatic premières and *Hedda Gabler*. This was more a postscript than a new show, being based on the Young Vic version, again with décor by Margaret Harris and a company consisting largely of former Vic School students. The main idea was to bring the poetry back to earth and restore the play from romance to folk-lore. Devine saw Oberon as a malevolent personage, and Powys Thomas played him as a bird of prey surrounded by hawk-like underlings. The firefly Titania was likewise accompanied by a troupe of grotesque little sprites. All the immortals were costumed as birds, animals, or insects: and to complete the purge on pretti-ness, Mendelssohn was ditched in favour of the spiky music of Roberto Gerhard. The show had collected glowing opinions for the Young Vic, but Stratford audiences were less prepared to make allowances for an immature company; and the general opinion was that it worked less well second time round.

Apart from co-directing Gielgud in *Much Ado About Nothing*, there remains the one production in which Devine really nailed up his colours. This was the 1955 *King Lear* with Gielgud in the title part and designs by Isamu Noguchi: invariably known as the 'Noguchi *Lear*'. It was Devine's last fling as a big-institution classical director, and for good or bad it has survived as a princi-pal Shakespearian landmark of the 1950s.

Much Ado and *Lear* were launched outside the regular Stratford season as a six-month tour, sandwiching a West End run between Scandinavia and Germany. Besides directing, Devine played Dogberry and Gloucester. Gielgud's *Much Ado* was an old favourite, dating back to 1949 and now enjoying its third revival. Stratford was therefore hedging its bet by coupling an experimental risk with an established hit. *Much Ado* reached the Palace Theatre on July 21: *Lear* a week later, with a pro-gramme note signed by the trio:

> Our object in this production has been to find a setting and costumes which would be free of historical and decorative associations so that the timeless, universal and mythical quality of the story may be clear. We have tried to present the places and the characters in a very simple and basic manner, for the play to come to life through the words and the acting.

The events leading up to that statement date back to the previous autumn when *Lear* was first being discussed. Gielgud and Byam Shaw met Devine for lunch and asked him what he wanted. Devine said, 'The one absolutely positive thing is that I want Noguchi to design it.' This, as it happened, was precisely what Gielgud wanted too: both men having seen Noguchi's work for the Martha Graham ballet. Noguchi was an American-born Japanese combining the professions of sculptor, and designer of furniture and stage décor. Sculpture as he practised it was a means of transforming performance and leisure space with elemental forms like his 'Soft Rock' settee or his hollowed glass table carrying a single long-stemmed flower. A pupil of Brancusi, he also had the instinct of a Japanese gardener. Theatrically he first made his mark with a 1934 design for Graham, consisting of two ropes stretching from the top corners of the proscenium and converging at an illusory infinity. It was with this kind of highly cultivated simplicity that Gielgud and Devine hoped to re-illuminate *King Lear*.

Devine's general attitude was obvious. He had had enough of the Shakespeare Memorial Theatre, which he regarded as 'a death trap'. 'There it is,' he said, 'that great lump of masonry, standing on the riverbank, imposing itself on everyone who has to work there.' *Lear* was an attempt to shake off this dead weight and liberate Shakespeare from the latest accumulation of Bardic débris. For *Lear*, Devine even coined the term 'essentialism' (uncharacteristically highfalutin for him) to suggest what he was trying to do.

In his brief to Noguchi, Devine necessarily left the precise forms up to the designer. But from the hints he did throw out, one can construct at least an outline of what he wanted. First of all, a permanent surround framing a series of fluid locations which, above all, would enable the play to expand beyond the confines of representational scenery. Second, costumes free of historical associations, which would define the essence of each character within the hierarchy of the play and also change so as to mirror the characters' development. 'The gloves', he wrote, 'are gradually removed, so that by the end of Part I no one is any more pretending to be anything but what he is.' Last, a symphonic division of the play into three movements: the first showing a blind pursuit of self-interest; the second showing the revenge of nature; and the third bringing a cathartic resolution. He saw Lear and Gloucester as the spiritual and materialist axis of the tragedy; and he saw Lear's enemies as animals – Goneril as a tigress, Regan as a leopard, Oswald as a weasel.

Armed with these suggestions plus a ground-plan, Noguchi

went to work on a model and in January dispatched his set designs by air-freight from New York. Opening the 'precious box' after extracting it from the customs, Devine found that his prayers had been answered. This was the world of *Lear* translated into the elemental shapes of the universe: egg-forms, triangular caverns, airborn prisms, a multi-faceted ramp, and other mobile abstract pieces, charged with a barbaric geometry fearsomely akin to the play. For Noguchi they carried definite meanings. He worked to a system of colour associations for different personality characteristics. Two moving screens represented aspects of the human will, and a large floating wall represented time. But these were matters of private notation, unimportant to the audience. What did matter to him was creating what he called a 'topography of counterpoint to movement'. Without that interplay, he said, his work would be meaningless. Photographs of the décor do no justice to moments like the storm scene when an ominous group of black shapes dilated and contracted like the iris of an eye according to mood and rhythm.

Devine had insisted from the beginning that scenery and costumes should be conceived together; but so far only the set designs had arrived. He ignored this in his cable of congratulations. He knew Noguchi had never designed costumes before. When they did arrive two months later it also appeared that Noguchi did not draw. Instead he sent paper maquettes, painted and cut to scale. Devine expressed himself pleased with them, but then added, 'you must feel uneasy about their realization.' Noguchi did not seem to be worried. From New York he went down to California, and it was not until the end of May, three weeks before the opening, that he finally arrived in London to survey his handiwork.

He attended a dress parade at the Scala Theatre where the costumes were at last unveiled to the company. 'We put them on', says Gielgud, 'with horror. I thought he'd adapt them and come back. But not at all. He went off to design a garden in Delhi!' Loud complaints resounded from actors caged in latticework armour, surcoats with lifebuoy-like waistbands and ponderous shoulder pieces requiring only to be topped off with a diver's helmet. Gielgud wore a cloak with holes that grew larger and larger throughout the play, prompting comparison with an ambulatory gruyère cheese. 'I went through with it', he says, 'but it killed my performance.' Peggy Ashcroft, as Cordelia, suffered the experience in a state of 'awful despair. With those clothes, I didn't see how anybody could act. Noguchi's intention had been that the clothes should be totally negative. But they were the most positive thing on the stage: you couldn't surmount them.' From the designer's point of view, Jocelyn Herbert's argument against the costumes hits the nail on the head. 'You can abstract a background, but you cannot abstract the human form. If you encase the human body in an abstract shape it becomes a robot.'

Gielgud roundly dismisses the production as a disaster. That is not my memory of it; but equally, the performance I saw bears little relation to the work Devine was hoping for. From his notes and letters, he was clearly trying to bring about a change in acting style no less than in staging. In place of heroic rhetoric, he wanted to match the orientally impassive décor with an equal detachment of movement and delivery. He refers periodically to the Noh, and to neutral facial make-up – 'marking the main planes of the face without "characteristic" detail' – duplicating the tragic mask. The intention, then, was a grand-scale application of the Saint-Denis style. It did not happen. The costumes partly explain this. Gielgud also says that Devine was too much under his control to assert his authority as a director. In the view of Byam Shaw and others, Gielgud retired into his accustomed style when the public arrived. For whatever reason, the two sides did not gell. There was a universal poetic setting with orthodox English classical acting going on inside it.

Quayle tells the story of a visit to the show by Nikolai Okhlopkov, the veteran director of the Moscow Realistic Theatre. Afterwards he went round to Devine's dressing room bubbling over with things to say while Devine was taking off his Gloucester make-up. 'George sat there like a cuddly old bear, smiling and nodding modestly through this enthusiastic torrent of Russian. In the end it came to a stop and the translator took over: "Mr Okhlopkov says this is a very old-fashioned production."' However, when Peter Brook came to direct his famous 'Endgame' *Lear* six years later, one of his first moves was to consult the Noguchi set designs in the Stratford archive.

This does not complete the record of Devine's free-lance years. He did some television and film acting: in 1953 he even went back to the Old Vic to direct Richard Burton in *King John*.

Margaret Harris who designed the show says that this return, barely a year after the Vic Centre collapse, came as a blow to Saint-Denis. The production attempted to cram the play into a three-arched Teatro Olimpico set which was being used for the whole season, and in her view it did not come off.

What did come off was her collaboration with Devine and Ashcroft in the 1954 production of *Hedda Gabler*: a Tennent's show which opened at the Lyric, Hammersmith, in September before moving on triumphantly to the Westminster and thence on tour to Norway. None of the company had played in Ibsen before, and they got off to a disastrously successful start in Dublin where the play was received as an uproarious light comedy. The original director was then dropped, and for the rest of the pre-London run they concentrated on getting to know their author. What finally arrived at the Lyric was a company production that did for middle-period Ibsen what Guthrie's *Peer Gynt* had done for Ibsen the young romantic. Its idiom was carefully situated between the world of mutton-chop whiskers and the present: stretched close enough for the audience to be able to identify with the characters, but not so far as to snap the formal nuances of the dialogue. It was still almost as much a surprise to see Ashcroft reclining with a cigarette as to see her blazing off with a duelling pistol. Individually each character was an intricate egoistic knot. Collectively, the production exposed them all to impartial scrutiny, inviting sympathy for none.

Devine played Tesman as a blinkered academic booby, 'but that label does not convey the weight of painful experience behind the performance. It was the work of someone who knew what it was like to have an ungainly body, and to become bookish as a substitute for being beautiful. It was a brilliantly intelligent study of an unintelligent character: a middle-aged juvenile, evidently fattened up on years of over-feeding by Aunt Julie, and now licking his lips over the one treat he never expected to get. The image of that aging mother's boy, desperately anxious to be liked, connects strongly with the early picture of Devine, the little boy with the photographer's train. It was as Tesman that I first saw Devine, and I can still see the beaming features and the bulging suit, and hear that fatuous yelp, 'Think of that, Hedda, think of that!'

With that memory, I must have seen the production early in its run, as it was around this time that he started dieting. Per-

haps it is a bit too neat to call this performance Devine's farewell
to his old self. But the Tesman who arrived in London in autumn
1954 was not the same Tesman who embarked for Norway in the
winter of 1955. 'That was the last time', Ashcroft says, 'that anyone saw George as a fat man.'

11

THE THIN MAN

After a certain time, when one has got rid of one's desire to exhibit oneself, the creation of conditions in theatre is the only interesting thing left.

George Devine, American *Equity*, February 1961

ONE day in 1955, Litz Pisk happened to meet Devine in the Zwemmer book shop in Charing Cross Road. She did not recognize him at first. Devine acknowledged her with a grunt and then opened a suitcase and filled it with books from the nearest shelf. 'Lift that,' he said. 'That's the amount of weight I've lost.'

Other old friends had the same shock when they met him around this time. It was not simply a question of physique. Something hand changed inside him as well. He was not jolly old George any longer. He seemed colder: and there was a new rasping militancy which some of them did not take to at all. 'He held all these intransigent opinions,' Quayle says: 'about fucking armies and bloody generals, and breaking these bloody institutions. All in that grating voice. I thought, Why argue? He's made his mind up.' This was how he struck colleagues who belonged to his past. It is not how he seemed to people who shared in the enterprise of his last ten years.

Some personal background is necessary to try and account for his transformation from the buffoonish uncle of the Old Vic Centre into the grizzled sage of Sloane Square. First, his marriage had gone wrong. The ten-year gap between himself and Sophie may not have mattered in their early days together, but it mattered increasingly when he came back from the war. Nor had he been a roaring success as a father. To begin with, he found it hard to get on with the four-year-old Harriet who saw him as an intruder and resented having the house swamped with grand visitors and being dumped on friends when he took her mother away on holidays. He used to amuse her by dressing up and cracking groan puns: and there was a running joke between them on the awful fate awaiting Harriet when she grew up, married to an office worker and living in a surburban semi with a brood of repulsive children. But once the Vic Centre got into its stride, both parents were too devoured with work to have much of a domestic life, and Harriet received a haphazard education, ranging from Victorian repressive to Bloomsbury progressive, before leaving school at fifteen. It was not until Devine's free-lance years and her adolescence that the two had much continuous contact, by which time a certain distance had been set between them. His tormented relationship with his mother, now living alone in a Camden Town bed-sitting room, continued as before.

It was in this situation, where his home life had become a bleak background to his working life, that he fell in love with Jocelyn Herbert, his former pupil at the L.T.S. Although Jocelyn had dropped out of the theatre to marry and have children, she and Devine had never lost contact. The two families were already on terms of close friendship at the time of Devine's move, early in 1954, to a house in Lower Mall, Hammersmith, which made him a neighbour both of Jocelyn and of her father, A. P. Herbert. But the new relationship did not begin over riverside dinner parties; it began in their working collaboration over a little Goldoni production for Frank Dunlop's Piccolo Theatre on the outskirts of Manchester.

One thing that brought them together was a shared loathing for the whole apparatus of well-to-do domesticity: they liked the *tréteau nu* as a living environment no less than on the stage. Like Devine, Jocelyn was devoted to Saint-Denis as someone who had shaped the direction of her life. And with his flair for divining the growth of talent, Devine recognized in her a potential stage artist of the first rank. As for personal feelings, it happened that both of them had reached the end of the marital road at the same time. Devine was forty-four, and Jocelyn seven years younger; but their lifelong attachment began with the torrential floods of letters and pains of separation that normally betoken a first love.

There commenced a double exit in agonized slow motion; Jocelyn was unable to walk out on her children and Devine could not yet nerve himself to leaving Sophie. It was not until the end of the 1950s that they had finally cut themselves free and were openly living together. It was during this time that Devine decided he had had enough of the fat man. But this was merely one by-product of the self-protective time-bomb which had exploded inside him. Very unusually for anyone in his mid-forties, he was getting a second chance.

Another relationship, theatrically of at least equal importance, was with an underworked young television director who rang him one day in 1952 to ask if he would play in an adaptation of a Chekhov story. 'I can't be bothered, the thing bores me to hell,' Devine said and put the phone down. Half an hour later it rang again with an appeal to meet the director for a drink: as a result of which, Devine did appear in Tony Richardson's production of *Curtain Down*. What surprised Devine more than Richardson's powers of persuasion was the fact that, on the day after the shooting, he put through yet another call asking Devine to tell him what was wrong with his direction. This was the beginning of what Devine called their 'great friendship'.

The friendship was a puzzle to some of his old friends. Why should a man of Devine's experience promote a complete beginner like Richardson into equal partnership? For Richardson was no docile protégé. In particular, he regarded Michel Saint-Denis as a baneful influence. 'I used', he says, 'to dread all that side of George.' 'I do not understand it,' was Saint-Denis's alleged response: 'George is in love.'

At Oxford, Richardson's college, like Devine's, was Wadham. Here, as it happens, I had a room immediately above his and often encountered his heron-like figure on the stairs and crossing the quadrangle to breakfast carrying our post-war butter and sugar rations in jam-jars. He had a penetrating reedy voice which could be heard from several tables away, uttering dicta like 'I cannot *bear* Antony and Cleopatra; they are my *noirest bêtes*.' He was, it seemed, an aesthete from Shipley; and with characters like Kenneth Tynan and Kingsley Amis on the scene, there was stiff competition in that department. However, Richardson soon made it clear (like Devne before him) that he had longer-range objectives than making it as an Oxford personality. He was in a tremendous hurry. Within weeks of his arrival he had taken a hall in Cowley for a production of Marlowe's *Faustus*, with the middle scenes quarried out and filled up with chunks of

Tamburlaine and news flashes of Faustus in New York. He followed this up with college productions, a vacation tour of *Romeo and Juliet* (with Nigel Davenport and David William), and then – as President of the OUDS – with a run of *Peer Gynt* at the Oxford Playhouse.

As a bit-player in some of these shows, I developed a grudging awe for Tony Richardson, as he seemed to be plugged into some source of energy denied to the common herd. He seemed never to get tired. At three in the morning, with a cast dropping with exhaustion, he would be ready to take a fencing rehearsal. He also seemed quite impervious to ridicule and incapable of losing his nerve.

Richardson stories often turn on his ruthlessness. As a boy in Shipley he had run an amateur theatre with William Gaskill. On one occasion they were trying to raise money for a show at the same time that Richardson's father was running for election to the Tory council. 'You've got to come canvassing for my father,. said Richardson. 'But I'm a Socialist,' Gaskill objected. 'Look' Do you want to do this production or not? It's the only way to get the money.' The Shipley Young Theatre got its show.

Between Richardson and Devine there was one strong personal link in their shared childhood memory of the misery of team games which had left a lasting sense of physical inadequacy. Otherwise it was an attraction of opposites. Devine, always very humble when he felt in the presence of a superior talent, was impressed by Richardson's fire: the sheer speed of his mind, his energy and his capacity for making lightning decisions. Richardson, in turn, saw Devine as an experienced man of the theatre with the know-how and connections to get things moving. As he puts it, 'Devine knew all about the organization side, and I knew the plays.' His idea at this time was to find a platform for work by Tennessee Williams, Giraudoux and other foreign playwrights then unfamiliar in Britain. Besides bringing ideas, Richardson also brought in a potential backer in the person of a wealthy middle-aged woman whom he knew from the Oxford stage. Devine sealed the alliance by engaging Richardson as his assistant at Stratford and giving him a flat in Lower Mall.

This was within a few months of the collapse of the Vic Centre; so throughout the free-lance years his real plans were ticking away in the background. What, precisely, did he want at that time? Richardson says that, besides admiring Devine as a master craftsman, he was also attracted by his 'vision of what the theatre should be in the largest sense'. That vision still had a lot to do with Saint-Denis. But one definite point of agreement between them was that their experiment should be conducted in the open. Hitherto, the kind of repertory they were interested in had flared up as a brief exception in the West End or lived a hole-in-corner existence in little theatre clubs. Practically every other country in Europe had had its Théâtre Libre or Freie Bühne where a regular public had been found for a regular programme of intelligent new work. In Britain, nothing essential had changed since Shaw's diagnosis in the 1890s of why sensible people steered clear of the West End's entertainment booths. Surely by now even the laggard British were ready for something better. To put this to the test, it must genuinely happen in public, not within the cocoon of an elitist theatre club. Clubs had served their purpose in the 1930s and had now outlived their usefulness. Hence Devine's antagonism towards the Mercury Theatre and its prize hothouse bloom, the poetic drama movement.

The theatres he and Richardson started exploring were straight commercial premises like the Royalty, the Kingsway, and the Royal Court. In support of their case they prepared a nine-page memorandum, plus a detailed budget, announcing their proposed repertory and general policy. It opened with a statement sadly familiar to British ears. 'Modern movements in music, sculpture, painting, literature, cinema and ballet all have reasonable circulation, but the comparable body of work in the theatre has no outlet.' To remedy this lack, the document offers a list of neglected writers (only two British out of a total of twenty-one) and a scheme for ten productions a season by a small permanent company. There would also be a permanent setting, an audience-building organization, and training courses for writers and actors. From all this, 'a truly contemporary style' should develop. Saint-Denis would have approved down to the last detail. Even the set was referred to as a *dispositif*, and the audience scheme was to be modelled on the *Associés du Vieux Colombier*. The grand objective, as ever, was 'style'.

The memorandum went through four drafts, and by the time it reached its final form in August 1963 the partners had lost their backer but found a theatre. As Devine tells the story, they went round to see Richardson's patroness who 'appeared in a kimono and we had brandies. Then Tony said, "This is the man who is going to run the theatre." Of course, the next day he got a letter saying, "I have thought about it and I don't want to have anything to do with it."' It was the old chestnut of the L.T.S. and the King of Siam; and, as in the 1930s, they followed it up with a blanket fund-raising appeal, circularizing their plans to baronets, biscuit firms, banks, chain stores, charities, oil companies, publishers, and leading members of their own profession including the Stratford management. Some people rallied round: notably Sybil Thorndike and O. B. Miller of the John Lewis Partnership.

Meanwhile, they were negotiating for a three-year tenancy at the Royal Court Theatre. Blitzed during the war, the Royal Court had been leased by the Cadogan Estate to Alfred Esdaile, a retired music-hall comedian and inventor of the microphone that comes up out of the floor. Esdaile's General Manager at the Court was Oscar Lewenstein, formerly a pillar of the left-wing Unity Theatre movement and editor of Unity's *New Theatre* magazine to which Devine was an occasional contributor. Lewenstein combined Marxism with an acute business sense and a flair for finding good new plays. He was as interested as anyone in creating an outlet for the new drama, including his own properties. Esdaile, another enthusiast for the new drama, was also interested in sub-letting his building to someone who could pay the rent. One early taker was Devine's old Oxford rival, Giles Playfair, who had already installed a company at the Court with the plan of launching a playwrights' theatre. This venture broke up acrimoniously after the resounding flop of *The Bride of Denmark Hill*, an American play about Ruskin with which he had seen fit to open the season.

By the time Devine and Richardson arrived on the scene, the Court was enjoying a breathing space with Laurier Lister's long-running revue *Airs on a Shoestring*, which Richardson describes as a 'stop-gap' production brought in to keep the theatre running until they were ready. They had £2,500 in the kitty, leaving – so they thought – another £5,000 to collect. Devine talked Quayle into considering an amalgamation with Stratford: and in October, the Arts Council unanimously accepted the Royal Court scheme. Then, in Devine's account, there came 'a historic occasion when Quayle and myself went to see Esdaile. He said, "Right, you can have it for ... " and he named some fantastic sum. Hopeless. So the whole thing collapsed.' When the Arts Council contacted Esdaile, it appeared that he was unwilling even to negotiate during the run of the 'stop-gap' show which continued for a highly profitable eighteen months.

Meanwhile, unknown to Richardson or Devine, another little cadre had entered the revolutionary field. It originated not in London but at the Taw and Torridge Festival in Devon and centred on the figure of Ronald Duncan, one of Britten's librettists and the author of two long-running West End plays. Together with Britten and two other friends – Lord Harewood and a local schoolmaster, J. E. Blacksell – Duncan had launched the festival in 1953. Among other things, it brought the English Opera Group down to Devon, not to mention Joan Littlewood in *Mother Courage* (which Lewenstein presented). But high on Duncan's list of priorities was the presentation of his own work; no easy matter, as commercial managements had no chance of recouping production costs in a fortnight's festival run. The answer, Duncan decided, was to set up a management for the performance of non-commercial plays; to which end he recruited an old Cambridge friend, Greville Poke, amassed a Council of impressive names, drafted an appeal to the Arts Council, and pursued the by now well-trodden path to the Royal Court where he broached the idea of the English Stage Company to Oscar Lewenstein. Lewenstein, as before, showed interest, even though the list of prospective plays had now switched from Brecht and Sartre to Cocteau and Montherlant.

At that time the four founders were aiming merely to set up productions that would tour arts festivals and, at the most, have a brief showing in some outlying London theatre. However, they lacked the capital even for that modest ambition. Lord Harewood says, 'I then performed the greatest service I ever did for the E.S.C. by refusing to be its Chairman. The Chairman must be someone who can raise money.' The next service was performed by Blacksell who, through an R.A.F. connection, suggested offering the Chair to Neville Blond. Blond was a Manchester businessman and a chief government adviser on transatlantic trade. Married to a Marks and Spencer heiress, he had lately sold his share in the textile firm of Blond Brothers and retired. In his late fifties, he was extremely wealthy and looking for something to do. But apart from backing C. B. Cochran revues, he was not known to have any interest in the theatre. Duncan and Greville Poke, not expecting much, took him to lunch, and by the end of the meal the E.S.C. had changed from a provincial festival service to a continuous metropolitan management. Won over by Duncan's argument, Blond agreed to come in, but only on the condition that the company leased a London theatre; leaving his hosts flabbergasted, he went out to get one.

The theatre in question was no longer the Royal Court but the Kingsway, also controlled by Esdaile. Blond's method of acquiring it was to raise mortgages by using the building itself as security. He also breezed into Esdaile's office and informed him that, as a member of the E.S.C. Council, he would be expected to guarantee £1,000 towards the purchase of his own premises.

With Blond's official arrival as Chairman in November 1954, the next step was to equip the company with an artistic director, as – with the exception of Esdaile – none of the Council members was a practical theatre man. (The first members were Duncan, Harewood, Blacksell, Poke, Blond, Esdaile, Lewenstein, Viscount Duncannon, Lord Bessborough, and Sir Reginald Kennedy-Cox – 'such an odd job lot', Devine remarked, 'that the company's bound to succeed.')

It was at this point that the two groups converged. Lewenstein, remembering the abortive scheme of the previous year, nominated Devine and went round to see him between the matinée and evening performances of *Hedda Gabler*. There followed another lunch at which Devine gave Duncan the impression of being wholly in sympathy with all his theatrical attitudes and plans for the company. He only stipulated that he must have Richardson as his associate. The Council swallowed this, and in March 1955 Devine became the English Stage Company's first artistic director at a salary of £1,560 a year. (In taking the job, he turned down an offer to become head of the Royal Academy of Dramatic Art.) To the Council it must have seemed that they had appointed an experienced and responsible man who would carry out whatever they required of him. 'In those days,' Lewenstein recalls, 'not everyone realized the implications of choosing an artistic director.'

The Kingsway campaign was now in full swing. Another victim of the blitz, the building was a derelict shell, its stage open to the sky and its auditorium full of rubble. The cost of renovation was estimated at £50,000. To drive home the point to potential donors, Blond held a cocktail party amid the débris, decorated for the occasion with ladders and pots of paint. During the party Blond asked Devine to outline the E.S.C.'s policy. Devine obliged by enlarging on the company's plans for touring arts festivals, taking English plays abroad, and encouraging new writers. After a few minutes, Blond had had enough of this; he began wandering round the guests topping up glasses, and finally silenced his artistic director in mid-sentence. Just as Devine had gone through the motions of agreement with Duncan, so he accepted the snub from Blond: it was all part of the price of survival.

If he had been allowed to finish his speech he might also have said something about the building. From his point of view its condition was almost an advantage. Here was the *tréteau nu* with a vengeance. No gilded caryatids, no antiquated equipment, no imprisoning proscenium. The stripping-down process over which he had been labouring for twenty years had been accomplished overnight by a German bomb. Here, at last, was the chance to build the theatre of his dreams. A series of notes he exchanged with Richardson and Margaret Harris give a good idea of what those dreams were. First, they were dictated by a moral attitude. The first priority was not to deceive the audience: the second was to turn the theatrical event into a mutually shared action between actors and spectators. Seeking for some architectural expression of this relationship, he proposed a return to 'air, freedom and space' as a substitute for the picture frame. He did not see the picture frame itself as the principal villain, but merely as a symptom of the whole attitude which had reduced theatregoing to a passive experience. The theatre's task now was to 'restate its milieu'; and this involved the paradox of creating open-air conditions within the confines of a building. In place of 'pseudo-solid architecture' the space must be liberated. The space would necessarily be contained within walls and a roof, but even so there was no need to conceive of the structure as a closed box. One escape route would be to clothe the interior in limiting planes illuminated from *outside*. These planes would form an unbroken line enfolding stage and auditorium into a single zone: in other words, the 'one room' effect. Also, plays would be performed in full light with actors *acting* darkness where necessary (an idea subsequently picked up by William Gaskill in his 1966 production of *Macbeth*). There was to be no 'illusion' in the old sense. Lighting equipment should be visible; pieces of scenery should be frankly inserted into the acting space. Most important, the stage should remain a stage: its sides masked in semi-transparent matting encircling a neutral outer space and an inner acting area. Instead of settings co-extensive with the stage floor, there would be a dramatic space within an actual space; and the presence of that impassive background, existing on the audience's own plane of reality, would guard against any pretence that they were actually looking into Tesman's living room or Ross's desert. Devine's criterion for stage design was whether a set was 'honest', whether it 'tried to cheat'. And, by this route, he had arrived at the point of merging Copeau's stage into the stage of Brecht (no direct copying can have been involved as he had not yet seen the work of the Berliner Ensemble).

Jocelyn Herbert prepared a model of the converted Kingsway, and when the E.S.C. Council turned up to view it, Devine explained that it would be necessary to acquire an adjoining bomb-site for store-rooms and workshops. The Kingsway was in Great Queen Street on an island site entirely surrounded by masonic property, and the Masons refused to budge. It then appeared that months might go by in obtaining the building permits. The estimates, meanwhile, had rocketed to £150,000. There was, therefore, no resistance when Esdaile (who had privately decided to sell out to the Masons) came up with an alternative proposal. Instead of the Kingsway, would the company be interested in leasing that illustrious home of Granville-Barker and George Bernard Shaw, the Royal Court Theatre?

When the news reached Devine, he says he 'flipped, naturally, with the history of that theatre, and said, Sure. "Will you go and look at it?" So I went round, and the place was in a frightful mess. It was very poorly re-installed. Esdaile kept saying, "It's a lovely theatre, beautiful condition, the switchboard ... " Well, you couldn't touch the switchboard without getting a 1,000 volt shock! There was water pouring through the roof. Then Blond said to me, "What sort of a state is the place in?" I said, "It's perfect, Neville, let's take it." I wasn't really going to be fool enough to tell them what it was going to cost.'

12

A WRITERS' THEATRE

WE are now approaching the year of 1956 in which the Royal
Court legend was born. For Devine it was a time of hope and
renewed vitality. Simultaneously two great opportunities had
come his way. The chance of attaining personal happiness with
Jocelyn Herbert; and the chance of carrying out his real aims in
the theatre. As yet, he had achieved neither. His personal life
remained unresolved, and at the age of forty-five, he had seen
and experienced enough of failure to be wary of the obvious
traps. He was a man of absolute integrity in defence of his main
values, and he was never a politician like Richardson. But behind that direct, plain-speaking manner, he could work his way
quite cannily around minor obstacles like the little matter of
Esdaile's switchboard. He played the relationship with Jocelyn
very quietly, and for the first few years there were few people
inside the company who knew about it. She was initially engaged
not as a designer but as a scene painter; there was no trace of
professional partiality. As for the E.S.C., there had been plenty of
similar ventures since Barker's time. All of them had collapsed.
Barker himself lasted only for three years, having made the
crucial error of burning his boats at the Royal Court and moving
to the Savoy (for which reason, Devine once told me, 'I'd never
give this place up.') The idea was not new. What must be new
was the way of making it work. 'If it were not difficult,' he wrote
to Blond, 'other people would have done it before.'

Devine had his own ideas about how to do it. He also had a
Board to deal with, including only one member – Lord Harewood – whom he really counted as an ally. After the Vic Centre
experience he was an old hand with Boards. He knew, if the
Board did not, that theatres are dictatorships, no matter how

festooned with democratic camouflage. But as artistic and financial control were interlocked, there was no evading the formalities of consultation. On some issues he would fight openly, but he very much disliked personal confrontation. Unless clashes of temperament were forced on him, he would more often achieve what he wanted through manipulation: a chance encounter with a disgruntled actor or director, an invitation for a quick drink, and within minutes he could win them back to his side. In his dealings with the Council and Management Committee of the E.S.C., he would preserve a mask of subservience behind which he kept his main purposes intact. 'There are two truths,' he remarked to Norman Collins; 'the truth, and what you tell Neville.' When an Artistic Sub-Committee was set up to vet the proposed plays, he turned it to his own advantage as a buffer between himself and the Council. If Blond were abominably rude to him, never mind, Blond was also capable of picking up the telephone and securing large overdrafts. If Ronald Duncan arrived from Devon bearing ominous manuscripts of verse drama, these must be considered with every token of respect, short of actually putting them on: without Duncan there would have been no English Stage Company. Subsequently he found an invaluable Management Committee ally in Robin Fox, a brilliant diplomat who was able to sell Devine's policies to Blond with effortless ease (this applied particularly to projects involving Oscar Lewenstein, with whom Blond was never on very good terms).

Of all these strained relationships, the relationship with Duncan was the most delicate. Devine had small regard for Duncan's work which he viewed as an irrelevant hangover of the club theatre decade. Duncan's high church attachments, his elitist attitudes and his literary bias stood for a tradition which Devine intended to supplant by establishing an alternative milieu for modern writing in the theatre. It is superbly ironic that the architect of the demotic writers' theatre should have received his brief from the high priest of the poetic drama movement. Each regarded himself as forward-looking; and as hostility built up between them at the Royal Court, each came to regard the other as a fossilized relic of the 1930s.

Devine hated the situation, and repeatedly told his colleagues how much he regretted being unable to talk to Duncan 'man to man'. But there was nothing he could do to stop the rift widening as his theatre proceeded on a course so remote from the one Duncan had planned. He was applying the lesson he had learned at the Vic Centre. He and his colleagues knew their trade: governing boards did not. He was there to carry out a mission: they were there (so he told an interviewer ten years later) for what they could get out of it. So the first rule was to hang on: to put up with anything rather than resign. 'How many times', he said later on, 'I had to eat shit to get what I wanted. But I was determined not to die. I wanted to survive more than anything.'

Repeated disappointments over the years had not shaken his belief in the supremacy of the writer. He was used to the stage's remoteness from the world outside, but this had now reached the point of complete dissociation. He wrote:

> Had we not seen six million Jews murdered? Were we not seeing McCarthyism in the United States, the emergence of the coloured races; were we not experiencing a scientific adjustment of all our values? ... There had been drastic political and social changes all around us; the new Prosperity State was more than suspect, both political parties looked the same. No man or woman of feeling who was not wearing blinkers could not but feel profoundly disturbed.

With these things to write about, the English dramatists had come up with *The Chalk Garden, Separate Tables* and *The Mousetrap*. The reason, surely, lay entirely in the facts of commercial production. Create one stable, non-commercial zone, and the intelligent writers who now ignored the theatre would return to it as their rightful territory, as they did in France. Devine, accordingly, placed an advertisement for new plays in the *Stage*. In drafting it, the one element he seems to have overlooked was the long-range effect of the 1994 Education Act.

The Royal Court was to pass officially into the E.S.C.'s hands in the following February. In August Devine held some preliminary auditions for the company which were attended by a young actor, late of the Derby rep, called John Osborne who mentioned to the stage manager that one of his plays had been accepted for production at the Royal Court. In September the Noguchi *Lear* went back on the road, severing Devine from his management committee until the tour wound up at Stratford in December. One stopping point on the tour was the Hebbel Theatre, Berlin, where Brecht and Helene Weigel came to a matinée and met the company. Ashcroft and Devine went out with them for beer and sausages, and extracted Brecht's permission for the Court to present *The Good Woman of Setzuan* with Ashcroft as Shen Te. Devine's party also went over to the East to inspect the Theater am Schiffbauerdamm where it was noted with interest that Brecht's stage was equipped with a permanent canvas surround lined with netting, and that the lighting bars were fully exposed; also that the auditorium positively dripped with gilt. To Devine, Brecht seemed like 'an intellectual peasant ... both shy and shrewd'; and he did not take unreservedly to the Ensemble. It had no school. Its stage management struck him as careless, and its actors 'like children playing'. But these objections were as nothing compared with his recognition that Brecht had created a people's theatre without making concessions to popular taste. The particular qualities he singled out in a production of *The Caucasian Chalk Circle* were its simplicity, beauty and honesty. But he valued it most for the attitude which had produced this end-product. Not for any particular ideological bias, but for its departure from the universalities of Stanislavsky to depict humanity 'through certain eyes, and for a certain society ... Brecht's theatre is above all a theatre of its time, of its place, and of its nation. This is its exemplary value.' So the example it offered to the Royal Court went beyond the physical details of stage design.

By the end of 1955, the foundations for the E.S.C. had been laid. With the aid of private donations (including £8,000 from Blond) and a pre-production grant of £2,500 from the Arts Council, the company had entered into an agreement for the purchase of the unexpired thirty-five years of Esdaile's lease on the Royal Court: the price was £20,000, to be repaid over ten years. From the scripts that had come in (100 of them read by Devine), the Artistic Committee in December proposed an opening list of six plays. In retrospect it seems ironic that they were still looking for a 'strong English play' to start with. Back in the summer they had bought the rights of Osborne's *Look Back in Anger*, together with two Duncan plays and Arthur Miller's *The Crucible*, all for £325. But they were looking for plays by established English authors. So in spite of Devine's subsequent claim that 'we had found a world dramatist for our first season', when it came to the point, Osborne appeared as number three on the bill. This detail is typical of the Court's opening phase. Devine and Richardson began with the famous policy of attracting novelists into the theatre and presenting seasons played in true repertory by a permanent company. When the vitality they had unleashed started pushing them in quite a different direction, they were able to bend to this pressure without sacrificing their essential aim. In this sense the English Stage Company was very English. Whatever its attachment to the doctrinaire French tradition, its own operation was pliable and pragmatic. Tucking Osborne away in the middle of the first season made excellent sense. The Court had to declare its identity without alienating too many respectable friends. To have lobbed that bomb into the stalls as an opening gesture would probably have been suicidal. 'I knew my country', Devine wrote, 'and I knew that ... we ourselves had to become part of the establishment against which our hearts if not our faces were set.'

Devine had proposed an eighteen-week period of preparation between the signing of the Court agreement and the start date. With the agreement made, he renewed auditions for the company. He already had some actors in mind: Joan Plowright, the ugly duckling of the Vic School, and Robert Stephens whom he had seen in a Library Theatre production while *Lear* was in Manchester. Others now appeared; Rosalie Crutchley, Michael Gwynne, John Welsh, with two last-minute arrivals – Kenneth Haigh and Alan Bates – who (together with Stephens) were most responsible for putting the term 'redbrick actor' into the reviewers' vocabulary. Looking through the final list of the twenty-two actors who played in the first season, one obvious fact stands out: very few of them had studied at the Vic School. The Vic School had been run to prepare its students for such a theatre as the Royal Court. Now that theatre had arrived and, with stray exceptions like Plowright and Sheila Ballantine, it had no place for them. Richardson, who did the initial screening for the Royal Court auditions, had seen them working for Devine at Stratford and considered them inferior and unsuited to the Court's 'realistic' repertory. 'They were doing mime and sub-Copeau jumping about, which wasn't at all the sort of acting that was required. The plays preceded the company; so we were looking for people who would fit.' Another link with the past had been cut. Also the ensemble ideal was compromised from the start by the decision to set up a two-tier hierarchy: a nucleus of versatile young actors, and a group of bigger names to be brought in for individual productions. The top weekly salary being £25 (half the West End average), there was no easy solution. But the answer Devine and Richardson arrived at already shows in which direction their priorities were moving.

In January 1956 Margaret Harris presented her model of the new stage. By now Devine had won his battle for a £3,500 new lighting system: a vital preliminary as one all-important feature of the new stage was its capacity to suspend the actor in a void with scenic statements made by lighting alone. In his brief to Harris, Devine had asked for the stage masking to be shaped so as to suggest that it led on to further space beyond; and executed in some non-associative material through which light and air could pass. 'We want something which will seem as impermanent and of the moment as the life that takes place on the stage.' Harris cracked this problem by making a divided surround, consisting of two S-shaped side pieces and a panel that dropped in connecting with the two upstage ends of the S. Viewed from in front, the effect was that of a wrap-round cyclorama equipped with six invisible exits. The panel, when not required, could be flown, opening up the full stage area to the back wall. The surround, as in Brecht's theatre, was executed in two layers of fabric, a solid backing of canvas and a transparent layer of netting, six inches apart. Finding the right netting put a strain even on the Motleys' ingenuity, but it was eventually run to earth in a fishing village on the North East coast. The result was worth the effort. It proved immensely responsive to light. It could present the hard brilliance of white canvas, or melt into a watered, *moiré* effect. In Devine's phrase, the surround was 'a box that flowed'.

Richardson denies that the Brecht stage had any great influence on the Court: and this certainly seems to be the case when it comes to lighting. Its productions did not make a fetish of Brechtian white light. And the exposure of lighting equipment was more an incidental occurrence than a positive design feature. Devine loved size and openness; and one of the first things he did was to get rid of the Court's old house curtain and take up the proscenium borders. This altered the proportions of the arch, which abruptly became tall and narrow, revealing some of the bars and vertical lighting positions, which, in England, was unheard of at that time. Devine's attitude, however, was merely that as it was no secret that stages were lit by electricity what did it matter if people saw the odd lamp? It was only gradually that visible lighting became an integral feature of design.

Getting the surround installed was a round-the-clock operation taking thee days in the freezing cold, by which time Devine had discovered the quality of his technical team. There was his Stage Director, Michael Halifax, imported from the *Lear* company; and Kevin Maybury, a tireless Australian master carpenter who had been a flyman at the Palace Theatre. Also there were several part-timers whom, Halifax says, it was hard to keep away. 'There was no division of labour in those days. There were so few of us that we all had to do everything. People at the Court knew their jobs because if they didn't there was always somebody who was willing to teach them. They felt "Gosh, I must learn because everybody seems to know so much". It was that sort of attitude.'

Besides installing the surround, the ropes had to be renewed and the interior repainted. There was also the job of extending the stage itself by filling in the orchestra pit and adding a fore-stage with flanking doors. This involved creating exits through what had formerly been stage boxes and matching up the timber. Devine insisted on this when he found that the Court still had its original 1888 stage, complete with slides and star-traps to left and right for the pantomime demon king and fairy godmother. Although it stood barely three feet above the front stalls, there was head-room underneath, and it was here that the production unit had its home (later it was also used as overspill dressing room space). For the first season, prop-making and scenery painting were done either under the stage or outside in the little yard between the theatre and Sloane Square tube station. Costumes were made at home in Lower Mall until the wardrobe was able to move into one of the cottages at the back of the theatre. But it was not until the following year that the Court acquired its own workshop, when one of the evening staff (a meter-reader by day) came in to announce that he had discovered a vacant first-floor workroom in Park Walk, a few minutes down the King's Road at the World's End.

If the acting company represented a break with Devine's past, there was no such break on the technical side. Virtually everyone in the production team came out of the L.T.S. or the Vic School. This included two of the main designers, Alan Tagg and Richard Negri: Margaret Harris and Sophie (who supplied the first company with a basic costume for the season): and the resident workshop unit of Jocelyn Herbert, Stephen Doncaster, and Clare Jeffery. A main reason for the Court's survival through its precarious first five years was the fact that board-room tactics and visions of the new drama never distracted Devine from the physical essentials of running a playhouse. He loved the fabric of the building, as visitors soon discovered if they stubbed out a cigarette on his stage or put their feet up on his Dress Circle. Towards the people who operated it and cared for it, he showed the proper respect due to the 'artist-technician'. The attitude of the stage hands mentioned by Halifax came down from Devine. He had done all the jobs himself. He knew what it was to put on a thimble and stitch all night: and he knew what could be expected of people and when the reasonable limits had been reached. Also he took care that the technical staff never formed a ghetto. When the workshops were set up he would bring parties from the theatre down to Park Walk with bottles of wine. He would also rope people in for picnics with the carpenters and scene painters. The time he could spend in this was necessarily limited, but it was enough to keep him in direct contact with everything that was going on. 'You took everything to him', Halifax says, 'because you knew he was going to give you an answer.' Quite apart from the non-commercial factor, Devine's method of running his theatre with a small technical and artistic team was then new to Britain.

They began occupying the theatre's offices in January. There followed a pre-opening run of *The Threepenny Opera*, presented by Lewenstein in association with the company. On April 2, 1956, the E.S.C. took the plunge with its first season of six productions: *The Mulberry Bush*, *The Crucible*, *Look Back in Anger*, *Don Juan* and *The Death of Satan*, *Cards of Identity*, and *The Good Woman of Setzuan*.

Devine's hope was that out of the 9 million people in Greater London he would find 3,500 a week to fill the Court. Others had no such hope. Theatrically the Court was right off the map. With a stray hit or a cast of stars it could siphon an audience out of the West End; but there was little passing trade. 'Chelsea' on headed writing paper was a good address, but it was a far from swinging area, immune even from the espresso bar boom in neighbouring South Kensington. The King's Road abounded in antique shops, but not in good restaurants or shops of any other kind. In fact, one of the area's few amenities was within the Royal Court itself where Clement Freud – to the management's mounting exasperation – ran a dining club on the top floor.

Hither the youth of the district would flock, heedless of the theatrical revolution being enacted beneath them. Debutantes were much in evidence. One of them, ascending the stairs to the club, was heard to emit a squeal: 'Oh shit! I've stepped in some yum-yum!' From such beginnings the E.S.C. was born.

13

FIRST SEASON

IN the autumn of 1955 Angus Wilson published an article in the *Observer* making the not unfamiliar point that the English stage was little frequented by the intelligentsia. Devine, he says, was excited by this piece which may have clinched his decision to launch his first season with *The Mulberry Bush*. Wilson can think of no other reason. The play had already been seen, and nationally reviewed, at the Bristol Theatre Royal. Wilson, before the publication of *Anglo-Saxon Attitudes*, was not yet an eminent author and was best known for his short stories. And the play itself, as he fully recognized, was no landmark in experimental dramaturgy: stylistically it drew on Barker and Chekhov, and could well have appeared in the West End at any time during the previous thirty-five years. What it did possess was an Oxford setting occupied by highly literate characters: a milieu familiar to Devine and hitherto neglected by the English stage. In that respect at least, it reflected his aim of introducing the theatre to life outside.

The two met. Devine found Wilson's manner 'viperish'. Wilson recalls Devine as a friendly, pipe-smoking paternalist. 'If I say that he reminded me of my second brother who is a headmaster of a prep school, it would not be unfair. There was a certain element of, "If we don't win this match against St Wilfrid's I shall be a very hurt man."' On Richardson's advice, Wilson cut the play; after which Richardson and Devine set about casting it. Having been assured that his play was a winner, Wilson was now disconcerted to be told that its prior production was a serious disadvantage, necessitating the engagement of a star. The star was Gwen Ffrangcon-Davies. She was recovering from 'flu when they went round to see her, and it appeared that she did not like the play. 'These people you're making fun of,' she objected, 'they're the salt of the earth.' The people were Wilson's family, the Padleys, a tribe of high-principled rationalists whose ruthless benevolence had already warped several lives and who were now being dramatically awakened to values other than their own tramline intellectual dogmatism. Wilson had based the role of Rose Padley on Beatrice Webb, and with Sybil Thorndike in mind. When Ffrangcon-Davies came to play it, he says she shifted it forward a generation and sweetened Mrs Webb into Vera Brittain.

At the time, though, he was incapable of criticism. Encouraged by Devine, he attended every rehearsal and made friends with the cast: a great mistake according to J. B. Priestley, who told Wilson, 'You should have gone every ten days and said "You're making a ruddy mess of my play."' What did surprise Wilson, after the fraternal introductions and Devine's invitation to the cast to discuss their parts with the author, was the fact that only Ffrangcon-Davies was permitted to ask questions. When Kenneth Haigh tried to do it, Devine squashed him flat.

Altogether, as Wilson saw things, Devine's heart was in the past even though his mind was fixed on the present. He wanted the theatre to make a serious contribution to British intellectual life. At the same time, he would cling to old friends like Gwen Ffrangcon-Davies, and be illogically reassured by congratulations from rearguard figures like Hugh Beaumont.

Wilson, however, is speaking as a disappointed author. He liked Devine and believed what he said. Devine had predicted success and then the play had failed. In looking for an explanation, Wilson hit on the very quality which, in other circumstances, kept the company afloat: the capacity for conducting a pioneer enterprise without cutting its lifeline to the past.

Not that Wilson was wholly disenchanted by the experience. After the initial revision, Devine treated the text as sacred. He had, Wilson says, 'a marvellous ear for the interplay of speech: the degree to which one speech should cover another or be separated from another. He would go over passages again and again to illustrate psychological nuance by getting a particular rhythm.' But again, he felt that Devine had cast him in the role of the intellectual and had adopted an over-respectful approach to the dialogue so that its pathos and bitchiness fell into separate compartments.

When *The Mulberry Bush* opened the obvious happened. Reviewers who had liked it in Bristol disliked it in London, and *vice versa*. Attendance was poor. The production itself attracted little comment, except from T. C. Worsley in the *New Statesman*:

> Mr George Devine's resident company made an excellent first impression and he has drawn from them acting of a subtle and convincing order in parts which do not, mostly, give very obvious opportunities and are certainly outside the stock range. He is dealing in this play with social and intellectual gradations which have seldom been charted in our theatre ... There is nothing ostentatiously 'experimental' about George Devine's direction and perhaps its very great merits may be missed. Sensitive is an overused word, but the right kind of sensitivity is the mark of acting and production here, senstitivity to the author's intentions, and a serious attempt to get at the subtleties. Mr Devine pushes the play just that little out of the conventional naturalistic framework – allowing his characters, for instance, at key points to come out of the proscenium arch ... He was helped by a most ingenious impressionist set by Motley.

Devine later returned the compliment by saying that Worsley was the only reviewer to have discerned his aims.

In the general haze of launching the new drama, author and reviewers alike had overlooked Devine's new stage. But for the stage crew it was the outstanding feature of the show. Viewed as an empty space under changing lights, the surround was exquisite to behold, but it was another story when the scenery came on. As the netting did not lie flat against the canvas and the stage space had been considerably reduced by the permanent masking, pieces had to be manoeuvred in with millimetres to spare. Or less, in cases such as that of the large revolving tree which dominated the set. Wilson thought it 'enormously pretty', but when it turned to reveal the house within, its twigs and branches ripped through the net.

The surround fared better in the second production, *The Crucible*, which joined the repertory a week later. For months before the season opened, Devine had been telling people that the Royal Court venture would give birth to a new style. In so far as that style ever did emerge, it was with this show in which he applied his 'essentialist' theory to a seventeenth-century New England Puritan setting. 'Essentialism', says Clare Jeffery (with memories of hammering away in the airless void under the

stage) 'meant that you made as few things as possible as well as
you possibly could.'

For *The Crucible* this meant reducing the set to five scenic
units: benches, a bed, a short flight of steps. A window was indicated by curtains on a pole. The designer was Stephen Doncaster
whose first ideas Devine had rejected as too elaborate. Doncaster
then came up with some pictures of a beamed ceiling and – working to Devine's specifications – used this as the permanant scenic
element: a massive piece consisting of two long members and
four shorter ones with Tudor bosses at the corners. Strong enough
to have held up a house, it was suspended over the bare stage
and hung in various positions. For the prison scene it came down
low over the actors' heads; in the farm house it was tilted to
suggest a roof. In the court room it was raised high, and Devine
lit through it so as to throw bars of shadow across the stage.

Inset within the grey neutrality of the surround, a few beautiful objects compelled your imagination to complete the picture.
In that sense the setting fulfilled Devine's theoretical intentions
to the letter. It also married perfectly with the play. Its sparse
sobriety reflected the values of historical Salem; but that same
sparseness also released the play from its period sufficiently for it
to make the allegorical jump to MacCarthy's America.

Having shown this degree of sympathy with the author's
intentions, Devine then took the wholly uncharacteristic step of
cutting out one of his characters. Richardson says this was done
simply because there was no money to pay for another actor.
But the principle of total respect for the writer's work was the
foundation stone of the E.S.C., and Devine made the cut without
consulting Arthur Miller. Nor was the character of Giles Corey
at all superfluous: he was there to expose the economic motive
behind witch-hunting, as a means of grabbing the victim's land.
Miller heard of the cut and cabled an ultimatum from New York
demanding for the part to be reinstated or for the play to be
withdrawn. Devine found the money and, at five days' notice,
engaged Peter Duguid for the part. Besides directing, Devine
was also playing the chief inquisitor, Darnforth, who shares
several scenes with Corey. Although a Vic School pupil, Duguid
had never played with Devine before, and he found their first
performance together 'the most exciting experience I've ever
had as an actor. He was very generous to play with: absolute eye-
to-eye tension. But after that one evening he never acted like

that again. There was only about 60 per cent of him doing it. He'd come off and start talking about key lines, and make-up and somebody's wig-join. You could see the cares of responsibility were already on stage with him as an actor.'

The Crucible (another importation from Bristol) aroused a good deal more critical enthusiasm than its predecessor, and notices ranged from the respectful to the ecstatic. But its appeal at the Box Office was almost identical: a chilly 45 per cent capacity. Devine had some reason to take his cares on stage.

Meanwhile, Tony Richardson was waiting in the wings with *Look Back in Anger* which issued in the new age a month later on May 8. The story of its rejection by the agents, its discovery by Devine and Richardson, their first trip to meet the penniless author on his Chiswick houseboat, and the play's decisive effect on the Royal Court's fortunes and the direction of the theatre at large, no more needs retelling than the fable of David and Goliath. Some of the letters of rejection are quite funny. One referred Osborne to an article in the *Daily Telegraph* deploring the modern playwrights' tendency to disregard plot, and complained that his characters were moving in a world of their own; another, admitting that the characterization was good, shot it down as 'utterly disagreeable'; a third rounded on the hero as 'just another neurotic who had not had the courage to take in his stride the youthful shocks and sufferings that most people experience, but is bent on licking his wounds'. Easy laughs now, but not so obvious in 1956. Lord Harewood recounts the typical response of a playwright friend to whom he had lent the script as a bedtime read. 'Well, it's very excitingly written, but you can't put that on in a theatre! People won't stand for being shouted at like that, it's not what they go to the theatre for.' Driving back from Stratford to London, Terence Rattigan spent two and a half hours telling Devine why the play could not be a success. 'Well it is,' he kept repeating, 'and it's going to make the Royal Court possible.' 'Then I know nothing about plays,' Rattigan eventually answered. 'You know everything about plays, but you don't know a fucking thing about *Look Back in Anger*.'

Out of some 750 plays submitted to the Court after the *Stage* advertisement, Osborne's was the only script that was so much as considered by the two directors. The remainder, Richardson says, were either bottom-drawer pieces by playwrights in decline or 'endless blank verse shit'. Devine, he says, saw the manuscript first. 'He read three pages and then brought it upstairs. "Look at this," he said. "This might be interesting."'

Writing about this moment six years later, he said, 'I knew this was the play we must do, even if it sank the enterprise.' As, by then, it had salvaged the Royal Court, he could hardly have said less. More to the point is the record of that initial contact with the script (which arrived by post direct from the unknown author); and the fact that Devine returned to it in the memoir he started dictating in the last weeks of his life.

'It's no good trying to fool yourself about love. You can't fall into it like a soft job, without dirtying your hands. It takes muscle and guts. And if you can't bear the thought of messing up your nice clean soul you'd better give up the whole idea of life and become a saint because you'll never make it as a human being. It's either this world or the next.' When I read this passage I felt so much in sympathy with it that I thought it must be said on a stage to a public. It is good luck to find such a thing.

This is the answer to the theory that Osborne's success diverted the Court from its chosen course; and to those, like Wilson, who thought that Devine's heart was still in the past. Osborne's appeal was entirely to the heart. If you did not respond to it in that way, then the objections of Rattigan and Harewood's friend made good sense. No one would have championed *Look Back in Anger* for its formal qualities. Osborne may have brought the tirade back into theatrical currency, but it was the content of the tirades that mattered. Osborne was enlarging the limits of the theatrically acceptable, he was not inventing a new kind of play. For Devine, the piece was a stylistic watershed. Hitherto he had been mainly interested in how things were said: henceforth this took second place to what those things were. This revised priority became evident from the physical change to his stage. For Tony Richardson's production, Alan Tagg supplied a cramped attic, littered with the dingy evidence of rented accommodation, and making it hard for the actors to move without colliding with the bed, the ironing board or the garbage bucket. It was not a completely naturalistic set: there was a sky-cloth instead of a ceiling, and all the props were still inside the surround. But you would never have deduced from the result that the company had set out to strip the stage of everything but the essentials.

It was not until the production of Barry Reckord's *Flesh to a Tiger* two years later that the surround finally vanished, but from the moment of Osborne's arrival it ceased to be a central design principle. It was emphasized or disguised according to the demands of each play, and designers adapted it as they saw fit. It was finally scrapped for the entirely practical reason that it was too cumbersome and that it devoured too much of the already tiny stage. But to Richardson, lukewarm about it from the start, it was a relief when the essentialist stage, and Sophie's basic costumes and other 'relics of George's past' were swept away by the demands of the new situation.

While Richardson was rehearsing *Look Back in Anger*, Devine was rehearsing the two Duncan plays. 'Don't produce a play unless you really believe in it,' he told an interviewer in June 1956, having just broken that rule himself. He had no alternative. There was no getting around the works of the E.S.C.'s founding father: they were the pound of flesh that had to be paid for putting on the season. The Court had only two directors and Richardson was otherwise engaged. It therefore fell to the Artistic Director to put himself on the chopping block.

As Duncan saw things, it was Devine who was wielding the knife. He had supplied the theatre with two full-length plays which his director then carved up to form a marathon double-bill. Duncan approved of John Minton's designs; but regarded the casting of Keith Michell and Rosalie Crutchley as outright sabotage, and felt that Devine poisoned rehearsals by instilling an atmosphere of wearisome contractual obligation. Duncan had to admit that the plays' technical problems, such as a ghost scene, had been solved neatly. 'I could not fault the surgeon though he was removing my guts and heart.' But when he arrived for the first night, he says he 'felt like a holed barge being towed out to be torpedoed'. His fears were answered. Attendance fell to a ruinous 18 per cent and the plays were withdrawn after eight performances.

If the poetic drama movement was moribund before, Devine's production gave it the death blow. He had no regrets about that. 'Mr Duncan's play failed abjectly and rightly as it was completely out of date,' he wrote to Saint-Denis some months later. What he did regret was his own part in the failure. Duncan's allegations of sabotage are flatly contradicted by Duncan's own friends who saw Devine after the opening, close to tears and bitterly reproaching himself for having 'ruined Ronnie's plays'. Duncan did not forgive what he saw as an insult to his work, and from this moment he and Devine became opponents in a struggle over Royal Court policy which reached its climax four years later.

In retrospect, the most interesting thing about the *Don Juan* fiasco is the strange similarity between Ronald Duncan and John Osborne: both elitist, both attracted to religious themes, both given to intemperate abuse, and, in these two productions, both saying much the same thing. Osborne got the credit for introducing the 'anti-hero', but he could well have shared it with Duncan. Don Juan and Jimmy Porter are both men of passion invading the territory of good manners. The message is the same. England has gone to sleep behind its mask of respectability; it would be better to wake up and feel something, even if that means treating your wife badly or being sent to hell. The all-important difference between the two is language. In Duncan it is so self-admiring that it gets in the way of what is being said: 'prose on stilts or verse in chains', Tynan called it. With Osborne you have no time to observe the stylistic pirouettes, because the sense hits you like a blow in the mouth. Of all the developments in the first year, this contrast was the most crucial in defining the Royal Court's identity. It was a writers' theatre: it was not a literary theatre.

After another month's gap, during which *Look Back in Anger* was at least keeping audiences above the half-way mark, the next pair of plays came into the repertory: *Cards of Identity* and *The Good Woman of Setzuan*. *Cards* was a Richardson project. Nigel Dennis's novel had been the hit of the 1955 spring book list. It was a cold, brilliantly executed comedy on the transformation of human personality. The author could have been an intelligent hyena. He also struck the Court directors as precisely the man they were looking for: a natural dramatist who had turned to novel-writing for want of a suitable theatre. In fact, Dennis's only theatrical ambition at that time was to write opera libretti, and when Richardson first approached him he was rather dashed to discover it was not for that purpose. Having spent five years on the novel, he had had enough of it. However, he succumbed to Richardson's enthusiasm and took on the job of adaptation. Devine was no less keen. He loved the quality of Dennis's mind. For all his admiration of Osborne's play he was apt to slip out of the theatre when the bears and squirrels came frisking on in the last act. There were no soft passages in Dennis: his work had the courage of its own scepticism and it was superbly articulate. Devine shared the scepticism, and vastly admired the verbal gift that went with it.

According to Dennis, the two directors were pinning their main hopes for the season on the success of *Cards*. 'The idea was that *Look Back in Anger* would be nursed along in its shadow. As it turned out, of course, it was exactly the other way round. *Look Back* paid for the huge losses on my play.' *Cards*, as I remember it, had its devastatingly funny moments, but the basic joke never got properly under way. The transformation of character, acceptable in the book, became implausible when acted out in flesh and blood. And in Dennis's two subsequent plays for the Court (*The Making of Moo* and *August for the People*), it became steadily clearer that he was far more interested in ideas than in people. He did, however, furnish Devine with the material for his best performance of the season in the character of Father Golden Orfe, resident chaplain of the Identity Club. Anti-clericism was a bond between them, both in this play and in *The Making of Moo*, in which Devine played a down-to-earth civil engineer turned high priest of a home-made religion. Devine had a violent distaste for institutional Christianity and for the current revival of superstition under artistic camouflage. Dennis, likewise, found Greene's and Eliot's plays intolerable, and wanted to strike a blow against the mumbo-jumbo of 'naked ladies being eaten on ant-hills for the greater glory of God'.

Hence, in *Cards*, the figure of the Rev. Golden Orfe, a whisky priest turned inside out, demonstrating the full length to which Christian sophistry can be stretched for ungodly ends. Devine played him with oozing sanctimonious gusto, perhaps drawing on memories of Uncle Minos in the pulpit. The centre-piece of the show was his ten-minute sermon which, at the time, aroused more hostility than anything in *Look Back in Anger*. 'I stink, therefore I am', the speech began, continuing through shouts of 'Get off' and 'Rubbish', and slamming seats. Alan Bates, who played in both productions, says that where there would be individual reactions to the Osborne, Dennis's play used to excite group protests, usually from the best dressed sections of the house.

The long-meditated Brecht première followed in October. Devine, like other British directors in this field, had been at

great pains to get it right. Besides his Berlin conversations with
the author, he had had a week's consultation with Weigel who
attended the Royal Court rehearsals in the aftermath of the
Berliner Ensemble's own triumphant Palace Theatre season.
The package involved engaging Brecht's designer, Teo Otto, who
(shades of Noguchi) dispatched sketches and handwritten German
notes from East Berlin. (When Otto arrived, only one of his
fifty costumes had been misinterpreted.) Brecht's composer, Paul
Dessau, was there as well, taxing the cast's patience with contributions in incomprehensible English.

Although Devine's starting policy was to fire off as much
material as possible to prove the company's vitality, he took an
unusual length of time over the Brecht, which went through
previews in Brighton and Oxford before opening in Sloane
Square. Even so, he had the task of getting an English cast
through the A to Z of Brechtian acting in a rehearsal period that
was ridiculously short by Continental standards. Here we enter
the territory of unverifiable legend. Some people, like Alan
Bates, were deeply impressed by the dress rehearsals. Peggy
Ashcroft says that by the end of the run, the style had been fully
achieved. All true, no doubt, together with the often-repeated
alibi that *The Good Woman* was a British casualty of the
Hungarian Revolution. The fact remains that when it did open,
no one was very enthusiastic. Designed at once as a path-finding
adventure and as a prestige event, it fell between the two
objectives. 'The edge was missing,' Bates says: a complaint already
made of Devine's productions.

While *The Good Woman* was in rehearsal, *Look Back in
Anger* returned for a solid eleven-week run at the Court. It was
not doing spectacular business, but the available alternatives
would have been worse. On October 16, a five-minute extract
went out on BBC Television, and within three days applications
for tickets were arriving in sackfuls. 'None of us thought we
were going to last through the summer,' says Michael Halifax.
'The houses were appalling. Then, after the TV extract, all these
people started arriving. People you never see in theatres. Young
people gazing around wondering where to go and what the rules
were. A completely new audience: just what we were trying to
find.'

Summing up the situation in a letter he wrote to Saint-Denis
shortly before this, Devine described his situation as

extraordinary. We have managed in four months to build up an artistic reputation which is far beyond the means at our disposal ... As my backers not only do not understand what we are doing but really dislike it, they are in the strange position of being obliged not to let down something which I think they would like to abandon ... Fortunately we have such a reputation that they dare not get rid of us – anyway just yet.

As that passage suggests, there are two ways of telling the story: not only of the first season, but equally of the seasons to come. Told from the Board-room level it is pretty bleak; the finances were always shaky and the company repeatedly found themselves on the rocks. If the only available source material were the Management Committee minutes, then the history of the E.S.C. would largely be one of gloom and impending disaster.

But for the people working in the theatre it was another story, if only for the reason that the sheer volume of work left no time for brooding. Beyond that, everyone, from the student A.S.M.s to visiting stars taking huge salary cuts, knew that they were engaged in a great adventure. It cannot be over-emphasized that the Court did not arise out of thin air. Generations of idealistic young actors had dreamt of such a place; and here it was, miraculously combining the most hard-headed and adroit administration with untarnished dedication to an artistic ideal. This is why so many people were ready to work there for very little money, or in some cases for no money at all. They were doing something important and also having the time of their lives. The stir which the Court made in London and the international reputation it soon developed went hand in hand with the domestic satisfactions of Sloane Square. Like the Vic under Lilian Baylis, the atmosphere of the Court was much coloured by the regular presence of a few kindly people doing humdrum jobs. Once a week, without fail, Devine went round the building, dropping into every department to sort out their problems. His door was open to anyone who wanted to see him. When groups of art college students were brought in to supplement the regular stage crew, he would take care to memorize all their names. On tour he would always ensure that the stage management were not left in the lurch; and that if the actors were going off to a night club, the backstage girls would be taken along. Whatever the cares of administration, he shouldered them himself and never allowed them to infect other people's working conditions.

Money apart, Devine sustained some serious policy defeats. The idea of playing in true repertory was one early casualty. Not only the general public were foxed by the repertoire system. Interested members of the profession, like the playwright John Whiting, would ring up inquiring if it was a conspiracy to keep people away. So repertoire was replaced by short runs. Allied to this, once the new plays started pouring in, was the question of the permanent company. If the Court was a writers' theatre, that meant casting the plays as well as possible: in other words, casting each show *ad hoc*. Also, as the Court could only keep afloat by exploiting its successful productions in other theatres, then casts must be available for long runs in the West End and Broadway. So, with immense reluctance, Devine snapped another link with Saint-Denis, and adopted the alternative of a friendly pool of actors for the ideal of a permanent troupe.

These changes were gradually forced upon him by the nature of the Court operation. During the opening season, he was still fighting to keep the original policy intact, while receiving a battering from the management committee: from Blond in particular, who had assumed chairmanship of the E.S.C. in a state of total theatrical ignorance. His job, as he saw it, was to market a product; the job of the 'artistic boys' was to supply something marketable, which they were palpably failing to do. Echoes still reverberate from those meetings in Mansfield Street with Blond pounding the table and shouting, 'Take it off, take it off!' Halifax stormed out of one meeting after hearing Devine denounced as a dictator and the company as vultures. To the first group of authors, Blond and the Council figured as ogres in the background. Devine sometimes took refuge in Nigel Dennis's cottage in Broxbourne Woods, but even there, 'Blond was still after him. He used to dread the phone going, and that hard grating voice saying "George, George!"' Wilson says he was sometimes roped in as a protective buffer when committee-members were looming. 'George would say, "You're so good with people, will you come to talk to them? They're terrible." And they were.'

To the outside world, as Devine says, the company seemed to be glowing with health. The E.S.C. famously came in on the Suez campaign; and Osborne's play was miraculously well timed to speak for the bloody-minded National Service generation and call the bluff of the smug old clubmen who were still presuming to run their lives. Amid all the noise about angry young men and kitchen sinks, the exploit of the Royal Court was viewed as heroic. A lot of people cared about it. The snag was that not enough of them expressed their feelings by purchasing tickets; and this was a problem Devine never resolved. He told the story of going to a 1959 Boat Race party 'full of journalists and architects, and they came up to me and said, "My dear fellow, you've changed the face of London." And just for fun I said to each of them, "Oh, I'm so glad. When did you last come?" And the whole damn lot said, "Well, actually, I've not been since you did Olivier in Feydeau." What do they think I live on – air?'

While the Brecht was limping through November, Devine estimated that his gamble on the new drama had so far lost the company £8,000. He had one card left to play: a Christmas revival of Wycherley's *The Country Wife*. 'This may surprise you,' he told Harewood, 'but I used to have quite a reputation for Restoration comedy.' He had a double purpose: to save the company's bacon with a popular show, and to launch Joan Plowright as a leading actress. This was not an easy equation to work out as Plowright was not yet a commercial name. To compensate, he built up the show in every other respect. Prominent company members from earlier in the season were relegated to small parts, and Restoration specialists like John Moffatt and Diana Churchill came in from outside. For the all-conquering Horner he reluctantly cast Laurence Harvey, no great exponent of eighteenth-century comedy but assuredly a star. He then framed Wycherley's steaming intrigue in the lightest and most antiseptic of settings. Anyone who found the dialogue filthy had to admit that the stage was clean. Motley's black and white set featured an ornamental gateway as delicate as icing sugar and a pair of equally insubstantial chandeliers. The surround was fully exposed, plus a few essential props echoing eighteenth-century design in modern materials. For the actors, the most important element was the chequer-board floor: a highly polished perspective walk-down built on a steep rake. This, coupled with high-heeled shoes, meant relearning how to walk, stand, and turn without looking unnatural or colliding with the breakables: which, in turn, enforced a particular choreography on the cast. They were not 'mannered' in an artificial sense: but there was no other way of moving with safety. The set was a stylistic gymnasium, like the outsize hats and crinolines of the Vic School's style parties. Some of the company, Alan Bates for one, did not get the hang of it at all. 'It's the only time I can ever remember having drunk before a first night to get myself on. I fell into every sort of trap, and I came on wishing I wasn't there. I remember George coming up to me in the wings and saying "For Christ's sake, boy, enjoy yourself!" It kept me out of classical plays for five years.' His was not the only makeweight performance. To save money, Devine played Pinchwife himself and lapsed into his bearish actor-managerial style. As in *The Crucible*, he was unable to shed his cares in the wings before he went on. Even his scenes with Plowright were mainly rehearsed through an understudy. 'He didn't take much account of his performance,' Plowright says: 'he took much more account of mine.' This time the gamble paid off. For all its blurred edges, the production scored decisively in its central casting, and Plowright fulfilled Devine's predictions by tumbling joyously into the character of Margery Pinchwife as a part she was born to play. The Court now had a show running to capacity business followed by a West End transfer to the Adelphi. 'The contemporary theatre', Devine commented afterwards, 'was saved by a classical revival.' That was the final lesson of the first year.

꧁꧂꧁꧂꧁꧂

14

VISIONS AND TACTICS

TOWARDS the end of 1957 a book called *Declaration* appeared in the shops. This was the brain-child of my astute publisher, Tom Maschler, who, noting that his generation were quite exceptionally dissatisfied with the state of the country, had decided to accord radical discontent the dignity of hard covers. He was quite right. For a collection of essays of uneven quality, *Declaration* had a rare success. Opening the book today it is hard to imagine the contributors making up any kind of Popular Front. Osborne is there with a fine autobiographical piece, plus his critical champion, Kenneth Tynan; also a sombre Rhodesian girl, Doris Lessing, the fiery young novelist John Wain, and the *Wunderkind* Outsider, Colin Wilson, trailing two acolytes, Stuart Holroyd and Bill Hopkins.

It was decided to launch the book with a publication party at the Royal Court, whither the contributors and a large crowd of friends were invited for a night in October. Within hours of this event, however, a majestic notice descended from the Council of the E.S.C. forbidding the party to set foot in the theatre. Just why still remains slightly obscure. One theory is that the Council had taken fright at the book's anti-monarchical tone (specifically, Osborne's reference to the Windsors as gold fillings in a mouthful of decay). Another rumour is that they had got wind of a plot to tip a bucket of whitewash over Colin Wilson (who had lately been kicking up a fuss because the Court had rejected one of his plays). After frantic telephoning, the party moved on to a drinking club up the King's Road and spent some happy hours denouncing the hypocrisy of the E.S.C. Council to whom they subsequently presented a £103 bill for the drinks.

I dredge up this hoary bit of gossip as indicative of the situation in which Devine now found himself. Through an extraordinary constellation of circumstances, the Royal Court had come to occupy a symbolic role quite beyond its theatrical function. The building had become a rallying point for the whole youth protest movement that exploded in the late 1950s and which centred on the word 'establishment'. It comprised such things as Free Cinema (a radical offshoot of the British Film Institute), *Encore* magazine (a radical offshoot of the Central School of Speech and Drama), and a complex of politico-educational attitudes variously expressed in the anti-institutional novels of Kingsley Amis, Richard Hoggart's *The Uses of Literacy*, and by maverick intellectual terrorists like Colin Wilson and his neo-Nietzschean comrades. Binding the whole thing together was the feeling that the country was being run by mad old men who had just committed the Suez folly and who had now signalled their fearful next move in the Defence White Paper on Nuclear Warfare. That, too, was in 1957, the year of the first Aldermaston march. It was more a mood than a movement. Its sympathies lay with the provinces and against London; with the autodidact (a popular word at the time) against the Oxbridge graduate; and, of course, with the idea of Socialism as expressed in the broad honest faces of Covent Garden porters to whom Free Cinema devoted much grainy footage. Its views were unstructured and its associates ranged from the ravenously opportunistic to the selflessly humanitarian. The one thing they all had in common was a determination to get the weight of established authority off their backs. Their spokesman was Osborne: and their centre, so far as one existed, was the Royal Court which had created an anti-institution to match the anti-hero.

The Council of the E.S.C. had no objection to seeing their organization bathed in fashionable publicity, but they were gravely embarrassed by the attitudes with which it was being identified. Its separate figures, like Harewood, a Leftist intellectual member of the Royal family, and Lewenstein, a Marxist entrepreneur, could not be fitted into any social category; but collectively they represented the same establishment against which their theatre had allegedly declared war; and the E.S.C. became polarized between the stage and the boardroom. Lengthy discussions took place on whether they should publicly dissociate themselves from the opinions of their authors; and as the Court repertory continued on its unrepentant way, terms like 'sink of iniquity' were apt to punctuate the Mansfield Street agenda.

Devine's stragetic position is all too plain. He was caught in the cross-fire between those who saw him as a catspaw of the rebels, and those who saw him as a lackey of the bosses. He swallowed this as an inescapable penalty of his main objective: which was at all costs to keep the theatre and its policy open, so that whatever was brewing up among the young could happen there. To this end he was all in favour of royal visits. Likewise, he was all for securing commercial backers for the company, even when they handed their cheques over requesting him to discover a 'new Shakespeare without sex'. He would raise no objection when the management committee exhorted him to find more optimistic scripts, and present work 'of a more wholesome nature', and when the Arts Council offered him its guidance in play selection. In February 1958 he donned the appropriate uniform and went along to Buckingham Palace to collect a C.B.E. 'for services to the drama': and then went on to a party where he showed it off. 'Look,' he said, brandishing the decoration with exaggerated awe, 'the Queen *touched* this!' He also went along to the *Declaration* party, and volunteered to foot the bill.

His aim in the prolific first season had been to put the E.S.C. on the map. That had been accomplished. The next task was to expand the company's operations. They were still in the same financial straits. In spite of the Adelphi transfer and Broadway offers for *Look Back in Anger*, their Arts Coucil grant was only £5,000 a year and survival depended on drumming up money from elsewhere and exploiting their product in theatres larger than the Court (its capacity was an uneconomic 455). One cheap method of expansion lay in the supporter's club, the English Stage Society, which had been formed on Duncan's suggestion the previous autumn. Devine began putting this to use for Sunday evening 'productions without décor' of the scripts which were now coming in at a rate of about twenty a week. These were to be 'rehearsed up to dress rehearsal point, but performed with only indications of scenery and costumes'. Where a three-week run might cost £5,000, a Sunday night could cost as little as £100. The first of these, Charles Robinson's *The Correspondence Course*, took place in May 1957, followed by a curtain speech from the author who said it was important to 'go on putting on plays regardless of whether they're good or bad'; which, at that time, was not quite as silly as it sounds. Drama was now becoming the

12–13 Andrey in *Three Sisters*, 1937: before and after marriage

14 Rehearsing Walton's *Troilus and Cressida*, 1954

15 John Gielgud in the
Noguchi *Lear*, 1955

16 Sophie Devine at Lower Mall

17 Breakthrough party in Sloane Square: (front row, extreme left)
Joan Plowright, (third from left) Mary Ure; (second row, third
from left) Devine; (third row, left) John Osborne, Tony Richardson;
(fourth row, left to right) Wilfrid Lawson, John Dexter, Michael
Hastings, Tom Maschler; (fifth row, second from left) John Arden,
(third from left) William Gaskill; (sixth row) Anthony Page, N. F.
Simpson; (back) Robert Shaw

dominant mode of expression for writers under thirty: they did not yet know their trade, and the theatre did not yet know what they were trying to say. In reaching an accommodation and nourishing whatever real talent there might be, it would have been pointless only to accept 'good' plays. The only way of teaching a playwright his business, Devine said, was to put his plays on a stage. No matter if the result was half-baked: 'the distinction between half-baked and half-formed is a subtle one.' However, if a hundred flowers were to bloom, somebody would have to do the weeding. Until now, play reading had been done largely by the two directors and by such new authors as they had already picked up. The first reader was Osborne, who had the kindly habit of marking anything he disliked as 'suitable for television'. But with this expansion, plus the prospects of West End and Broadway transfers and festival tours, it was becoming imperative to take on new artistic assistants as well as new writers. When this question cropped up in committee Devine replied that he had found no one of suitable talent. He never did. It was Richardson and Osborne who found the extraordinary group of young directors who began, that summer, to take over the Sunday night shows. The first to appear was John Dexter, a friend of Osborne's rep days and the model of the unseen Webster in *Look Back in Anger*. He was followed by Richardson's Free Cinema associate, Lindsay Anderson; and by William Gaskill, the former fund-raiser of the Shipley Young Theatre and an Oxford contemporary of Richardson's. Anthony Page arrived in 1958, another Oxford director whom Richardson recruited from the Sandford Meisner workshop in New York. Others came and went, but that was the main group. And with the exception of Dexter, who describes himself as 'totally un-lettered' at the time he joined, they formed an exclusively Oxford club. Anderson even shared the same college with Devine and Richardson. 'One thing you must understand if you're going to work in this theatre', Devine told one of his recruits, 'is the difference between an Oxford man and a Cambridge man.'

However, the club was some time in coming together (Anderson was not taken on to the staff for two years after his début); nor, when it did, was its atmosphere particularly cosy. The close equal partnership between Richardson and Devine did not extend to the newcomers, even after they had proved their professional worth. Through their eyes, Devine appears in what had become his most famous role – the father figure of the Royal Court. Anderson in particular, found the sense of hierarchy and exclusion from the theatre's inner councils hard to take. Dexter found Devine 'very forbidding', but managed to fox out a comic Captain and N.C.O. routine with him based on their mutual detestation of the Army. 'Tell me, Dexter, how did you rise from the ranks?' 'I didn't, sir, I stayed as a Staff Sergeant because I wanted to be with the boys.' But he never dared tell Devine that he had looked up the audition card for the occasion when Devine rejected him as an actor: 'Nice little chappie; not greatly talented; looks like Noguchi.' The assistant artistic directors were taken on like midshipmen: clamped into the A.A.D.'s room, a tiny windowless box, and left to get on with script reading, sorting out audition files, or embarking on lonely trips in search of promising material in the provinces. Starting pay was £15 a week.

Meanwhile, they were absorbing the rules of the writers' theatre as laid down by Devine. Plays were to be known by author, not by title. It was *the* Wilson, *the* Dennis: and when it happened that *Look Back in Anger* and *The Entertainer* were playing simultaneously, they became 'Osborne I' and 'Osborne II'. Bureaucratic efficiency was encouraged (memos used to bounce back inscribed 'Date and signature, please'), especially when it came to scripts, which were filtered through two readings before being passed to Richardson or Devine for a final decision. According to Keith Johnstone, the mainstay of the script department, the preference was for plays that seemed rooted in personal rather than theatrical experience. Or, as Devine put it to his A.A.D.s, 'There are plays that you do out of passion. There are plays that you do to express your beliefs. And there are plays that you do because the author needs that support at the moment. You are in the third category.' In other words, they were not there to make it as young geniuses; any more than the actors were there to make it as stars, or Devine himself to imprint a house style on the repertory. For all practical purposes, he had abandoned that ideal. Nothing obscured the main intention of doing justice to the individual demands of each play. On the other hand, once anyone had been allotted a task, he was given total responsibility for carrying it out. This applied to young directors no less than to carpenters and electricians. They had control over casting and all other aesthetic matters; and if Devine gave any help it took the form of rapping out a few brisk

orders to the stage staff or conducting the director through a
Socratic interview to discover his intentions and his chances of
achieving them. 'He was', says Dexter, 'the only man I know
who could help without interfering.' A good half of Devine's
life was spent in his office, and he said that he had never had the
time to teach his directors anything, beyond involving them in
the day-to-day operation of the theatre. 'I have never said "No"
to anyone. I have said "If you do this, that will happen: do you
want that?" If they insist, I allow them to have their way and
take the consequences on my own shoulders. I think this is the
best way to bring them up. If I say "No" they will never be
convinced they were wrong or I was right.'

One of the myths of the Royal Court is that through its
Oxonian directorate a savage horde of proletarian authors were
smuggled on to the stage. In fact, only two of the first-wave playwrights – Michael Hastings and Arnold Wesker – could lay
claim to non-university working-class credentials; and they came
from Jewish families where learning was valued. Nor were they
starting entirely from scratch. Wesker was a student at the
London School of Film Technique as well as a qualified pastry-
cook; and Hastings, then an eighteen-year-old tailor's apprentice,
had had a play published and performed at the New Lindsay
Theatre. Keith Johnstone came in through films. Of the others,
Kathleen Sully and Doris Lessing entered the theatre from
novel-writing, and Christopher Logue from poetry. John Arden
was a graduate architect; N. F. Simpson was a teacher at a private
London college, and Ann Jellicoe an ex-public school girl who had
run her own theatre company. All these writers had achieved
some kind of recognition before they gravitated to the Court.
The Osborne romance of receiving dazzling material from out of
the blue was not repeated.

Nor was the close friendship that developed between Osborne
and Devine. Towards most of his writers, Devine remained a
benign background presence who radiated encouragement without intruding into their rehearsals or their private lives. Hastings
is an exception. Devine went along to the New Lindsay production of *Don't Destroy Me* and discovered not only that its
author had a talent but that he was in some danger of destroying
himself. Besides his eight-to-six tailoring job, he was drunk
nightly in the Fitzrovian company of Colquhoun and MacBryde
(well known to the director of the Redgrave *Lear*). Devine

thereupon 'in a most fatherly manner' warned him off the literary life and the Beaverbrook Press and advised him to get on with writing and finishing his apprenticeship: telling 'me in no uncertain terms that Radiguet was a finer writer at this age than I was and young Raymond never required a Colquhoun or a MacBryde to carry him home at night'. After that, Devine secured him a £500 Arts Council grant for which he made him line up with the rest of the company on Fridays for a £10 payment. All that came out of this for the Court was a Sunday night production of Hasting's rape study *Yes – And After* (also Dexter's début); though that was certainly an amazing performance for a boy of nineteen. Once the Court had accepted a play, it was assumed that the author would keep on writing for the company. Another statement to Hastings goes to the root of Devine's commitment to writers. When his young protégé had accused him of over-indulging in theatre of emotions, Devine 'shouted at me: "All plays are plays of ideas. It is my job to pull the thought out of the flesh, like a tooth." '

Devine did commonly impress his writers as a father figure, but it was only towards Hastings that he assumed a directly paternal role. Although he was unshakably loyal to Arden (whose plays invariably emptied the house) the two were shy of each other: Arden 'found him rather intimidating, and he may have found me uncouth'. He had little contact with Simpson, who suspected that Devine regarded his plays as curious Acts of God which he had been inscrutably called upon to bring forth. Not showing that their relationship was heavy-going, Simpson says, was heavy-going for him: 'he felt he ought to be drawing me out, and the thing was manifestly impossible.' Logue carried the Court banner with Devine on the first Aldermaston march, but otherwise kept his distance: 'I was a standoffish, arrogant greenhorn, and never sought to gain his confidence.' Wesker, the least standoffish of the writers, also found the relationship strained. He was living in a council flat in Clapton at the time of his Court début with *Chicken Soup with Barley*. Devine went there for dinner and tried to put the Wesker family at their ease by telling them stories about his eccentric uncles; but to them he seemed a member of the ruling class who had come along to inspect the social background that had produced the play. To Wesker, 'paternalistic' is a pejorative term; and at the Court he felt he was entering a traditional authoritarian set-up, despite all the efforts to create a friendly atmosphere where outsiders could feel at home. On an occasion when he brought his wife to the theatre, the atmosphere was rudely shattered by Devine's shout, 'Get that woman out of here!' on discovering Mrs Wesker breast-feeding young Lindsay in his office. Their relationship was complicated by the fact that although Wesker was precisely the type of writer the Court was searching for, his work was not really to Devine's taste. Wesker might be putting an unfamiliar bit of England on the stage but – to a sceptical veteran of the 1930s – he was also bringing back some clammily familiar sentiments.

Ann Jellicoe, already a member of the profession, was in a different case. Not only was Devine excited enough by her ferociously unorthodox first play, *The Sport of My Mad Mother*, to risk it as a main bill production: after its failure at the box office, he took her into the Court family as a friend and regular free-lance colleague. Sometimes he would suggest projects to writers. He commissioned Hastings to adapt *The Dybbuk* and Mayakovsky's *The Bed Bug*, and tried to interest Gwyn Thomas in translating the Spanish Golden Age dramatists. As a rule, nothing came of these approaches, but they succeeded with Jellicoe who followed up her violent jazz-idiom original work with scrupulous new versions of Ibsen and Chekhov. She was also one of the first newcomers to discover that Devine really liked women. He liked them sexually, and – from his memory of the Motley Studio – he liked them as working partners: hence the key appointments of Doreen Dixon and Helen Montagu as successive General Managers and Miriam Brickman as casting director. In Ann Jellicoe he found a tough professional competence as well as an experimental writing talent. 'I regard myself', he told her, 'as your mad uncle.'

Next to Osborne, his main friend among the writers was Nigel Dennis. But when he visited Dennis in the country it was to get away from the theatre, not to talk about writing. As Dennis saw him, there were 'two Georges'. The first was the gruff, white-haired patriarch who held the Court together and made such a forbidding impression on some of his juniors. The second was a hypersensitive fugitive who would collapse into a garden chair and slowly recover from his latest collision with the management committee. Once unwound, he would soak in the country gossip and news about the local hunt, and tell his old army stories until it was time to go: when he would linger at the side of his **big**

green Alvis, polishing the headlamps with his sleeve. Whither
the writers' theatre was not a topic than came up much.

These separate notes on some of the Court's first writers give no
impression at all of the impact the writers made collectively. It
was as though Devine had hit an oil well in Sloane Square: an
unstoppable gusher of pent-up energy that had at last found an
outlet.

Although most of the new writers had already made some kind
of a start, none of them would have stood much chance of artistic
survival without the Court. Either they would have languished
obscurely in the shrinking wilderness of the little theatre clubs,
or they would have reached the West End at the price of crippling
self-censorship. What the Court gave them was an open platform
where they could say exactly what they wanted, and the result
was a dramatic revival of a kind that had no precedent in English
theatre history. Never before had a public theatre unreservedly
handed itself over to the writer, and subordinated every other
priority to that of doing justice to new texts.

Devine would not have held with the pop ethic that everyone
is an artist. He did believe that centralized metropolitan culture
excluded a lot of talented people who happened not to have
the right educational or class background, and who spoke in the
wrong accent. Hardly an original idea: what was original was the
fact that he really meant it, and that he let the outsiders into his
building on the assumption that they might know what was good
for the theatre better than the blinkered old pros who were used
to making the rules. As in his comedy classes, creative originality
came first: there would be time for discipline later on.

This atmosphere was passed on to the audience. In no theatre
have I ever felt anything like the exhilaration of the Court in its
early days. There was a feeling that the fetters had been struck
off. If the West End traded like an Edwardian grocery shop,
selling a number of approved brands to its regular customers,
Sloane Square was like a marvellous street market, with battered
old trucks arriving from the wilds laden with unknown delicacies.
You never knew what was coming next. The 'kitchen sink' and
'angry young man' labels, and the myth of an exclusively
proletarian repertory, were desperate attempts to pin down an
unclassifiably various output. The only safe generalization about
the Court's first authors is that they were inventing their own

kinds of play and drawing on first-hand experience, rather than following literary models. And that the English stage, for so long 'hermetically sealed off from life' (in Arthur Miller's famous phrase of 1956), was now grabbing it in handfuls.

Devine was by temperament a teacher, but even if he had had the time it is most unlikely that he would have tried personally to teach anyone how to write plays. Part of his admiration for people with verbal skill derived from the feeling that he lacked it himself. Also he was a team man: writers were strange solitary creatures whose isolated activity was indispensable for the operation of his team. The thing to do was to involve writers in the team without infringing the private area in which they did their real work. Hence the system – valued more by some than by others – of the 'writer's pass' which gave them admission to rehearsals and to free seats at Court performances. Arden counts this as one of the two most important presents he had ever been given. 'The other was a job of reading manuscripts, at a flat rate of ten bob a script. I was accordingly able to leave the architect's office I was working in and spend all my time in or around a theatre. The point is that the theatre had come out and asked me in. I don't suppose I would have ever really got going as a proper playwright if this had not happened.'

Another of Devine's early innovations was the Writers' Group, which began holding weekly meetings at an old paint shop in Flood Street in 1958 and later moved to Anne Piper's house on Lower Mall. The early meetings lapsed into aimless discussion on the state of the theatre. Some months later the group re-united with a sense of purpose. In succession, *The Sport of My Mad Mother*, Arden's *Live Like Pigs* and Pinter's *The Birthday Party* (not a Court show) had flopped; and it seemed that a new area of drama was in danger of being stifled at birth. This gave the Writers' Group a common cause, and when they resumed meetings under Gaskill and Keith Johnstone, discussion gave way to enactment. Anyone suffering from writer's block could bring material into the group where it formed a starting point for improvisation. Every Wednesday for two years, writers including Jellicoe, Wesker, Wole Soyinka, Edward Bond and David Cregan turned up for these workouts, and passages in their subsequent plays (such as the bedspring piano scene in Jellicoe's *The Knack* and the birth game in Wesker's *I'm Talking about*

Jerusalem) arose directly from improvisation. Devine's mask classes (described in a previous chapter) stimulated Arden to write *The Happy Haven* and Johnstone to form his mask troupe, Theatre Machine.

Side by side with the Writers' Group was the Actors' Rehearsal Group, formed by Anderson and Page to pass on American workshop techniques to English actors. But the group to which Devine gave most of his time was the Actors' Studio. This was a later growth. It developed out of Gaskill's classes at the City Literary Institute and then found a home at the new Jeannetta Cochrane Theatre, which was lying empty because Princess Margaret could never find time to open it. The Studio was set up as a joint training ground for the Court and the National Theatre, but anyone could go, and few of its seventy-odd members were Royal Court actors. For Devine, this was like a return to the Vic School, and besides teaching the mask he also resumed his comedy classes. As the fountain of new drama began drying up in the early 1960s, he spent more and more time at the Studio, initiating a new generation into the mysteries of cleft palates, lisps, farts, tricks with screens and ladders, and the systematized anarchy of the Keystone Cops. The Royal Court never gained its own school, but Devine never lost his dream of founding one. When his assistant John Blatchley asked for permission to run the stage course at the Central School of Speech and Drama, Devine at first refused. Then he relented and confessed to envy. 'I couldn't take it', he said, 'when you said, "I'm going to have *my* school."'

If you compiled a credits list for the main events of the first decade, Devine's name would not come at the top of it. The obvious peaks in the company's history – Olivier in *The Entertainer*, Plowright in *Roots*, N. F. Simpson's *One Way Pendulum* – were the work of others. With the exception of *The Country Wife*, he directed no Royal Court production on Broadway. One of his achievements was to set up fertile marriages between playwrights and directors. Beginning with the Osborne–Richardson partnership, these continued with Simpson and Gaskill, Wesker and Dexter, Logue and Anderson. The negative side of this is that he found no partner for himself. He had launched a theatre for new English writers; but, after the first season, only once did he take full responsibility for directing any of their plays. He intended to direct *The Sport of My Mad Mother*, but when it came to the point he handed the production over to Ann Jellicoe. He commissioned Arden's *Live Like Pigs*, and began co-directing it with Anthony Page, but again he dropped out (to replace Alan Webb as Undershaft in *Major Barbara*), leaving Page to shoulder responsibility for the show's failure. Osborne pleaded with him to direct *Inadmissible Evidence* and he refused. The one exception was for a play written by someone of his own generation, Nigel Dennis's *August for the People*; and that 1961 production was the unhappiest single experience of his life at the Royal Court.

'In support of the young writers', he said, 'one must use young actors and directors;' and then corrected himself. 'By young, I mean young in attitude, not in age.' So that hardly explains why he handed his discoveries on to others. In any case, he was only forty-five when the Court opened. 'If I didn't have white hair and smoke a pipe,' he told Gaskill, 'no one would pay any attention to me.' There is the obvious fact that he was grossly overworked. Besides administration, he also made himself available as an actor to save the company money. He was usually cast as an authority figure at a salary of £10 a week, and was then criticized in the committee for neglecting administrative duties. No wonder that fellow actors could sometimes see him counting the house. He directed five productions in the first season. Over the next decade his output went down to an average of one a year, and he preferred to allow happy marriages to blossom between authors and A.A.D.s – especially in the case of work he respected without totally sympathizing with it. The Wesker partnership is the outstanding instance, summed up in Dexter's remark, 'Shut up, Arnold, or I'll direct this play as you wrote it.' Dexter could operate like that and 'pull out the tooth': if Devine had tried it, perhaps he felt he would have drilled it away to nothing.

Another consideration is that the Court stage was not exclusively occupied by new English writing. The repertory had two other important departments: work by modern French dramatists and 'pylons', and Devine was heavily involved in both. The 'pylon' policy developed out of the success of *The Country Wife*. It was a scheme for periodically arresting the headlong flow of untested novelties and bringing in a sober, resplendently cast classical revival which could be anything from Middleton to Shaw, designed to keep the E.S.C. financially afloat by transferring to the West End. The snag was that star casting on a shoestring was apt to mean that stars choose the plays. And that success could no more be predicted for revivals than for premières. Stringing out risks between certainties would be a foolproof formula if you could be sure of the certainties. Not surprisingly, the pylons had a hit-or-miss record.

Their most resounding hit was Devine's 1959 production of Ibsen's *Rosmersholm* with Peggy Ashcroft as Rebecca West. This was a sequel to their *Hedda Gabler*, with the difference that it was not a popular play. As before, their method was to ransack the text for clues and double-meanings; and then, having decided on what Ibsen was saying, to slice away some of the obtruding symbols. Devine had a practical explanation for Ulrik Brendel's supposedly Freudian challenge to Rebecca to cut off her right ear; Brendel was drunk. On the other hand, he and Ashcroft read Freud's essay on the play and accepted the incest motif and the diagnosis of Rebecca's case as the Electra complex. Jellicoe made the translation, which included the line, 'He's not in the back passage.' '"Ha, ha, ha," said George, "We'd better alter that."' That was his only textual alteration, and the production was greeted as a marvel of the dramatic force that can reside in detailed, low-key acting. 'Every character', wrote Harold Hobson, 'has the bright, alert hostility of a duellist.' Worsley in the *New Statesman* said, 'This performance is in sum as near perfection as you are likely to see in this imperfect world.' The show played to capacity and transferred to the Comedy Theatre with advance bookings of £3,000.

Devine was less fortunate with his 1958 *Major Barbara*, in which Plowright failed to repeat her *Country Wife* success; and Richardson's 1962 *A Midsummer Night's Dream*, with a cast of brilliant newcomers, was a classic case of the pot-boiler that refused to boil. Pylons in general involved trafficking with West End managers, accommodating the whims of stars, and meeting the middle-class public half-way. As such, they were viewed with deep suspicion by the more radical occupants of the A.A.D.'s room. The Court was supposed to be storming the commercial citadel, not doing deals with it. These mutinous rumbles came to a head over the 1959 production of the Feydeau-Coward *Look after Lulu*, a supposedly sure thing starring Vivien Leigh in white cambric pantalettes and compromising the Court in a liaison with Laurence Olivier Productions and H. M. Tennent Ltd. Devine succumbed to this passing infidelity in the hope of repairing the company's £11,000 deficit: but although *Lulu* packed out the Court it did not fill the New Theatre on transfer and in the end the production lost the E.S.C. £1,500. Transfers were an indispensable source of revenue, but of the shows that made the jump, pylons were outnumbered by the new plays of Osborne, Simpson, Willis Hall and Gwyn Thomas, none of which Devine directed.

The French repertory was a continuation of the abortive scheme of 1953 when Richardson and Devine had hoped to alert London to the Paris *avant-garde*. By 1956, *Waiting for Godot* and Ionesco's *The Bald Prima Donna* had already appeared at the Arts Theatre, and the Court had missed its chance of getting in on the ground floor. Nor was Sartre's *Nekrassov*, which Devine directed in 1957, a British première. For ideological reasons, Sartre had rebuffed commercial offers and entrusted his farce to the Marxist amateurs of the Unity Theatre where (as I well recall) it blew the roof off. At the Court, as Richard Findlater pointed out, it was as politically ill-timed as *The Good Woman of Setzuan*: 'The jokes about choosing freedom echo less heartily against the background of Kadar's Budapest.' Other complaints centred on the miscasting of Robert Helpmann in the title part: to have a swindler masquerading as an escaped Soviet diplomat was quite enough without making him a ballet dancer as well. Even in farce, a con-man should inspire confidence. The general feeling was that the play's satirical edge had been blunted by ponderous caricature. However, *Nekrassov* was the first E.S.C. production to play at the Edinburgh Festival, and it established a connection with Edinburgh that was strengthened by Harewood's subsequent appointment as festival director in 1959.

Devine's own French cultural sympathies, dating back to his boyhood and his years with Saint-Denis, were not eclipsed by developments at home. Paris was still important, in spite of John Osborne; and, he wrote, 'it was our deliberate intention to promote this parallel influence in the choice of our repertoire.' In spite of the committee's objections that the English Stage Company should be devoting itself to English plays, he pursued this policy doggedly through to the three-month French season of 1961, when, in fateful procession, Ionesco's *Jacques*, Sartre's *Altona* and Genet's *The Blacks* passed over the Court stage and lost the company just under £14,000 (the Arts Council grant for that year was £8,000). Even so, Devine counted the season an

artistic success and the last production of his life, in 1963, was of
Ionesco's *Exit the King*.

It was also with Ionesco that his French work began in 1957
when he and Plowright appeared as the ancient couple in *The
Chairs*, and here, for once, he escaped the run of authority roles.
For Devine, no less than for the partner half his age, it was a
complete disappearance into character, and also an occasion when
counting the house could be turned to advantage. Amid the
walkouts and cries of 'Surrealist rubbish', the two decrepit figures
treated the actual public as an extension of their invisible throng
of stage visitors: issuing garrulous instructions to the house and
responding to abuse by asking each other 'What did he say, dear?'
and other quavering *ad libs* which, for all the public knew, might
have been in the text. Plowright says she had never seen him
happier. 'When people went out shouting and grumbling into
Sloane Square, George would watch through his window and
smoke his pipe and think "That's what I'm here for." He would
never look out of his window when they were all gliding out into
their Daimlers after a Restoration revival.'

Before this production, the French alliance had already been
sealed by a much more important event. Hearing that Roger
Blin was having difficulty in raising Parisian money for a new
play by Samuel Beckett, the E.S.C. set about acquiring this production to open the 1957 season and dispatched Devine to
negotiate the world première of *Fin de partie*. This was Devine's
first meeting with Beckett, and he described what it meant to
him in a note dictated a few days before he died.

> I spent half an hour with him in his flat in Paris. We talked, drank
> whiskey, and decided nothing. In that half hour I felt I was in
> touch with all the great streams of European thought and literature
> from Dante onwards. This man seemed to have lived and suffered
> so that I could see, and he was generous enough to pass it on to me.

The statement that Devine found no partner among the new
writers must be qualified by this huge exception: he found
Beckett. He had also found another master as austerely in-
corruptible as Michel Saint-Denis, and this new friendship was
likewise shaped by Devine's humility towards anyone he regarded as wiser than himself. His attitude to Beckett and his
work was one of reverence. Beckett repaid the compliment by
giving him control over all English productions of his plays.

When it came to presenting them at the Court, their relationship differed from that of the other author-director teams. Beckett was always the senior partner.

Blin's production of *Fin de partie* opened at the Court in April 1957 as part of a French Fortnight organized by the Union Française des Industries Exportatrices: an official occasion, in short, attended by the French Ambassador. As such, it met with no official obstruction, and all the Daimlers rolled up. Notices of the week's run hinted that the author of *Waiting for Godot* had gone over the top this time, but generally they treated the play with frigid courtesy.

The E.S.C. paid for the French production. In return, Beckett agreed to translate the piece and allow the Court to stage its English première. But when the translation arrived a year later, it hit an official rock. *Fin de partie* might be a distinguished cultural event, but *Endgame* was another matter. The Lord Chamberlain's office refused to license it without a cut of twenty-one lines in the prayer scene including the celebrated snub to the Almighty: 'the bastard, he doesn't exist.' Devine tried to break the deadlock by gathering a small audience of writers and staging a rehearsed reading of the piece for the benefit of Lieutenant-Colonel Sir St Vincent Troubridge of the Lord Chamberlain's office. Besides reading Hamm, Devine was giving the stage directions *sotto voce*, and when he reached the offending passage he threw it away in the same undertone. However, the effort was wasted on Sir St Vincent who sat through the reading like a graven idol with his convictions unshaken. 'It's because it's in English,' Devine told Ann Jellicoe afterwards: 'you can get away with much more in French. Think what you could get away with in Japanese!'

The comedy of the situation was not lost on the press who also noted that the ban practically coincided with the announcement of Devine's C.B.E.: honoured at the Palace, he was being smeared in Stable Yard. 'Does this mean', asked the *Evening Standard*, 'that the Lord Chamberlain considers all people who understand French beyond hope ... Or does he believe that knowledge of the French language bestows immunity from corruption?' Negotiations dragged on for six months and ended with Beckett's consenting to the substitution of 'swine' for 'bastard'.

Failing to engage Alec Guinness, Devine took on the role of

the blind paralysed Hamm as well as directing the Court production of *Endgame*. He was in total sympathy with the piece
and as his stage partner, Clov, he had the superb Beckett actor
Jack MacGowran. The censorship campaign had created a climate
of goodwill towards the play, and in any case the sequel to
Waiting for Godot was a matter of public interest. *Endgame*
started with a good prospect of success, but when the production
opened on October 28, something had gone wrong. Reviewers of
the old guard, like Alan Dent, leapt to the task of dismissing it as
'weird and wanton drivel'. But neither was there much approval
from the Court's friends and Beckett's sympathizers. Tynan
reviewed it in the form of a dialogue parody. The case was more
fairly put by Harold Hobson who said: 'There is nothing positively wrong ... the cast simply have not that element that will
radiate through the language, giving it body and soul.'

Beckett supervised the last two weeks' rehearsals. Up to that
point, Devine and MacGowran had been working on extracting
the ghastly comedy from the Hamm–Clov relationship. Beckett
did not approve what he saw and asked for stylistic corrections.
Another director might have asserted his own authority, but
Devine accepted Beckett's instructions, with the result that
when the production opened the cast were still striving to achieve
the 'toneless voice' required by the author. One cannot say that
the production would have been 'better' without Beckett's
assistance, though perhaps it might have been more popular. But
what the episode illustrates is that Devine's respect for Beckett
and his work was such that he would surrender professional
control in Beckett's presence.

Believing the play to be a masterpiece and well aware of the
derision it might arouse, he was exceptionally nervous of his
responsibilities towards it. He sensed that his performance was
not right, and in trying to correct it he became more nervous
than ever. Preparing for the show was a nightly ordeal. He
would take his seat alone in the centre of the stage with the buzz
of audience conversation coming through the curtain. The rug
would be tucked under his feet, the black glasses put on, the
handkerchief draped over his head, and by the end of this process he would be shaking with fright. The sound I remember
from his performance is one of grating determination. He himself felt that he had failed in the part.

Six years later, the same situation recurred in his production of *Happy Days*. Plowright, originally cast as Winnie, discovered she was pregnant and abandoned the show shortly before the start of rehearsals. Brenda Bruce took her place and began learning the immense part in under a fortnight, at which point Beckett arrived and started giving microscopically detailed notes. It was as if someone battling with the scale of C major were suddenly placed under the baton of Karajan. Peter Duguid, playing Willie, reports that the distracted Miss Bruce was staying up until three in the morning trying to learn the part from a text which Beckett had annotated with as many as eleven inflections in a single line. Meanwhile, he says, Devine had stopped directing and virtually handed the show over to the author. Jocelyn Herbert saw a disastrous run-through and gently suggested that Miss Bruce needed some time to herself; after which Beckett volunteered to stay away for a few days.

As it turned out, *Happy Days* was an artistic success and Devine's trust in Beckett was vindicated. It is easy to recognize that now. We have the testimony of Martin Held, Madeleine Renaud, Alan Schneider, Billie Whitelaw and other artists on the enormous value of Beckett's participation in rehearsal. And his Schiller Theater production of *Waiting for Godot* (which reached the Royal Court in 1976) conclusively proved him a master exponent of his own work. But at the time of the early Court productions he had no such credentials to offer and lacked the confidence to take on the full responsibilities of directing a show himself. Actors like Duguid, accustomed to the straight professional transactions between cast and director, were apt to view him as a meddling amateur.

Devine from the start believed that Beckett was the best guide to staging the plays; and he proved this in his own lifetime with the 1964 National Theatre production of *Play*, which was the occasion for an acrimonious correspondence with the theatre's Literary Manager, Kenneth Tynan. Tynan wrote:

> Before Beckett arrived at rehearsals, *Play* was recognizably a work we all liked and were eager to do. The delivery of the lines was (rightly) puppet-like and mechanical, but not wholly dehumanized ... It seems that Beckett's advice on the production has changed all that – the lines are chanted in a breakneck monotone with no inflections, and I'm not alone in fearing that many of them will be simply inaudible ... The point is that we are not putting on *Play* to satisfy Beckett alone ... I trust the play completely, and I trust

your production of it. What I don't especially trust is Beckett as co-director.

Devine replied:

The presence of Beckett was of great help to me, and to the actors ...
I assume you read the stage directions: 'voices toneless except where
indicated. Rapid movement throughout.' It was always my intention
to try and achieve this, as it is, in my opinion, the only way to perform the play as written. Any other interpretation is a distortion ...
You do not seem to realize that rehearsing a play is an organic process ... To play the play as you indicate would be to demolish its
dramatic purpose and turn it into literature ... You'll have to have
a bit more guts if you really want to do experimental works, which,
nine times out of ten, only come off for a 'minority' to begin with. I
certainly would never have leased the play to the National Theatre
if I had thought the intention was to turn it into something it isn't,
to please the majority.

The rights and wrongs of the dispute were settled by a production
which was greeted as a stylistic triumph, in no way diminished
by the presence of Sophocles in the same programme.

I have attempted by this roundabout route to explain why the
father of the new English drama should have directed so few new
English plays. But there is no point in dwelling any longer on
contributory factors when the main reason is self-evident. For
its first five years, the theatre was always sinking; and it was not
until the big film money began to roll in from the Osborne-
Richardson *Tom Jones* and the subsequent increase in Arts
Council grants that there was any sense of security. It was during
those five years that most of the new writers appeared; and
Devine's priority was to keep his theatre open and get their
work on – a task that left him with little surplus energy for
staging it himself. His main interest, as he told a New York
audience in 1960, was in creating the conditions in which other
people could work. This became a lonely process. He had begun
in equal partnership with Richardson, who promptly built up a
fashionable reputation with Osborne's first plays. Even Richardson's flops, like Faulkner's *Requiem for a Nun* (with two
American stars) and Barry Reckford's *Flesh to a Tiger* (London's
first West Indian play) were spectacular flops. Richardson's
career then extended to Broadway and into films when he and
Osborne formed the Woodfall production company. All of which

18 Devine as the Baron von Epp
   in *A Patriot for Me*, 1965

19 Jocelyn Herbert

20 Devine taking a class at the Royal Court Actors' Studio

21 Noel Coward with John Osborne (right) in the benefit performance
of *The Kitchen*, June 1966

22 Devine saying goodbye to Helene Weigel on the day of his
heart attack

brought money into the Court, but at the expense of Richardson's increasingly prolonged absences. Even so, he kept all his original influence over the company; and it was a standing complaint among the A.A.D.s that whatever they planned with Devine was likely to be capsized when Richardson returned from foreign parts with his own plans for what they should do next.

Thus, besides his running battle with the management committee, Devine also found himself at the centre of a group of conflicting artistic egoisms from which he could only preserve his authority by remaining aloof. And to say the theatre was sinking is no idle metaphor. The new drama comes a poor second to roofs and drains in the E.S.C. minutes. When Gwyn Thomas drove up from Wales in a rainstorm to see a Sunday night performance of *The Keep*, Devine greeted him on the steps of the Court and informed him that his play was off. The auditorium was awash; and, Devine said, 'while he had heard of extravaganzas like *Cinderella* being done on ice, he had never heard of a straight play being done in sewage.' There was also the matter of Clement Freud's dining club, still rooted like a mandrake on the top floor, and denying the company rehearsal space and the chance of enticing some of the bar sales from the pub next door.

These are not matters that attained much prominence in critical discussions of the 'breakthrough' movement, but they loomed large for Devine, especially when he felt his assistants were joining the gang of left-wing snipers instead of getting on with the job. He wrote to one of them:

A man in my position responds to dynamism almost more than anything else ... When I announce the building of a mingy hut in the yard (after many months of struggle) most people ... look gloomy because it is so small. But who, may I ask, has done anything else? We discussed ages ago the erection on the piece of grass behind the London Transport Board canteen of a tent theatre by Sean Kenny. Has anything been done? Has anyone been to me to urge some action? Has anyone volunteered to inquire into the possibility of leasing the land, the cost of a tent, of seats, of making a working budget? The answer is no. It is left to me. And if, for reasons which even a blind man could see, I have no time or energy to pursue such a project, the Royal Court is blamed for lack of initiative and drive ... I had hoped that all of you would do such things ... Instead I find you remain as a figure-head that talks and bellyaches but does nothing. You wear a workman's cap but you don't work. You look like a workman but despise people who work.

Nor did he find it helpful to the organization when young directors, who saw themselves as truer Socialists than he was, started pulling rank over the secretaries and stage staff; or when they struck their own blow against the establishment by defying management committee decisions. He had somehow to reach an accommodation between a Council that refused to have *Private Eye* sold on the theatre bookstall, and directors who got up to tricks like foxing the audience with joke replays of the National Anthem. So any attempt to define that mysterious thing, 'Royal Court policy', must begin by recognizing that it grew out of an unending sequence of financial crises, and collisions between those who found the money and those who put on the plays. Gaskill once gave me a weary smile when I asked him for a policy definition. 'Policy', he said, 'just means the people you're working with.' And in Devine's case, the spectrum of tempera-ments amounted almost to a self-destroying machine. The one thing that held everyone together, from the most die-hard Council member to the fieriest A.A.D., was the censorship issue. It was in their financial as well as aesthetic interests to see the Lord Chamberlain's powers abolished. On that issue, Devine came out into the open, advocating the introduction of an X-Certificate in place of the arbitrary rulings of Stable Yard, and presenting public debates on censorship at the Royal Court. On other public issues, he took the view that statements should be expressed through the plays, and that demonstrations on the side were a dangerous luxury. He was not pleased to find a C.N.D. contingent waiting outside the theatre to serenade the first-night audience for *Rosmersholm*. He even forbade the appearance of a skiffle-group on the steps which had been planned for the opening of Logue's *The Lily White Boys*. Personally, Devine was shy of demonstrations in any case. During Dexter's trial on a homo-sexual charge, he gritted his teeth and went along to Bow Street as a character witness: which, Dexter says, cost him a consider-able effort as he loathed any form of parading. Dexter knew this already from their conversations over the first Aldermaston March. 'I'm going, boy,' Devine said, 'but I always feel a fool in these situations. I've bloody well got to, but I have to tell you that I hate it. I hate demonstrating in public.' Aldermaston, even so, became a regular date in the Royal Court calendar: among other things, it was one point of contact with the young public for whom Devine would dearly have loved to exchange the Daimler trade.

So politically, too, he held an isolated position: though, aside from the fact that he voted Labour, there is not much agreement on just where he did stand. Keith Johnstone saw him as 'an anarchist who happened to be an English gentleman'. To Dexter, he appeared a Socialist who would have liked to keep the revolution on paper. Anderson thought him intellectually naive and apt to chip into discussions with conversation-stoppers like 'I don't really know what a Socialist is. Tell me, am I a Socialist?' It seems that what touched him most was the spectacle of any kind of injustice. Like his father and Lex, he was a champion of the underdog, and would remain obsessed by particular cases like the Craig-Bentley murder trial long after they had dropped out of the news. He also subscribed to causes like the anti-apartheid movement, the abolition of capital punishment and C.N.D.; but when Bertrand Russell invited him to join the Committee of 100, he replied by proposing advertising campaigns instead of civil disobedience. 'If we want to combat this great evil of our time, we have to use the means of our time with all the cunning that they are employed against us': the same principle, in short, on which he ran the Royal Court. 'I do not remember George ever being interested in politics,' remarked the bewildered Saint-Denis when the Sloane Square barricades went up. The truth seems to be that, for all practical purposes, politics for Devine still meant what it had done at the OUDS. It meant theatre politics; but with the crucial difference that he now had his own theatre, and was enaged in building a miniature of the just society as well as devoting his cunning to its defence.

He would adopt underdogs like Hastings and the near-destitute Osborne, fully prepared for them to achieve success and leave him behind: or, in the case of the A.A.D.s, push them firmly out of the nest when he felt it was time for them to go. Dexter, Gaskill and Page were all expelled in this way. 'Justice', Dexter says, 'had to be earned; which made it more appreciated when you got it. All of us wanted his approval very much. If you could prove your belief in a play, then you would get your production. But he did believe you should be able to defend anything with your mouth. He never held a disaster against you if it was something that had gone right to the extreme. What he couldn't bear was a disaster that stayed in the middle.'

Devine, on his side, had no great regard for the ideologies that were sheltering under his roof. It was an area he specifically excluded in summing up the achievements of the Court. 'These young people', he wrote in 1962, 'woke up everything they touched except (alas) politics, which is an older man's game.' He might well have sympathized with John Whiting's dismissal of the new drama as a monster with a big heart and 'a little tiny head'. What he would not have agreed to was cutting the head off. He was placing his bet on talented idealists, no matter how naive, rather than on wise old birds who know that ideals are always defeated. And if he found a talent he believed in, he was ready to wait for it to mature and for the public to accept it. He would maintain a dogged support for some non-writing writers, convinced that they would produce something of real value five years ahead. His enthusiasm for Arden's plays was only increased by their disastrous box office record. When Blond exploded over the third of these, *The Happy Haven* (Arden now having lost the Court £14,757), Devine wrote back defending Arden as 'probably the next most important dramatist to Osborne we have produced ... We must support the people we believe in, *especially* if they don't have critical appeal ... *Lulu* did our reputation more harm than all the plays of Arden put together.' After the opening of *The Happy Haven*, he dumped a pile of newspapers in front of the author and said, 'Well, boy, they're even worse than *Serjeant Musgrave*', and then immediately began talking about Arden's next play. In a *Guardian* article written around the same time, he said, '*Serjeant Musgrave's Dance* is now an O.K. play (they are studying it in schools), even if it did lose us a cool £5,820 in 1958.'

With this aspect of Devine's policy, his assistants were in full agreement: and out of it there grew, if not exactly an indiscriminate contempt for criticism, at least a conviction that they knew more about new drama than did the current batch of London reviewers. The Court consistently refused to play the old game of mock-subservience to newspaper judgments. And although Devine never went to Gaskill's subsequent extreme of locking a critic out of his theatre, he did exact stinging reprisals for any breach of journalistic ethics, and challenged adverse reviews by drumming up support from spokesmen outside the first-night list. He enlisted Alan Sillitoe in defence of *The Happy Haven*, and for *Musgrave* he brought out a pamphlet as a counterblast to the notices.

From episodes of this kind, the separate personalities fused into a common identity, creating something distinctly visible as an artistic policy. Hard though it is to pin down, 'Royal Court policy' was not an empty phrase. It was easy to spot the shows that did not conform to it. *Lulu* and the Duncan plays were obvious outsiders; so were middle-of-the-road popular pieces like Willis Hall's *The Long and the Short and the Tall* and Gwyn Thomas's *The Keep*. 'Director's theatre' (which Devine hated) also felt wrong in the building, even when it tackled an issue that needed to be dragged into the open, like the Johnstone–Gaskill *Eleven Men Dead at Hola Camp*. Star performances, on the other hand, fitted in quite naturally, and with one exception the visiting stars followed the lead of Ashcroft and Olivier in accepting the discipline of writers' theatre along with the reduced pay. Class-warfare was an obsessive theme on the Court stage, but among the people who worked there class barriers were set aside. Anthony Page, after Oxford and America, found he was moving in a 'wider spectrum of people' than ever before when he came to Sloane Square. And, from the spectators' viewpoint, one of the big attractions of the Court was that it drew on all available resources from folk singers to West End names to project the new drama.

These are some of the factors that gave the Court its recognizable signature: but the key factor, obviously, was the choice of plays – another issue over which Devine had to employ his wits against the E.S.C. Council. When the company began its operations, all plays had to be passed by an Artistic Sub-Committee consisting of Harewood, Duncan and Lewenstein. Between that group and the Management Committee, therefore, Devine was tied hand and foot. He had control neither over the budget nor the repertory. During the first season the system worked well enough as Harewood's committee raised no obstruction to the choice of plays and even Duncan was enthusiastic over the discovery of *Look Back in Anger*. The trouble began with Osborne's second play, and Olivier's desire to appear in it. Osborne finished *The Entertainer* at breakneck speed so as to fit in with Olivier's dates, and there followed a meeting with the Oliviers to discuss the possibility of Vivien Leigh also gracing the Court stage in a rubber mask as the dilapidated Mrs Rice. To the relief of the Court contingent, this idea was dropped, and it was agreed that Richardson's production, starring Olivier with a Royal Court company, should follow *Fin de partie* into the theatre early in

April 1957. At this point, the Artistic Sub-Committee rejected the play by two votes to one. After two hours of discussion, Harewood says, 'I remember going icy cold and thinking, "My God, we're going to make the most appalling bloomer, out of well-meaning democratic principles." I was buggered if we were going to do that, so I went off to see Neville Blond first thing the next morning.' Blond came down firmly on Harewood's side, and the production went on. As Devine found then, and on other occasions, the Chairman was a good friend in times of crisis, even if he did treat his artistic staff like factory operatives. However, it was no thanks to the E.S.C.'s constitution that *The Entertainer* got the go-ahead to pack out the Court, the Palace, and the Broadway Royale. Something would have to be changed.

The change took place in two stages. First, with Blond's consent, Devine brought Osborne and Peggy Ashcroft on to the committee. As he described this move: 'I put my own people in': after which there were no repetitions of the *Entertainer* deadlock. But as every script now had to be read by a minimum of five people, this created an exasperatingly prolonged delay during which the play might be snapped up by another management. After enduring this for some months, Devine demanded the right to choose his own plays without consultation. The Council, with some grumbling, yielded to an unanswerable case, and the Artistic Committee lost its powers of veto. Thus, by 1959, Devine had gained his artistic freedom even though he remained firmly hedged around with financial safeguards.

Harewood and Lewenstein, who trusted him, surrendered their control without complaint. Not so Duncan who viewed the episode as evidence of a plot. Even before any official change had been made, he felt the committee were being out-manoeuvred by Devine, in that the only plays they received arrived via Devine's office. And heaven knows what acts of secret murder might have been done in there. It was a known fact that Christopher Fry's *Curtmantle* had been turned down: without doubt there were other equally grisly cases. No playwright stood a chance unless he followed the dictates of the 'new establishment' and gave his work the approved 'polemical slant'. Should a member of the committee dare to propose a play, then (said Duncan) Devine would block it by reporting that it was impossible to cast or that the rights were unavailable.

Eliot, Whiting, Ustinov, John Mortimer and N. C. Hunter

were some of the writers who figured on this alleged blacklist.
In fairness to Duncan, none on that weird assortment of names
would have raised much of a cheer from Devine's readers.
Devine himself considered some of them to be second-rate; also,
of course, he found verse drama unacceptable; and he stated with
regret that the Court had arrived too late to be of any help to
senior playwrights of the Priestley–Benn Levy generation.
Otherwise Duncan's charges read like a malicious distortion.
Very little outright polemical writing got on to the Court stage.
Indeed, in the case of Duncan's particular *bête noire* John Arden,
the main problem for audiences was the playwright's resolute
refusal to take sides or tell them what to think. Wesker's work was
polemical, but Wesker had most of his premières not at the
Court but at the Belgrade Theatre, Coventry. Duncan's description of the Court repertory as an illiterate working-class jamboree
is too obviously untruthful to need detailed denial.

The irony of the situation, as he presents it in *How to Make
Enemies*, is that of an autocrat entangled in a democratic process.
'Anything', he writes, 'is to be preferred to the fumbling caution
of committees ... Give me an editor suffering from dipsomania
in preference to a sober editorial board.' At the Court he was a
member of such a board, and matched against an adversary who
wholeheartedly shared his views on committees. He was in a
false position, and whatever he did to change it only made matters
worse.

By degrees, he elevated his rancour to a philosophical level.
There were, he said, two kinds of human problem: those that
could be cured by social or political action, and those, like old age
and death, for which there was no cure. Only the second was the
proper province of the drama; and Devine had trivialized the
Court through his bias in favour of the first (an odd charge to lay
against the main British exponent of Beckett). Whether Duncan
really believed that a theatre of grand universal themes might
have emerged with the aid of Peter Ustinov and N. C. Hunter is
a moot point. He certainly viewed it as his own territory, and
bitterly resented the non-production of his work. The feud
simmered on with waspish notes from Duncan on the latest
show he disapproved of, and weary answers from Devine.
Duncan submitted a new play, *The Catalyst*, carefully drained
of religious content and typed to obscure the fact that it was
written in verse. Devine headed it off to the Arts Theatre.

In the end, Duncan complained formally to the Management Committee over the treatment of his plays and was invited to come in and put his case. In January 1960 he accepted this invitation. He also composed a 1,500-word statement on artistic policy, addressed to Blond for the attention of the E.S.C. Council. The substance of this document was that, under Devine, the company had betrayed its original aims; that Osborne's commercial success should not be confused with artistic achievement; and that the famous Sloane Square breakthrough merely echoed 'a revolution which took place when Auden was twenty-three'. As for Devine, he was an able administrator, 'but the ideal Director for the E.S.C. should have a more creative bent'. In any case, Duncan concluded (having just held up the inexhaustible Diaghilev as the ideal), any director would be creatively bankrupt after two years in the job.

To Blond's anger, the statement was leaked to the Press and widely reported early in March, which from Duncan's point of view was quite good timing as the Court had lately been losing money on such left-wing investments as Logue's *The Lily White Boys*, and the Wesker trilogy was looming in April. Devine, as at the time of the Vic Centre crisis, observed a strict public silence, leaving the field clear for Duncan to inform reporters that the Court had fallen into the hands of a blinkered Socialist clique, and to call on witnesses like John Mortimer to testify that 'this theatre is not for pleasure. You feel that you have to go to it as a sort of duty.' Not that Duncan affected to care how much support he got, as he was staging the 'showdown' as a personal last stand. Two months passed. Then, in May, the E.S.C. Council issued a statement affirming their support for the theatre's existing policy and declaring their 'complete confidence' in Devine. Once again, Blond had proved a loyal foul-weather friend. But even after this defeat, Duncan clung to his position in the company, and it was not until after Devine's death that he finally resigned.

Viewed as a bit of theatre history, this episode shows the Royal Court catching up with the battles which the rest of Europe had fought half a century before. Mortimer's complaints precisely echo the pre-1914 criticisms of the Vieux-Colombier, and there could be no better defence for the Court's sorties into working-class naturalism than Karl Kraus's 1905 remarks on the Vienna première of Wedekind's *Pandora's Box*: '"Backstairs poetry" becomes a real poetry of the back stairs which can only be condemned by that sort of official weakmindedness which prefers a badly painted palace to a well-painted gutter.' The fact that London's club theatres had occasionally staged such work in the 1930s did not disqualify a theatre of the 1950s from bringing it out into the open. In any case, where were the Osbornes, Ardens, and Weskers of the 1930s? The Duncan dispute clarified two vital principles: the authority of an artistic director to shape artistic policy; and the need to conduct in public the kind of experiments which formerly took place only for minority audiences. This was the real meaning of 'the right to fail'; and the point Duncan seems never to have grasped is that the circumstances of production mattered just as much as the choice of plays.

15

⁂

SECOND WIND

By 1960, then, Devine had won most of the main battles. He had created a theatre that counted in the intellectual life of the community. He had opened the door to a generation of outsiders and escaped enslavement to the box office. He had convinced the Council that there was no more safety in committee rule than in allowing an artistic director to back his own hunches. And he had learned that he could trust his Chairman. Blond might say, 'Take it off,' but he would never say, 'don't put it on.' 'Don't tell the artistic boys,' he once confided to Greville Poke, 'but I'll never let them down.'

However, there was still no sign of any financial respite, and Blond's promise would have been in vain but for the continued success of Osborne's plays which earned the theatre £50,000 during its first five years (compared with Arts Council grants of £30,000). And while Devine had gained a stronger position, he had spent much of his own strength. Besides his basic struggle to keep the theatre running, he had been pouring energy into side activities, such as a stylistic overhaul of posters and production photographs, a schools' scheme for week-long visits by sixth-formers, plans for foreign tours and for a network of provincial theatres linked to the Court, lecture engagements, and work for the various studio groups.

In the autumn before the Duncan row blew up, he had directed both *Rosmersholm* and the 1959 Edinburgh Festival show, Sean O'Casey's *Cock-A-Doodle-Dandy*, which involved two casting trips to Dublin and the engagement of the Paris-based dancer, Berto Pasuka, in the Dionysian role of the Cock. In choosing this play, neither a pylon nor a new work, Devine seems to have been honouring a debt to the past. One of his first statements on joining the E.S.C. was that he hoped to emulate the example of the Abbey Theatre, where the public 'beat each other over the head with shillelaghs'. *Cock-A-Doodle-Dandy*, a bog-Irish *Bacchae* which had been waiting eleven years for a professional performance, definitely belonged in the shillelagh department, and O'Casey told Devine, 'that if I put it on in Dublin, I would be stoned'. As there was no prospect of putting that to the test (given O'Casey's ban on productions in Ireland), Devine also wanted to challenge the conventional belittlement of O'Casey as a two-play author whose talent had withered in his self-imposed exile. Originally planned for the Berlin Festival as well as for Edinburgh and London, the production was a last-minute act of recognition towards the 79-year-old playwright.

The outcome was inconclusive, as the Berlin plan fell through and English reviewers were more impressed by Devine's success in staging an apparently unstageable text and showing it off as 'a maypole dance rather than a propaganda tract' than by any revelation of unsuspected powers in late O'Casey. It was not a show that changed anybody's mind; but O'Casey was pleased, and made one of his rare visits to London to see it. Devine threw a party for him on stage where he was photographed, posing with Osborne among the pseudo-stone walls of Sean Kenny's set as the Angry Old Man exchanging fraternal greetings with his youthful counterpart.

After that production and the ensuing *Rosmersholm*, Devine did not direct again for almost a year. He was exhausted. The problems of his personal life were still unresolved; though he had begun the process of moving out by taking a studio in Flood Street, near the theatre, where he and Jocelyn Herbert could briefly disengage themselves from outside pressures. On his doctor's advice he also started regular visits to a gymnasium, as he was often so tired that he found it difficult even to get out of his car.

But after four years in which he had 'fought myself to my knees', he needed to clear off the scene for long enough to re-charge his batteries. Two means of doing so cropped up. Richardson, who had undertaken the simultaneous production of the film of *Sanctuary* and the American stage première of *A Taste of Honey*, invited Devine and Jocelyn to a working holiday in Los Angeles. Another proposal came from the Institute of Advanced Studies in the Theatre Arts who invited Devine to spend six weeks in New York holding 'master class' rehearsals in Restoration comedy. Devine accepted both invitations, although they virtually coincided with his one and only Court production of the year: the October 1960 opening of Rex Harrison in Chekhov's *Platonov*.

As with Olivier's *Entertainer*, this was another case of a middle-aged star taking his plunge into the modern theatre, and it seems to have been prompted by Olivier's example. Harrison, returning to London after a prolonged spell in America, telephoned Kenneth Tynan to ask whether he knew Devine and 'those other chappies at the Court' as he wished to associate himself with the new movement in Sloane Square. Were there any playwrights who could do for him what Osborne had done for Olivier? This was a tricky question as the writers' theatre militants were not turning out many parts to fit Harrison's high comedy upper bourgeois style. However, Tynan did suggest the name of Nigel Dennis, and brought him together with Harrison and Devine to discuss the idea. 'It was', he says, 'a very uneasy affair: none of them had ever met, and Rex was not used to the role of suppliant.' However, Devine had no difficulty in envisaging Harrison in the Court context, and he immediately commissioned Dennis to write a play for him. This led to their eventual collaboration in *August for the People*. That production did not take place until 1961. As an immediate project, Harrison agreed to make his Sloane Square début as the Don Juan schoolmaster hero of Chekhov's first play.

Whether or not Devine's production counts as a première is a doubtful point as the piece had cropped up under various titles. Chekhov wrote the piece as a medical student, and filed it away untitled and forgotten until it came to light during the 1920s. The manuscript, written in home-made exercise books, runs to 134 pages, and the Court's *Platonov* is among various attempts to carve a workable text out of the monstrous original.

The translation was made by Dmitri Makaroff in collaboration with Devine and his assistant John Blatchley. Makaroff fed the text, act by act, to Blatchley who weeded it of 'dmitri-isms' and then dispatched it to Devine in Los Angeles where it occupied whatever time he could spare from directing Plowright in *A Taste of Honey*. When he returned to England, the day before the first rehearsal, there was still a long way to go in reducing Makaroff's script to manageable length. Also he had just stumbled

on the play's first act, omitted in most versions, including that of
his own translator. It struck him as a vital means of framing the
play 'as a social commentary on the young intellectuals who had
failed to take their responsibilities in the changing political
climate of Russia'. So it became necessary to re-examine the
structure of Makaroff's text so as to accommodate the new
material, and bring the playing time down to three hours.

Rehearsals were sandwiched between unravelling sessions to
which Harrison and Devine devoted the evening and early
morning. The cutting went on until the last minute, with a final
fifteen minutes being sliced out between the dress-rehearsal and
the first night. Another complication was that Harrison had a
strong say in the casting and had to be persuaded to accept
actresses like Elvi Hale and Rachel Roberts whose work he did
not know. Devine, besides directing, was also standing in for the
women during the early readings and, Harrison says, 'we were
getting a bit sick of him playing Anna Petrovna all the time.'

Before first rehearsal, Devine assembled the cast for an opening
talk on the play. This was his standard practice, and a point of
directorial technique on which he differed from the Court's
A.A.D.s. He once told John Dexter, 'I like to get all that out of
my system, and then be prepared to scrap the lot of it.' To which
Dexter replied, 'Yes, I like to scrap, but not to change my
position in front of people. It's hard enough keeping people's
confidence anyway without setting them a false objective.' In
the case of *Platonov*, he did not win everybody's confidence.
Peter Duguid, returning to the Court after four years, says he
was 'shattered' by the change in Devine from the ebullient
pioneer of the first season to the careworn figure he had become:
'*Platonov* should have been an absolute gift for him, but he
simply didn't know the play.' Nicholas Selby, who had not
worked with Devine before being cast as Vengerovich, briskly
dismisses the opening talk as 'waffle'.

Harrison, however, claims to have enjoyed this 'terribly
instructive lecture ... Under normal conditions, I wouldn't want
particularly to be sat down in the stalls while the director sat on
the stage and told you how rotten you were. But he didn't do that.
He'd be frightfully witty and entertaining, about the piece and
where we'd gone right or wrong with it. This went on all through
rehearsals. I thought it was beautiful.'

Quite apart from the fact that Sloane Square had introduced

him to his future wife, Rachel Roberts (again echoing the Olivier-Plowright marriage), this was the honeymoon period for Harrison and the Court. 'It wasn't the same as acting in the West End in those days. You weren't on tour, you weren't in the provinces, and you weren't in London either. There was a marvellous atmosphere of freedom in that little theatre.' Other members of the company were somewhat less impressed by this atmosphere, as it was not Harrison's way to waive his usual privileges as leading actor, and his charm was based on the deference of others. Still, he was a wonderful artist from whom there was much to be learnt; and it was to everyone's advantage that he knew he had been superbly cast.

It was also very much Devine's play, as he proved (even to Duguid) once he got into his stride. As the work of a prodigiously gifted novice, it fell into line with his E.S.C. policy; and as the novice was Chekhov, there was a particular fascination in sorting out the derivative elements from those presaging his maturity. The young Chekhov once remarked that the only effective ways he knew of ending a play were to get the hero married or kill him; but *Platonov*'s debts to nineteenth-century melodrama were no drawback from Devine's point of view, as he loved the old melodramatic devices, and if there was one thing that impressed everyone who saw the production it was Sasha's Second Act escape from under the wheels of an approaching train. A red eye grew out of the darkness, and momentarily it did seem that a ton of metal was hurtling towards the auditorium. This effect was jointly achieved by Devine, Richard Negri (the designer) and Richard Pilbrow (the lighting consultant); a partnership demonstrating Devine's continued exploration of stage lighting. It was not limited to this one effect. The whole production amounted to an exercise in revitalizing traditional scenery. Negri employed a surround including a Victorian backcloth, and detailed representational sets, but coupled these with a rear-lighting technique which enabled Devine to conceal certain areas in darkness and reveal only selected vistas to the audience. Also, while the forms of the scenery remained traditional, their materials – cotton ducks and filled gauzes – were chosen for their responsiveness to atmospheric light.

When it opened in October 1960, the production caught most reviewers off their guard. Nurtured on the Chekhov of *Uncle Vanya* and *Three Sisters*, they were unprepared for Chekhov the

young humorist and follower of Ostrovsky. Their bewilderment
was summed up by Milton Shulman who called the production
'an outrageous burlesque ... with as much resemblance to
Chekhov as Sweeney Tod.' There were also complaints that it
lacked a sense of period and social tone: and – the root objection –
that it failed to guide the spectator into a 'stable emotional
position'. As I remember it, *Platonov* was not the most polished of
the Court's shows, but its supreme virtue was that it did avoid
fixed emotional positions. In place of the expected journey
through the flat Chekhovian landscape, it substituted an ex-
hilarating switchback ride between the extremes of melodramatic hysteria and broad farce. A year or two later, the piece
would have been labelled a 'black comedy'. On paper, it might
appear a jumble of incompatible styles. Devine's achievement
was to assemble these into an expressive kaleidoscopic pattern.
Just as his performance in *The White Guard* had convinced
Agate that taking a footbath and going into battle were matters of
equal importance to a Russian, so his production of *Platonov*
made sense of a Russian society in which landowners, Jewish
businessmen, retired Army officers and peasant horse thieves
could meet on shared terms of merciless candour: and in which
a failed suicide is presented seriously and a successful killing in
the midst of laughter. Emotionally, one was thoroughly prepared for Ronald Barker's stunned inquiry to the lifeless
Platonov: 'Who am I going to drink with now at your funeral?'

In his introduction to the published text, Devine wrote that
at the time of the Court production

> an extraordinary idea was put about with considerable vehemence
> that the play was meant to be entirely serious ... The trouble with
> genius is that people like to adopt it, make it their own and then
> accuse of vandalism anyone who does not comply with *their* adopted
> conception of this genius.

However, the show certainly got through to some people, like
Tynan, who saluted its 'general success' in harvesting the 'first
fruits of Chekhov's life-long curiosity about the symptoms and
causes of human boredom'. Unlike *Cock-A-Doodle-Dandy*, it
was a production that changed people's minds.

It also filled the Court to 86 per cent capacity at increased
prices, and ranked as a personal triumph for Harrison whose
'febrile and wild-eyed satyr' tied with Alec Guinness's Ross in
the *Evening Standard* Award for the best performance of the

year. He departed for Portofino with Rachel Roberts; and thence to Spain to make a film with Rita Hayworth; but with an understanding that he would like to come back. The honeymoon was still on.

With *Platonov* out of the way, Devine returned to America early in November. His first visit to New York had been for the brief run of *The Country Wife* in 1957 when Plowright had been replaced by a Method actress whom the show's producers considered to be too fragile to take direction. This time there was no money at stake, and he was working *in camera* with actors who wanted to learn. I.A.S.T.A. existed partly to exercise Americans in foreign styles, and Devine arrived to direct *The Way of the World* in the wake of 'master directors' from the Moscow Art Theatre and the Comédie-Française. His visit had been set up by Michel Saint-Denis whose wife (formerly Suria Magito) was already in New York. As Plowright and Richardson were already there with *A Taste of Honey* and Olivier was playing in Anouilh's *Becket* there was plenty of familiar company even though he had left the Court behind. By day he was doing what he enjoyed most – working with keen young actors in a non-commercial situation: by night he was dining with old friends and touring the Manhattan jazz spots he had discovered with Jocelyn on his last trip for the Broadway opening of *The Chairs*.

One complication was that thirty actors had enrolled for a play calling for half that number. The only way of using them all was to split them into two companies and rehearse two separate productions. Devine gave in to this 'crazy idea' and shouldered the double assignment with the aid of a young soap-opera director, Joe Hardy; and towards the end of rehearsals, he had come to see some advantages in the system as a means of giving the actor a mirror-image of his own work. As he was working in good physical conditions and with a cast of intelligent novices, this obscure event (which played only to festival audiences) has the interest of highlighting his general approach to Restoration acting. Instead of using the kind of directorial shorthand familiar to British casts, he had to spell everything out and quote bits of basic advice, like Edith Evans's 'Don't work through the line; pull the end of the line towards you like a fish.' Also he had to convince Americans that virility could be projected through the apparently effeminate attitudes of the eighteenth-century silhouette.

Rehearsals began with warm-up dances which then became the basis for dramatic movement within the play thanks to the virtually circular stage. As Devine put it, 'When we taught kids about the eighteenth-century theatre, they used to learn it through the dance: and all the dance movements are in the round, so there was air between you and the audience. Even the things people say go round in a circle.' This links up with the 'open air' principle he tried to apply in the first designs for the Court, and goes to prove that he valued the Restoration stage for what it could still give to the modern theatre rather than as a closed stylistic category. 'I am not interested in the past but only in the future,' he told a New York audience, 'but I do believe in the inspiration of tradition.' Besides preparing a show, the I.A.S.T.A. programme involved a certain amount of campus lecturing which still afflicted Devine with stage-fright. It came as a big surprise to I.A.S.T.A's President John Mitchell that his distinguished guest should need to stop for repeated slugs of whisky on his way up to Bronxville to address a bored group of 'new American mothers' at Sarah Lawrence College. As a university speaker, Devine sometimes offended people by playing the plain man of the theatre confronting a pack of intellectuals: his shyness was mistaken for ill-disguised contempt. But no such misunderstandings arose when he was addressing members of his own profession, judging by the most widely reported of his American lectures. This was delivered to an Actors Equity meeting at the Morosco Theatre, held at midnight for the benefit of Broadway's working actors. Nerves or no nerves, it was a fighting performance. Through his past dealings with Broadway managements he had become deeply suspicious of American producers and all his suspicions had been confirmed by five weeks in New York. Broadway struck him as a horribly magnified replica of all that was worst in the British system. There was a total absence of intellectual drive. 'I see a theatre where the tail is wagging the dog and the dog is lying down and taking it.' The artist was being devoured by parasites. 'I do assure you that the people I have mentioned are an absolute enemy to us – to be studied like the enemy ... Who ever heard of an agent dying in his office? But actors have died on stage.'

He went on to recommend some form of artistic collective, pointing out that individual careerism in the acting profession and the traditional fight between the actor and the writer were two elements that played into the enemy's hands. Theatre people 'should not think, as I did between the wars, that all that was necessary was to do the work to the best of one's ability'. Another mistake was to wait for premises, like the Lincoln Center, to arrive. Equity should start hunting for premises in converted cinemas and studying the legalities of non-profit-making performance. As a collective undertaking, this would mean compromise. 'If we want to change things we have got to be as cunning and knowledgeable as the people we want to defeat.' The material obstacles were obvious, but these were never the primary causes of failure. In any case, the enemy had a weak spot:

> You have an affluent society and a lot of very guilty people. Coronary thrombosis is on your side. What I'm urging is art with an attitude. Don't worry about geniuses, because they will take care of themselves ... If you want an alive theatre you will get it. I have never seen utter and entire determination defeated. Never.

The *New York Times* reported this speech under the headline 'American Stage Scorned by Briton', and according to Harold Clurman it had an impact that split the audience down the middle. No speech can do any more than boost morale; but Devine needed no reminding of how effectively it could do that after Arthur Miller's famous 1956 statement that the British theatre was 'hermetically sealed off from life'. The timing of that observation was worth a mint to the English Stage Company. Devine's appearance at the Morosco was no less well timed. It was shortly followed by the emergence of anti-commercial groupings like the American Place Theater and Edward Albee's Playwrights' Unit, not to mention the whole off-off-Broadway explosion. So one can at least say that Devine repaid the debt to Miller.

He returned to London in mid-December, having laid plans for presenting Mort Sahl and other American stand-up satirists at the Court. I.A.S.T.A. sent him off with a champagne birthday party. London, of course, closed in immediately. Within a few days of his arrival, his mother died in her Camden Town bed-sitting room. The Court was at a low ebb, following an internal row over Lindsay Anderson's production of *Trials by Logue* which had been withdrawn a week before the end of its scheduled run. Notice to quit the workshops had been served on the company by the Park Walk landlord: true, they were rat-infested, but there were no other premises in sight. Plans for the spring French season then hit a rock when Laurence Harvey broke his contract to appear in Sartre's *Altona*. An obvious means of repairing morale lay in Osborne's *Luther* which had been awaiting production since the summer; but as Albert Finney was considered indispensable in the title part, the wait had to be prolonged until Finney's release from the long-running *Billy Liar*.

During Devine's absence, plans had taken shape for touring seven West European countries and finishing with a non-commercial foray into Czechoslovakia and Poland. The commercial impresario was Jan de Blieck, now President of the Association of European Festivals. Prague and Warsaw depended on the British Council. Both sides of this plan now caved in. De Blieck's views on stars and repertory did not coincide with those of the E.S.C., and the British Council announced that they were out of funds. However, the star in question was Rex Harrison and the collapse of the foreign tour left him available to appear in the New Nigel Dennis comedy. So, coupled with *Luther*, the Court was in a position to face 1961 with two potential trump cards to play.

The script of *August for the People* had been accepted by the Edinburgh Festival, and Harrison agreed to rejoin the company for the festival première followed by a five-and-a-half week run at the Court. In the same month the *Luther* deadlock was resolved. Richardson's production, starring Finney, was to open at Nottingham in June and proceed to London via the Paris, Holland and Spoleto festivals.

The Court, meanwhile, was occupied with its big French season, but as Devine was not artistically engaged in it he had a breathing space to start setting up a transfer scheme between the Court and selected provincial reps, and to introduce a profit-sharing system at the workshops for outside commissions. He also went down to Park Walk as an actor when Richardson took the cameras in there to film *A Taste of Honey*. The real pressures of the year began in March when the Lord Chamberlain refused to license *Luther* and Osborne declared his readiness to withdraw the play rather than make alterations. The Italian censor promptly followed suit with a blanket prohibition on the play which dished its chances for Spoleto.

Devine considered *Luther* to be a 'giant step forward' for

Osborne, and to get it on somehow he even suggested reversing a basic principle of E.S.C. policy and turning the Court into a club. At the same time, he was assiduously arguing the point with Stable Yard, and by early April he was able to report that no drastic measures would be needed as the censor had ceded his eight most important objections to the script, and – Albert Finney's tonsils permitting – the production was free to go ahead as planned.

As Devine was playing in *Luther*, this meant simultaneous involvement in the two major productions of the year: rehearsing and touring in the Osborne for two months from June and then embarking on the Dennis rehearsals when *Luther* reached London at the end of July. This was Devine's first stage appearance in an Osborne play (on television he had played in Osborne's *A Subject of Scandal and Concern*), and he was very keen to make it, even though the part of Vicar General Staupitz was another of the authority figures he seemed doomed always to play.

After two international hits and then the flop of *The World of Paul Slickey* there was an intense build-up of expectation around the delayed and censor-scarred première of *Luther*. Beyond that, Osborne still exercised a mesmeric hold over his generation, akin to that of a hell-fire preacher, and *Luther* marked his zenith as rebel custodian of the national conscience. *Time* magazine got hold of the text early enough to print a notice in Chicago and come out in Britain the day after the Nottingham première. Devine had recently been proclaiming the right to fail to his New York audience. But for once, it was intoxicating to be working in a play he believed in and which, from the start, was clearly a whale of a hit. After Nottingham he went out with the company to the Paris and Holland festivals. Money, as always, was tight. 'If this doesn't go, we can't pay the actors,' he said before the Paris opening. But it was a joke. Peter Duguid remembers him in a bar with some of the cast: 'He was really relaxed, sitting there with Jocelyn. Just an actor among actors, telling funny stories about the Young Vic and what it was like on tour, and crying with laughter. It was super: something one hadn't seen for years.'

A month later he was back in London, running the Court, appearing nightly as Staupitz and rehearsing Harrison in *August for the People*. When the idea of this production was first discussed, it promised a marvellous convergence of interests. For Harrison, it offered a tailor-made part which would also give him a stake in the new drama movement. For Dennis, it was a means of repaying the money which the Court had lost on his previous plays. And he was very keen to write for Harrison whom he saw as a virtuoso using only a small part of his range: 'instead of a few notes, I wanted to give him a whole keyboard.' Devine, who was devoted to Dennis and his work, saw the project as an opportunity by which the author of *Cards of Identity* and *The Making of Moo* might finally get through to the big public. Having commissioned the play, he had promised to direct it himself, as in this case he had no stylistic misgivings: he and Dennis were of the same generation and he understood the rhythms and comic pointing of Dennis's dialogue. He saw another advantage in the service the production might perform in demonstrating the breadth of E.S.C. policy. When accused of left-wing working-class bias, his habitual response was: 'Oh, if only they knew how much we're looking for the other stuff.' A really successful modern high comedy could decisively silence the kitchen sink gibes.

These were the starting hopes in mid-1960: and they all depended on the quality of the script which began thudding in, act by act, from the Broxbourne woods. *August for the People* tells the story of Sir Augustus Thwaites, a retired colonial governor and now Chairman of a Stately Homes Association whose blue-blooded members turn an honest penny by opening their country seats to the tireless British sight-seer. The play begins with a celebration banquet where Thwaites, arising to deliver his Chairman's speech, launches into a contemptuous description of the average population as a flock of sheep. The press, duly appalled, report the speech with pious horror, thus turning Thwaites into a celebrity and doubling the queues at his stately turnstiles. So far so good. The problems arose in the last act which forsakes satiric comedy for expressionist farce, and we see Thwaites being lectured on the evils of colonialism by a visiting African and setting up a school of philosophy with an old boxer before finally going mad in red velvet.

Dennis had trouble with this act and was late in delivering it. At the time of the E.S.C. tour negotiations, there was some doubt as to whether Harrison would be available, and the script was offered to a number of other leading actors who all turned it down.

Dennis's theory is that they were nervous of becoming indentified with Thwaites's unpopular views, particularly his scorn for the press. One star returned the script with the remark, 'I like my morning paper.' Not only actors responded in this way. Oscar Lewenstein, normally a principal link between the E.S.C. and the West End, informed the management committee that, for ideological reasons, he wished to be released from participation in the Dennis production.

August is not a straightforward right-wing piece. Thwaites, after all, does go out of his mind. The problem was not so much content as form: the gear-change, as one critic put it, from *The Apple Cart* to *Timon of Athens*. As Dennis saw it, this development was implicit in the violence of Thwaites's character: as Harrison saw it, the play had a lousy last act. They were therefore at loggerheads from the start. Devine was in no position to reconcile them, for (as he told his designer, Stephen Doncaster) he could not understand what Dennis was after in the play.

After a week's rehearsal the atmosphere had worsened to such an extent that the author and star were barely on speaking terms. Dennis's impression was that Harrison approached the text in a state of innocence, and horror gradually descended on him as he listened to what he was saying. It might be all right for an author to make himself unpopular, but for a leading man it was quite another matter. It appeared to Dennis that the virtuoso had turned up his nose at the Emperor Concerto and was keen to revert to 'Chopsticks'. Dennis retired to the woods and wrote Harrison a letter, arguing that it would be fatal to try and pass Thwaites off as an amiable diplomat but that if he let rip and played him as a real Tartar who finally goes down fighting, he would at once make sense of the play and retain a measure of the spectators' sympathy. Harrison complied with a vengeance, at least in his off-stage performance. Enraged by what he considered amateur interference, he demanded that Dennis should be exluded from the theatre. Devine, he says, backed him up. 'George said, "You're absolutely right. I think it's always wrong to have authors in theatres when the actors are trying to bring their words to life."' This is in flat contradiction to all Devine's past policy at the Court; but, whether or not he said it, he gave way to Harrison's demands rather than risk a walkout. There was, he assured Dennis, no alternative.

Dennis was sceptical about this and saw it as symptomatic of

Devine's general exhaustion, of which others were equally aware. With Dennis on one side urging him to stand up to Harrison, and Harrison on the other demanding a professional closed shop, it is not surprising that Devine suffered a loss in artistic energy. His only relief during the miserable weeks of rehearsal was his nightly escape into the role of Staupitz. Dennis says, 'He fled into that like a wife who can't face the washing-up.'

At the end of August, the play opened for its pre-Edinburgh tryout at Newcastle where it packed out the cavernous Theatre Royal for a week. The company's unhappiness was not dispelled by full houses, and agents descended in a flock on Newcastle to hover protectively over their clients. At this point, Harrison let it be known that Twentieth-Century Fox had offered him the role of Caesar in the Burton–Taylor *Cleopatra*, and that he intended to accept it at the price of abandoning the Court production in mid-run. Dennis demanded that he should be held to his contract. To which Devine, unarguably, replied that there was no way of holding on to an actor who had decided to leave. When the production arrived at the Edinburgh Lyceum, Tynan, the instigator of the project, delivered the *coup de grace* in the *Observer*. The play, he said, recalled the declining years of Shaw:

> a neglected Aunt Sally determined at all costs to attract hostility ... How can one blame the sins of the tabloid Press on democracy, as Mr Dennis does, when the tabloids are not democratically controlled? Oh that Mr Dennis's style might have been allied to a more interesting mind.

Thanks to Harrison, the 'dead duck of the Edinburgh Festival' withstood such attacks well enough to wing its way to Sloane Square where the first night public, rolling up to witness an aristocratically articulate massacre of the mumbling herd, were greeted on the steps by Lindsay Anderson holding a banner listing the playwrights gaoled in the cause of C.N.D. Again, Harrison's name brought in the public; but after a fortnight he bought himself out of the show and departed for Rome. The money from Fox enabled Devine to pay compensation to the company and the author, but his humiliation was intense. Nor did Dennis regard a cash payment as adequate compensation for the dispersal of the first box office queues his work had ever attracted. There was no way of salvaging the play. But Dennis, bewitched by his full houses, did not accept this situation and asked Devine to take on the part. Devine refused this impossible request, and for the disappointed playwright that was the last straw. 'I quarrelled with him,' Dennis says, 'I don't think he ever quarrelled with me.' So, besides losing a star and a production, Devine also lost one of his dearest friends. Richardson, who watched it all happening, described the episode as 'the nastiest thing that's happened in the history of the Royal Court'.

Devine's annual holiday was due, and he went to ground in the South of France with Jocelyn Herbert. Their destination was an old farmhouse at Valbonne which Osborne and Richardson had rented for the summer when planning the film of *Tom Jones*. It was from here that Osborne, in one of his fits of negative patriotism, had just dispatched his hysterical 'Damn You, England' letter to *Tribune*; followed shortly by his elopement with Penelope Gilliatt: so the atmosphere was hardly less tense than that of the Court. On arrival, Devine collapsed with a nervous breakdown which took the form of uncontrollable weeping, inability to make decisions, and paranoid suspicion that his friends were patronizing or attacking him. In this state he wrote a last, almost illegible, letter to Dennis apologizing for everything that had happened to the play. Dennis did not reply.

Richardson's doctor put him under deep sedation. After ten days in bed, he started getting up to sit in the sun and swim in the pool, and by the third week he had recovered sufficiently to make the return trip. Jocelyn drove him back through a violent storm in the mountains in Richardson's Thunderbird, and got him home to London where his own doctor told him to take three months off. Blond agreed, on condition that Richardson took over the Court during his absence.

It so happened that Devine and Jocelyn had just acquired a bit of property. The previous year they had come across a derelict farmhouse close to the Redgraves' Hampshire cottage. They were hard up and they were at the end of a queue of prospective buyers. But thanks to the prohibitive cost of installing electricity, the other deals fell through. Jocelyn and Devine, who had no objection to oil lamps, were the vendor's last hope. Then some money came their way. Richardson gave Jocelyn her first film job as costume designer and colour consultant on *Tom Jones*, and offered her a fee which was the exact price of the farm, which became theirs shortly before the opening of *Luther*.

Andrew's Farm appears in the Domesday Book, complete with

a map showing its barns and pigsties which, to the fury of Devine and Jocelyn, had just been demolished by a local builder. It had been empty for ten years: there were no chimneys, all the windows were broken, and there were gaping holes in the wall and roof. There was no road to the farm, and the surrounding land was densely overgrown with high nettles and cow-parsley. One of the first jobs was to create a practically invisible private driveway from the main road, just wide enough to take the old green Alvis. The place promised perfect, inviolable seclusion. Devine had never particularly valued property, but in the case of Andrew's Farm he felt he had at last discovered his own place.

While the farm was being patched up he stayed with the Redgraves, coming over every day to muck in with the builders; and as soon as it became habitable he moved in and started making furniture. Jocelyn came down at weekends and he always had something new to show her: solid country carpentry that looked entirely at home in the 900-year-old building with its gigantic fireplace and dwarfish doorways. Later on, when Saint-Denis came to stay at the farm, he summed up this side of Devine as the *côté Saint Joseph*. In different ways throughout his career Devine had always been a builder: a man for whom vision and intellect had to be justified through manual skills. But he was not quite the same man at the end of the Andrew's Farm convalescence. Henceforth, the more alienated he became from the world of contractual haggling and box office percentages, of actors crying on the stairs and friendships being ruined for money and artistic vanity, the more important it became to him to escape into the country.

16

PROTEST AND PROFIT

DECADE divisions are supposed to exist only for the convenience of historians, but there is nothing artificial in the contrast between the 1950s and the 1960s in the British theatre. Even at the time, you could feel the climate changing. An age of endeavour was giving way to an age of instant success. Art with an attitude subsided into random satire. Convictions dwindled into fashionable attitudes. Yesterday's rebels turned into today's beautiful people; and the 'redbrick' artists of 1956 became the focus of glamour-struck West End tributes like Elaine Dundy's *My Place* (1962), wherein an actress of the 'breakthrough' generation is pictured camping out in a theatre attended by an exclusive group of new wave chums every bit as sealed off from life as the hot-house swells who so offended Arthur Miller in the 1950s. The English middle classes, Osborne wrote in 1959, 'disarm revolutions by simply not appearing to fight them'.

For someone like myself, whose viewpoint was shaped by the experience of the 1950s, it is extremely hard to describe this period without falling into cant. Even as I put them down, I know that terms like 'establishment', 'breakthrough' and 'vital theatre' are as dead as a door-nail, and that the battlefield metaphor of *avant-garde* outposts lobbing revolutionary missiles into the commercial stronghold tells one precisely nothing about the realities of theatrical change. I can only record that, at the time, the rhetoric of the 1950s did mean something; and that the meaning drained away during the next decade as it appeared that the most conspicuous achievement of the campaign had been to link protest to the profit motive.

Devine, who believed in hard work, long-term planning, and the possibility of changing people's hearts, had good reason to feel disenchanted with the 1960s. And if he was an altered man when he emerged from his three-month hibernation, the Court too had outlived its heroic phase. Its pre-eminence in the 1950s derived in part from the fact that there was simply nowhere else for writers like Osborne and Arden to go. By the end of the decade, it had lost that monopoly. How could the Court maintain its path-finding role when, for instance, Harold Pinter had arrived through commercial production and David Mercer through BBC Television? In any case, the new drama movement had gone off the boil. Many of the first writers had fallen by the wayside and no comparable second wave had appeared. To keep up the flow of material, Devine brought in plays by Theatre Workshop authors like Shelagh Delaney and Henry Chapman (although he fought for Theatre Workshop with the Arts Council and respected Joan Littlewood's aims, he was no enthusiast for her work). He still had the same reservations about Arnold Wesker, but he went in with a commercial management to stage *Chips with Everything*. The Sunday night productions continued but, with the exception of David Cregan's *Miniatures* and Edward Bond's *The Pope's Wedding* (which Devine, who considered Bond a 'second-string dramatist', failed to exploit), they turned up no new writer of importance. Economically, too, it had been discovered that the Sundays cut both ways. If little need be put into them, there was not much to be got out of them either; and critical approval for a production without décor was no guarantee of favourable reviews if the show were promoted to the main bill. Osborne alone retained undiminished dramatic power and unswerving loyalty to the theatre.

Summing up the situation when I met him in 1963, Devine said: 'I can't disguise from you the fact that the position of this theatre has changed. We are supposed to be the spear-head; but how do you keep sharpening the spear? After an explosion like 1956 it's not surprising there's a hiatus now. Everybody wants to be with it. But there must be a place where people who don't want to be with it can go, because they are the people who create the with-its.' He then ran through a list of his past assistant directors at the Court: some working in television, some attached to other subsidized companies in London and the provinces; all entrenched in some organization or other. 'All these guys are in work. Any one of them, in the old days, not having an outlet, might have started a theatre; and the funny thing is that there probably isn't one among them who wouldn't subscribe to the idea that one should try to reach a more popular audience. Indeed, some of them at one time used to come to me and say, "We've found a place in Battersea." And I used to say, "Fine. Let's get a budget out." They'd say, "Budget?" So I'd help them with a budget and how to get hold of a lease: but unless I actually drove the thing right through to the end it somehow disintegrated because something else always came along. Frankly, I think you've got to have an obsession to make anything happen; because if you're not obsessed somebody comes along and says, "What about this?" and you're hooked.'

In spite of all this, it would be false to picture Devine as a tired man presiding over a declining enterprise. He did not know he had only four years to live. 'Fifty-two today,' he noted in November 1962, 'and sound as a bell.' The breaking of the Court monopoly in the 1960s was a direct consequence of its success, and if Devine lost a good many of his assistant directors it was often because he himself pushed them out of the nest. He was not so much concerned with loss as with replacement, and never did he hatch out more dreams than in the period of his return to the Court. Among the plans that failed to come off were those of taking over the Chelsea Palace and the old Metropolitan Music Hall as 'popular' extensions of Sloane Square. There were schemes for running a touring service to universities, for mounting annual seasons of plays by young writers, and creating a link with the American National Theatre and Academy. There was a two-pronged comedy project, involving star Restoration revivals on one hand, and on the other the importation of American satirists and the appearance of clowns like Zero Mostel as Ubu and Tony Hancock as Brecht's Galy Gay.

Through these, and through the plans that did work out, two main purposes appear: to increase the scale of promotion and rewards within the Court's own organization; and to return to the original task of building a new audience as well as a new theatre.

One scheme was in full swing when Devine returned in January 1962. Four years previously, the Court had run an anniversary season to mark the foundation of the British repertory movement. Four provincial reps contributed to it, but the only successful show had been Wesker's *Chicken Soup with Barley*, which Devine had placed with the Belgrade Theatre,

Coventry. From this experience he concluded that in the case of any future links with the provinces, the Court must not simply be on the receiving end. Subsequently he developed the idea of a Court-based regional circuit following the French decentralization pattern. It would consist of resident companies run by his own A.A.D.s and exchanging productions on a weekly rota, thus allowing adequate rehearsal time and giving provincial companies the chance of working in Sloane Square. Early in 1961 he made a trip to East Anglia. Norwich and Cambridge nibbled at the bait, and in July the Gulbenkian Foundation recommended a £3,000 guarantee towards a pilot scheme. A month later Norwich faded out, leaving the Cambridge Arts Theatre to Sloane Square's undivided attentions.

The scheme got under way in October during Devine's absence. It began with Jellicoe's new play, *The Knack*, which was enthusiastically reviewed and transferred to the Bath Theatre Royal. This was followed by an Edward Albee double bill, Henry Chapman's *That's Us*, Gwyn Thomas's *The Keep* and Max Frisch's *The Fire Raisers*, which all transferred to the Court after a week's run in Cambridge. With one exception the season was directed by Devine's assistants, and thus relieved the eternal headache of finding enough for the A.A.D.s to do.

At the end of the season, the Cambridge General Manager, Andrew Blackwood, was refusing to pay his theatre's guarantee for the final production on grounds of faulty stage management and last-minute programme changes. Some defence was found for these criticisms, but there was no answer to Commander Blackwood's complaint that the Court was merely using Cambridge as a tryout for London. This was indeed the case. The original idea of a network of regional companies working for each other's benefit had shrivelled into the old pattern of a London management exploiting a provincial house for its own advantage. The scheme, thereupon, came to an end and was not renewed.

One lesson of this experience was that, no matter how much goodwill is involved, it is extremely hard to avoid the big-fish-little-fish relationship in any working alliance between theatres of unequal resources. It was a message that Devine took to heart when the National Theatre began casting hungry glances towards Sloane Square.

Dreams and long-term schemes apart, he resumed the Court's day-to-day business with all his old vigour. Practically the first thing he did after his return was to snatch success out of disaster by recasting the company of Richardson's much-abused *A Midsummer Night's Dream* in his own morale-repairing *Twelfth Night*. Later in the year, he saved the bacon again by stepping in to supervise the rehearsals of Tennessee Williams's *Period of Adjustment* which had proved too much for its young American director. This came at a low point in Williams's British reputation but the show vied with Wesker's *Chips with Everything* as the only two financial successes of 1962. This was also the year of his production of Beckett's *Happy Days*, and his appearance in George Tabori's collage programme, *Brecht on Brecht*, which brought Lotte Lenya to the London stage for the first time since the early 1930s. Devine went through the show as Brecht's spokesman stabbing his points home with a cigar butt and coming forward at the end to deliver a wry *envoi* on the futility of trying to describe a house by holding up a single brick. Playing another theatre director whose practice had done much to shape his own, he was working well within his range. Brecht, no less than so many of his previous roles, was a middle-aged authority figure, but this time there was no external assertion of power. The impression was simply that of a man speaking the truth. Playing a director, he gave the opposite of a 'director's performance', betraying none of his habitual strain. With outstanding exceptions, such as Andrey and Tesman, he had previously excelled only in grotesque parts and there was something masked and almost toad-like about his acting. But with this performance he began to look beautiful on the stage and to find the means of revealing himself through a role rather than using it as a disguise.

Less interesting artistically but important for other reasons was his performance as Squire Allworthy in Richardson's film of *Tom Jones*. This, famously, was a family project, directed, co-designed and largely acted by Court artists. To Devine, even so, it was just another job. He had no film ambitions and small interest in film technique: and he persistently turned down Richardson's efforts to involve him in film directing. It is ironic that on the one occasion that his writers and actors really reached a popular audience it should have been through a medium he rather despised. With his committee's permission, he took odd days off during the summer to join Richardson's company at Weymouth where the film was being shot on

location. On release, it proceeded to make a fortune for Woodfall
Productions and win an Oscar. Osborne and Richardson, to their
lasting credit, then approached Devine and Jocelyn and made
them a joint offer of 1 per cent of the gross profits, which worked
out as a gift of £25,000. It was the first big money either of them
had ever made.

In November, after the opening of his production of *Happy
Days*, Devine took off alone on a British Council lecture tour of
Brazil, his first such engagement since the tour of Greece and
Turkey eight years before. On this occasion, he also kept daily
notes on his month in Rio, São Paulo, Belo Horizonte and
Brásília. The other difference was that the fame of the Royal
Court had preceded him, and he arrived in Brazil as the founding
father of the British new drama movement, to be lionized alike
by the expatriate establishment, by young experimental groups
and by student audiences. The one exception was in Brásília
when he drove through a rainstorm to the remote campus of the
new university to deliver a lecture only to find a totally empty
auditorium. Even so, he put Brásília down as 'a great experience';
and he fell sufficiently under the country's spell to plan to take a
university job in Rio after his retirement from the Court. The
Brazilian mystique of achievement in the face of impossible
obstacles held a powerful fascination for him.

Devine was not exactly British Council material. He went to
Brazil to teach and to learn, not to perform the cultural genu-
flexions of the official visitor. Unavoidably, he had to spend
much of his time with the well-to-do dilettante society he most
despised; particularly the expatriate British community who
aroused his withering contempt. At the Cultura Inglesa in Rio,
he addresses an audience of 'middle-aged ladies and sad self-
important gentlemen. Not a student in sight. Awful. Dreadful.
Nearly all the women's breath smells.' Cocktail party at the
same address: 'Over 200 invited – NOT one professional theatre
person!'

Meanwhile he was casting the same cold eye over the official
Brazilian theatre, finding a repertory of feeble national plays
and imposed Western classics; a series of 'appalling' drama
schools; and a popular theatre of 'petit bourgeois' bum and tit
shows. Reading Devine in this mood, you feel quite glad not to
have crossed his path. But, as always, he reserved his intolerance
for the dead weight of respectable mediocrity. It vanishes

instantly in the presence of individual talent and of the young. When he appeared before them as a V.I.P. lecturer, he built his arguments around one morale-boosting message: 'You are not alone.'

Outside the official programme he had a number of fruitful encounters with the young artists and experimental groups who were at the centre of the indigenous theatre movement. Based mainly at São Paulo, this took the form of a 'black theatre' celebrating modern guerillas under the historical mask of Spartacus-like slave uprisings; and direct Marxist treatments of the peasant *flagelados* in the north-eastern famine areas. This movement came to an abrupt end in 1964 with the military coup against the socially reformist régime of President João Goulart. But in Devine's time it was still in full swing, and it was here that he had most to teach and to learn. His first contact was with the Teatro Officina group and their twenty-year-old director, Ronaldo Daniel, who had built their own open stage in São Paulo, and whose American repertory had led them into trouble with both Left and Right. Other contacts followed with young choreographers, directors and playwrights, and the notes begin to take on a sadly experienced tone: 'Sat up talking till 1 a.m.: the usual desire for panaceas.' 'The problem of political corruption seems to stop them at every turn.' To begin with he was unimpressed by the new political theatre. He then encountered the Teatro Arena of São Paulo – a sophisticated Marxist repertory company recently set up by the writer Gianfrancesco Guarnieri and the director Augusto Boal: a Brechtian partnership which specialized in discovering historical parallels for immediate political realities, and presenting them through their own form of folk-theatre montage, known as the *ferias de opinião*. Devine saw the Arena troupe in an extract from Machiavelli's *Mandragola* and commented: 'Really *political* theatre, with a four-year plan, going towards non-subjective production. Makes me feel out of date for the first time.'

His closest personal friendship was with João Bethencourt, a young playwright-director who arrived in London the following year to work as Devine's assistant on the production of Ionesco's *Exit the King*. At their first meeting, Bethencourt was complaining about the difficulty of getting any help from those in power. To which, he says, Devine replied: 'What do you think it cost me to build up the Court company? How many times did I have to eat shit to get what I wanted?'

The interesting thing about the Brazilian experience is that it highlights two sides of Devine's temperament. As a visiting theatrical pundit, he was talking the kind of language he had used in New York. 'If, as a nation, you feel that you need a theatre that should be more than a distraction, you will have it and it will be Brazilian.' It is the message of a man who sees achievement as the reward for will-power. On the other hand, his notes are interspersed with quiescent proverbs like 'While Brazilians sleep, Brazil moves on', which clearly appealed to that side of Devine which had lately awakened to Zen Buddhism and enabled him to relax and discover his centre as an actor. It seems that the fascination of Brazil was that it mirrored his own temperamental polarities on an unimaginably vast scale.

During his month's absence, Richardson had been running the Court as he had done over the period of Devine's nervous breakdown. This produced quite an administrative jolt. 'My natural rhythm', says Richardson, 'was quick; and his natural rhythm was measured.' Which meant that whereas Devine came in most days and worked long office hours, ploughing through correspondence and the appalling stack of scripts and readers' reports, Richardson would turn up in plimsolls on a Saturday morning and depart after an hour's strenuous decision-making. Among his decisions this time were the choice of an Israeli mime, Samy Molcho, and a double bill by Keith Waterhouse and Willis Hall to follow the production of *Happy Days*. This programme was under way when Devine returned early in December, and it gave him a gloomy homecoming. Fog kept the pantomime audience away and the takings for the Waterhouse-Hall plays (*Squat Betty* and *The Sponge Room*) were so poor that they were withdrawn three weeks before the scheduled end of the run.

In spite of larger Arts Council grants, costs were rising so steeply that the hazard of mounting untried work was greater than it had been in the 1950s. Back in May 1962, Devine had decided that the best way of subsidizing the repertory was, wherever possible, to go into production on a sharing basis with another management. The highly profitable co-production of *Chips with Everything*, in alliance with Bob Swash, was one instance of this policy. But there was no sequel to match that success and the policy's main effect was to raise star casting to a first priority.

In terms of new plays, 1962 was a depressing year for the Court. Elsewhere new writers like David Rudkin, Giles Cooper, Fred Watson and David Turner were arriving on the London stage. Devine's hope of introducing the new American satirists to Britain had been thwarted by the founding of the Establishment Club and the Chicago Premise group's début at the Comedy Theatre: and in spite of his early support for the unknown Edward Albee, Albee's representatives now dropped the Court and gave *Who's Afraid of Virginia Woolf?* to a West End management. The E.S.C.'s initial attempt to bring novelists into the theatre was yielding plays from writers like Muriel Spark and Edna O'Brien – but, again, on other stages. Sunday nights apart, the company launched no new writer during 1962. Devine also had doubts about one real winner from his regular stable – Ann Jellicoe's *The Knack* – with the result that its star, Rita Tushingham, accepted a film contract which prevented the show from transferring.

Finally, 1962 was the first year in which the Court lost money on John Osborne. Even that magnetic name failed to overcome the English playgoer's resistance to double bills. Devine's contribution to the two *Plays for England* was to negotiate a budget increase of £500 to film the wedding scene in *The Blood of the Bambergs* (much the weaker of the pair); and to find a brand new director for its brilliant sequel, *Under Plain Cover*. True to its title, the script arrived unannounced through Jonathan Miller's letter-box with an invitation from Devine, who then went through the rehearsals with Miller, knowing that he had never directed professionally before. 'George confined himself entirely to giving technical help: he never said anything to affect interpretation. You weren't anxious when he came in. There wasn't that terrible feeling that you were going to be questioned or hauled over the coals. It was life-enhancing support.' Devine thus released one of the most original directorial talents to have appeared since the war, but it was a gift to the theatre at large, as Miller never worked at the Court again.

At the turn of 1962–3, Devine was much depressed by the quality of the work that was coming in. Another source of despondency was the loss of the World's End workshops which, after a lengthy search for new premises, had moved to an address in Blackfriars on the other side of London, thus severing a vital link between the technical and artistic staff.

There remained one plan on which Devine was grounding his hopes of renewal. In November, he was telling Brazilian friends that the Court had won its first round and that it was now necessary to begin again. In Sloane Square, this intention took the shape of a first meeting with the architect Elidir Davies to discuss the reconstruction of the theatre. This was not simply a question of coming to grips at last with the recalcitrant drains and the coffin-like gents' lavatory: it was a grand-scale attempt to solve the problem of both plays and audiences through architectural means. The 1960s were the great years for British theatre building, when not only the Arts Council but hitherto philistine municipal authorities began investing in housing the arts. The novel idea that theatres had something of value to contribute to the community was, in turn, another bequest of the Court's pioneer work of the 1950s; and by the time city councils came to embrace it, the dramatic movement that had generated the idea was already in decline. Devine must have known this; but he also saw it as a means of turning the 'Edifice Complex' to his own theatre's advantage. His attempt to diversify the Court's activities along French decentralist lines had foundered with the Cambridge venture. He now proposed to extend the company's work through a transformation of their metropolitan base. This plan had nothing in common with Arnold Wesker's parallel campaign to involve the trades unions in the Centre 42 arts centre – a scheme which Devine privately dismissed as 'batty'. Rather, the new Royal Court would have effected a marriage between the aesthetics of Saint-Denis and Devine's own brand of Socialism: a fusion of his theatrical past and present. Outlining his ideas to the Management Committee, he said he wished the scheme 'to be considered in conjunction with an entirely new image for the theatre aesthetically, whereby he hoped to present plays in a style which would attract new writing'. It was in just such terms, fifteen years before, that he had tried to interest the Vic Governors in the EXP project.

Side by side with this he wanted to strengthen the Court's civic identity by opening it up for daytime and early evening exhibitions, films and discussions. This would have involved constructing a studio on the site of the old cottages and gutting the interior of the Court so as to expand its auditorium and create a single sweep of seats which would be entered at street level through an enlarged foyer. This plan was linked with the idea of acquiring a permanent second house which would enable the E.S.C. to operate its own ladder on which artists could ascend from the Sloane Square nursery into commercial success without breaking their ties with the parent company. Training and educational work was also to be developed with courses for actors, directors (under Devine) and designers. As for repertory, he wanted to discard 'piecemeal' productions in favour of coherent four-month seasons built around a single author, period or style.

I have tried, so far, to dwell only on the plans that came off and skate over the innumerable unrealized dreams. But the reconstruction was Devine's last big dream for the Court, and he had achieved so much there that one must speculate on what the undefined 'new image' might have been if it had materialized.

It clearly had a lot to do with his developing belief in the theatre as a force in society. The problem is that where the aesthetic principles he shared with Saint-Denis are clearly inscribed in theatre history, his subsequent theatrical Socialism is a nebulous and undocumented area. Aside from the facts that he declared himself a Labour voter and a professional dissenter, and said he was more interested in content than in form, the public evidence is pretty sparse. Hard-line political acquaintances, as we have seen, sometimes became impatient with his technique of survival through compromise. Others, measuring his work by results, found him 'profoundly Socialist' and 'purer than those bitten with the purity bug'. What makes him especially hard to grasp is that he was an idealist with his eyes set on distant goals, and also a man with no intellectual pride. That combination makes him unique among major theatre reformers, and leads to a series of lesser paradoxes: the democratic father figure, the non-pedagogic teacher, the non-competitive artist who regarded ravenous egoism as a mark of artistic health.

One explanation of his particular gift was that it underlay conscious thought and operated as innately as vegetable tropism: making him incline towards talent and ideas like a plant towards the sun. It was observed that where other directors of his generation would instictively shy away from work with radical implications, Devine would shy towards it. As many people noticed, he retained the intellectual openness of a man half his age: and it was this same undefensive quality which left him vulnerable to personal attack.

These observations make sense in relation to Devine's daily life in the theatre, and to his work as a catalytic agent among his artistic juniors. To some people, he did rank strictly as a catalyst, possessing nothing original to compare with his powers of releasing the buried talents and co-operative potential of others. This view ignores the idealistic factor; and I would dispute it on the simple grounds that it is contradicted by the tenacious coherence of his whole career. That pattern was not created by someone swayed exclusively by day-to-day impulses.

In the absence of manifestoes, one has to fall back on secondary evidence to approach the question of what political theatre meant to Devine, and why he gave himself over as an organism to be devoured by the Royal Court. These were not matters for daily discussion with his colleagues in the theatre, but he had at least one friend with whom he was ready to drop his intellectual guard. This was George Goetschius, an American sociologist who shared a flat with Richardson in Lower Mall from the mid-1950s and stayed on there when Devine left the house. He was privy to the Court's inner councils and to the marital crack-up without being personally involved; and was thus a person in whom Devine could confide.

According to Goetschius, Devine underwent a change from gentlemanly liberal into Labour activist, but he still saw the theatre as his exclusive field of action. Also, 'his Socialism was more interested in the release of individual human capabilities than in abstractions about redistribution of income. So he leapt past the whole dirty work of creating a new society to methods of enriching the personality once we had it.' His main preoccupation was not with the structure of a non-competitive society, but with the accompanying change in human personality. 'The question that was always murky', says Goetschius, 'was "Change in what direction?" And here he hung on to two myths. One, that universal education would produce geniuses from the lower classes who had been silent under the former system (which was a myth to which his own organization had given some credit). And two, that any cultural regeneration would come about largely through the theatre. He cared about the theatre being a central profession, because he really believed that it had an effect on the personality.' This was not simply the effect of dramatizing ideas. It was a question of using texture, sound, colour and other theatrical elements as a means of 'orchestrating the senses' and thus influencing human relationships.

It is quite clear that no amount of theatre-going will have any such influence on the hardened middle-aged minority who make up the regular audience; so anyone who believes in the theatre's life-changing properties must equally embrace the cult of youth. Not that Devine needed any pushing in that direction. Goetschius's testimony rings true because it offers such a natural link between Devine's artistic and social attitudes. It takes account of the sensory education he owed to the Motleys. It picks up the thread from Lex's schools for social rejects to Devine's theatre for rejected playwrights. It explains how he converted a mystical French tradition into a pragmatic British policy. The educationally reformist element runs straight through from Clayesmore and Saint-Denis's schools to the unique operation of the Court where productions thrived on the reciprocal exchange of new vision and old professional skills. Finally, it accounts for the fact that although Devine was attracted by cultures, like those of Germany and Brazil, that threw up genuine political theatres, he made no attempt to transform the Royal Court into a Socialist platform. His politics were implicit in the way he ran the company. Beyond that, it was up to the playwrights to lead the way. He cared about what ideas they expressed: passionately in the case of Osborne and Nigel Dennis. Dennis's onslaught on organized religion in *The Making of Moo* was, he said, 'exactly what I want to have said in my theatre.' But his own political action lay in rescuing them from silence and putting them in a place where their voices could be heard; not in confining them within ideological guidelines. He would have regarded this an unnecessary as well as impertinent. So much of the programme came true: the playwright did lead, his voice did have immense carrying power, and – for Devine – he was saying the right thing without any need of guidance. All of which, in good times and bad, confirmed his faith in the writers' theatre. 'This place', he told me in 1963, 'must stand or fall by its plays, because that is the only real *raison d'être* that we have.'

So, to Goetschius's two myths I would add a third: namely that Devine was offended by much of what he saw in English society and took it on trust that this offence would be shared by the young artists he rescued from the system and by the public who turned up to applaud their work. He assumed that they still wanted to change the status quo rather than settling for success inside it. 'The one thing I don't think he could grasp', says Goetschius, 'was that society was no longer looking for that change. Until his dying day, he was still looking for young authors to say things the way Osborne had done.'

Returning, therefore, to his dream of the reconstructed Royal Court, it seems to have had a double objective: to revitalize dramatic writing by cultivating the missing element of a vital audience. 'Piecemeal' productions had hitherto attracted a piecemeal public with no special loyalty to the Court. The same Osborne or Noël Coward public would have turned up at any other London theatre. And whatever the radical content of the piece, they would still be segregated by an architectural form perpetuating nineteenth-century class division. In proposing the Court's 'new image' Devine was aiming to approach the audience on several fronts. The new auditorium, with its single sweep of seats and its stage shorn of the proscenium, would have demolished the hierarchy of stalls and circle. The E.S.C.'s architect, Elidir Davies, had in fact created such an auditorium at the Mermaid in 1958, and Devine was very conscious that whatever the vagaries of the Mermaid programme, the building itself attracted a much larger regular public than the Court's. In 1963, Bernard Miles was claiming regular weekly houses of 1,500: 'if we knock off 500 for fun,' Devine told me, 'I still couldn't say I had a regular 1,000 a week here.'

The plan for thematically organized seasons was another move in the same direction. If audiences could be persuaded to stick with the Court for four months, there was a chance of persuading them to stick for good. Meanwhile, with other activities spreading through the building and filling the new studio and foyer, the net would be cast beyond the normal theatregoing public.

For years artists and technicians had treated the Court as a home where they could drop in to see the work going on and meet friends. What they spent in the pub next door and the adjoining London Transport Canteen must vastly have exceeded the Motleys' tea bill. What Devine wanted now was to make the general public feel at home there as well. The basic purpose of the reconstruction was to create space. In that sense, Devine's

architectural ideal would have been something like the Agora
at Leylistad in Holland: a covered multi-purpose performance
and community centre simulating the open-air conditions of a
Hellenic market-place. Nothing on that scale was ever within his
reach, but with all the means at his disposal he did champion the
idea 'that this place should become what it is: Chelsea's theatre'.

One plan canvassed at this time was that the Court should
lease the Chelsea Palace as its second house; another, supported
by some local councillors, was that Chelsea should start com-
missioning plays. Devine did not imagine that by such methods
he could conjure a new writers' movement out of thin air.
(Even at this exploratory stage, the Chelsea council were already dropping hints about some of the Court's plays not being
very nice for young people.) What he was doing was preparing
the ground. 'Even if the plays aren't there at present', he said,
'they may pop up at any minute. It isn't a thing you can force.'
But the reconstruction plans were there to help it along, and to
assist writers at various stages of development. At Gaskill's
Actors' Studio, Devine wanted to re-activate the pattern of Obey
and the Quinze: 'if we can produce a group of actors with a
certain approach and certain skills, we could then say to writers,
"Well, there's an instrument for you."' The new studio itself
would supply them with a more attractive platform than isolated
Sunday night performances. And for main bill playwrights,
experimentalists and novices alike, it would be a huge advantage
if the Chelsea marriage came off, and they found themselves
addressing a familiar community rather than an audience of
fly-by-night strangers. Finally, to solve the snag of personal
ambition on which theatrical ideals so often come to grief,
Devine proposed the formation of a larger second company permanently installed in the West End, and presenting Court
plays in straight commercial terms. 'The idea of the West End
is still attractive to people,' he said. 'You and I may know what
success means there: but if you've never had it, it's very difficult to say, "I don't like the bourgeois audience and all that stuff;
I won't have my plays done there." Find me the people who'd
say that!'

Before recording what became of the dream in Devine's lifetime, it is worth noting that some of it came true after his death.
Under Gaskill, the Court acquired its own studio, and for six
years the Theatre Upstairs flourished as the most productive

experimental centre in London. The attachment of writers to acting groups became a common feature in the fringe movement of the 1970s, achieving some of its finest results in Gaskill's collaborations with Heathcote Williams and David Hare. Again under Gaskill, the Court auditorium was gutted for the 1971 *Come Together* season which brought in a lot of people one has not seen in the theatre before or since to sample a variety of fringe treats and demolish the exhibition of coloured food.

If the plan had materialized it would have been Neville Blond's supreme gift to the Royal Court, financed through his family business connections. But Blond, even in his role as the good fairy, always left his colleagues with plenty to do. And besides the captial he proposed to inject, it was still necessary to raise money from other sources, not to mention negotiating for a longer lease, keeping the architect to his brief, and maintaining the flow of E.S.C. product while the building was dark. The task of juggling with these equal priorities fell principally on Devine who, since Gaskill and Dexter's departure to the National Theatre, was running the company single-handed.

A general sigh of relief greeted 1963 as Clement Freud at last surrendered the upstairs club on the expiry of his lease. From its leaking roof to its overflowing drains, the Court was now the exclusive territory of the E.S.C.; and the club was instantly taken over as a rehearsal room. The lease on the theatre itself was due to run out in 1991, and the company's next move was to seek some assurance that their investment would not simply vanish after twenty-eight years.

The theatre belonged to the Cadogan Estate. And in February a deputation put the company's case to Lord Cadogan who informed them that 'he did not see his way that afternoon to agreeing to the extension of the lease.' However, he was conscious of the company's importance 'as a potential branch of the National Theatre', and for that reason he was prepared to help.

Evidently what weighed with Lord Cadogan was not the company's own artistic record but its embryonic attachment to an official institution which, as yet, had produced nothing. For the E.S.C. it was a question of achieving what they wanted by presenting it as something the establishment could approve. None of which would have come as news to Devine. It was a fact of British life that art suddenly becomes visible to the ruling class once it is housed in the National Gallery or the Royal

Opera House. So, when the National Theatre in 1963 began making overtures to Sloane Square, Devine did not discourage them. He set up the Actors' Studio as a joint venture with the National, and agreed to a reciprocal exchange of new plays. He attended a series of lunches to discuss the idea of an amalgamation (ominous word) which would have turned the Court into the National's experimental annexe. He also told Kenneth Tynan that he had more than once privately contemplated a liaison with the National Theatre, but the only tangible result of the 1963 courtship was the appearance of one or two Court texts (like Arden's *The Workhouse Donkey*) under Olivier's management, and Devine's 1964 production of Beckett's *Play* in Waterloo Road. There was no question of his surrendering his autonomy: and whatever the attractions of the National, the immediate advantage of the association was that it strengthened the Court's independent bargaining power. Hence the white marriage that took place in July 1963 with the public announcement of a federal agreement between the two theatres and the setting up of a joint committee to work out details of co-operation. Having voiced this resounding declaration, the committee never met again; but thereafter, whenever advantageous, the Court was able to flash the credentials of a major State institution.

The association was obviously useful when it came to fundraising. As a figurehead to impress a finance committee, Olivier was an ally above suspicion, whereas anyone who knew anything of the Royal Court must have suspected that beneath Devine's good grey exterior there beat the heart of a radical. Thus, well before the Cadogan Estate had announced the result of their deliberations, the Arts Council had chipped in with a capital grant of £5,000 towards the rebuilding, followed by an offer from the London County Council of between £5,000 and £10,000 provided the balance could be met from other sources. An offer of £7,500 over three years also came from the Gulbenkian Foundation for the Artists' Training Scheme. In the hope of persuading neighbouring councils to follow the lead of the L.C.C., Devine then instituted an approach to Kensington, Westminster and – ever optimistic – to Chelsea, which in the past had supported the Court to the tune of around £150 a year.

In April, the grand scheme suffered its first setback. Devine discovered that the Grosvenor Estate and London Transport were planning a development of the island site behind the theatre where he had hoped to erect the experimental studio. It was therefore necessary to abandon any idea of extending the premises and confine the work to the existing building.

Together with this, the company scrapped the idea of widening the auditorium and settled for a more modest plan providing an enlarged foyer and extra bars within the theatre's given shape. The cost of this, plus various technical improvements and the installation of an adjustable forestage and a new stalls floor, was estimated at £80,000. These plans were then transmitted to the Cadogan Estate, and it was agreed to close down the Court on November 1 and operate from the West End during the eight months of rebuilding. That was how the scheme stood in mid-April: somewhat battered, but more or less intact.

The Court resumed its planned repertory with Gwyn Thomas's *Jackie the Jumper*, a piece written with the encouragement of Devine who had hoped to lead the errant author of *The Keep* into paths closer to normal Sloane Square policy. Thomas, however, was not attracted by themes of contemporary social protest: 'the people for whom I wished to speak had long since shut up.' So he compromised with a ballad drama on the Merthyr Riots of 1831 in which he adopted an Ardenesque stance while firmly confining his attention to the past. Thomas was not the man to impress the dignity of this local tragedy upon the metropolitan public. He was an incorrigibly cheerful writer, and every move to elevate his outlaw protagonist into a folk hero or justify the rioters' cause was apt to be doused in cascades of comic rhetoric. Besides which, Thomas once again fell victim to the London climate. The play opened on February 1: and 'on the second day of the run there began a series of blizzards unique in the history of foul weather. Plays died like flies and mine got to the bone-yard first.'

Other new plays were Frank Hilton's *Day of the Prince*, a domestic political prank rashly promoted from a Sunday-night showing, and Henry Living's *Kelly's Eye* which gave Nicol Williamson his first lead on the Court stage but disconcerted Living's admirers by exchanging highly individual farce for carelessly plotted melodrama. The only new piece that outlived the season was Barry Reckord's *Skyvers*. This study of a comprehensive school malcontent was one of the closest exercises in British social analysis ever to appear at the Court, and it is ironic that such a work should have come from the author of *Flesh into*

Tiger, originally recruited to impart an exotic flavour to the repertory during the 1950s boom in West Indian writing. The subject of *Skyvers* was one after Devine's heart, and he considered Reckord's play as by far his best; although at the time, in spite of a meteoric début by David Hemmings (who instantly vanished into films), the production fared little better at the box office than the other new shows.

In Management Committee post-mortems Devine classified the company's achievements in three grades. There was 'Success', which meant something in the Osborne class which could be exploited in other markets. There was the 'Royal Court Success', which meant a production that had run satisfactorily in Sloane Square but did not warrant a transfer. And there was the 'Artistic Success', which meant that certain expressive intentions had been fulfilled no matter how empty the house. Of the new British plays of 1963, only *Skyvers*, a clear artistic success, qualified for any of these categories. The other material was far from worthless. But what became increasingly apparent over the year was that the slogan 'the writer leads' only made sense when there were writers capable of leading. There was a place, perhaps, for minor novelists. But there was no place for the competent minor playwright.

Official policy was shortly to be revised along these lines. In the meanwhile, the new order was reflected in the increasing proportion of foreign classics. These had no inbuilt popular appeal, but two of them came with star names attached. The adaptation of Gogol's *Diary of a Madman* was the product of an alliance between Lindsay Anderson and Richard Harris. Pirandello's *Naked* was a package deal offered to the Court by Diane Cilento, featuring herself as translator and as the servant girl heroine. Both were interesting projects, but both seemed addressed more to collectors than to the general public who confirmed this impression by staying away. The one foreign play that captured public imagination was Wedekind's *Spring Awakening*. This was the case of a European masterpiece that had been withheld from the British stage by half a century of censorship and its importance was at once recognized even in Desmond O'Donovan's starless Sunday-night production. From Devine's point of view, it also formed a monumental German counterpart to *Skyvers* as another study of the mistreatment of the young.

Among the year's Sunday-night shows, the educational motif

cropped up again in an April programme, *First Results*, demonstrating the work of Gaskill's recently formed Actors' Studio. This opened with some elegantly formal pantomime, but its main fascination lay in a series of half-mask improvisations as alarming as they were funny. Half-masks promote regression into an unformed creature that has to learn like a baby. And the point about the *First Results* group was that they had reached the half-way stage: the masks had discovered who they were and how to express themselves in movement, but they were still in the process of learning speech.

They had names: Henrietta Hedgehog, a wrathful dervish called Splodge, and Daisy Bum, a waddling outsider with a love of 'oo' sounds terminated with a pert pelvic flick. The exercises consisted of switching the masks on to a given situation, and switching them off at the moment when conscious invention started replacing imagination. And in comparison with the Method class improvisations (then fashionable in London) the speed with which the masks launched themselves into unprepared situations was uncanny.

This was the only occasion during the Court years when Devine came before the public as a teacher, and he used it as a pretext for dry self-mockery; supplying basic information and introducing comic tricks in a straight-faced classroom manner, and then coming a cropper over invisible banana skins. Like his Brecht, it was an authoritarian performance turned inside out.

However good for artistic morale, this was of no help at the box office and Devine set out to stop the rot by returning to two authors with whom he had scored in the past: Ionesco and Tennessee Williams. The bet was hedged with stars. Alec Guinness was available for *Exit the King*, and Ruth Gordon for *The Milk Train doesn't stop here anymore*, added to which its American producer, David Merrick, offered to put up 50 per cent of the capitalization. Neither project was financially ideal, as Guinness had only two months to spare for the Ionesco, and the film rights of the Williams were already tied up. However, here was a chance for the theatre to make a fighting recovery before reaching its close-down date, which the architects had now pushed forward to the end of November.

Following the trail he had pursued in misery with *August for the People*, Devine took the Ionesco company up to Newcastle and the Edinburgh Festival before installing the production at the

Court on September 12. Guinness found him still smarting from the Rex Harrison experience and decidedly on his guard against star visitors. 'He was expecting the same trouble he'd had before. I made no trouble, but I got no thanks for it. He never gave me a word of encouragement.' In general, Guinness thought Devine's direction 'meticulous, schoolmasterly, and a bit dispiriting'. In Edinburgh, where I saw the production, it did seem that Ionesco had fallen into the hands of a Beckett specialist.

Admittedly, the play contributed to this impression. A ninety-minute march to the coffin, it elevates Ionesco's old friend Berenger (the bourgeois individualist hero of *Rhinoceros*) to the throne of a derelict kingdom and shows him coming to terms with death in a desolate palace with cracks advancing across the walls. Having wound up this fine bit of comic mechanism, Ionesco simply allows it to run down, with comedy surrendering to fear and desolation as it ticks on towards the moment of extinction. No doubt another production might have given the play more of a lift. But Devine's version did contain some brilliant tangential comedy from Graham Crowden's wizard-like Doctor, and Eileen Atkins as the mutinous palace drudge; and Jocelyn Herbert's throne-room, a mud-daubed chamber with self-sealing doors, beautifully intensified the metaphor of the stage as a body in decay. As for central casting, Guinness was partnered by Googie Withers, returning to the British stage after a prolonged absence. Star casting turned the balance, whatever Devine's suspicion of stars. 'With the notices that play got,' he told me, 'I think I would have played to about 700 a week. With Guinness in it, I played to absolute capacity for seven and a half weeks and made money.'

The first half of the programme had worked out perfectly; and with solvency restored by full houses and a £10,000 Arts Council guarantee against loss, Devine again turned his attention to the future. The rebuilding plan had run into two more snags. The appeal for funds had drawn a blank with the Kensington and Westminster councils, and Chelsea had not even replied: and this, in turn, cast doubt on the L.C.C.'s conditional offer of help. Also the West End season was being delayed by casting problems and there was likely to be a two-month gap between the closedown date and the beginning of rehearsals: meeting the extra expenses of the delay meant imposing redundancies including most of the workshop staff.

Partly to offset this sacrifice, Devine proposed a series of interim projects to keep the company's name alive during the closure period, including a universities' tour with two productions and lecture-demonstrations. With those plans laid, he accepted an invitation from the International Theatre Institute to visit Tokyo in November, and disappeared into the *Milk Train* rehearsals.

These began in the first week of October. On October 8 he went home complaining of a headache and pain in the elbows and wrists. It was the first warning of a heart attack, and he was moved that night to the Middlesex Hospital where the cardiac spasms continued over the next two days. On his discharge, he retired to the farm for a three-month rest. He was not an invalid. He could get up and 'indulge in light activity'. But he could no longer describe himself as sound as a bell.

He cancelled the Tokyo trip and withdrew from the play; and as Ruth Gordon refused to accept any alternative director, the production was abandoned. Added to which the rebuilding date had moved on again, and it was now necessary to keep the theatre running until January.

With their programme in ruins, the company learned that the Cadogan Estate had entirely approved the architectural plans and agreed to extend the lease. But by the time Devine returned to work in November, the bottom had dropped out of the scheme. The money which Blond was to have raised for it now proved to be unobtainable. Also, as Devine told the Management Committee, it seemed that the final cost was likely to be twice that of the original estimate; nor would the builders be able to complete the job within the agreed eight-month period to which the West End season had been geared.

As a drastic remedy, Devine offered a new scheme of his own under which the essential work could be carried out for a fixed cost and within a fixed length of time. There was no question under 'Scheme B' of any architectural transformation. No shred remained of the original dream. There would be virtually no change to the existing building; but it would be in less danger of falling down, and the price could be met without any windfall of fairy gold. In December, the company accepted the inevitable and communicated their changed plans to the Cadogan Estate who promptly withdrew their offer to extend the lease.

'Scheme B' went into operation with the grim resolve that

this time there must be no mistake. Devine drew up a list of essential improvements and instructed the architect to proceed on a cost-plus basis of £20,000. As for timing, a new closure date was set ahead in March, allowing the builders six months to complete before the company's return from the West End in September. Devine's schedule of improvements included some basic structural changes, such as the installation of a bar at the back of the stalls and a properly equipped lighting box in place of the old makeshift arrangement of lighting from the corner of the Upper Circle. A new stage floor was also laid, and counterweights were brought in to replace the hemp flying ropes. None of which really touched the main problem of the theatre's lack of space: its cramped dressing rooms and offices, its lack of a Green Room, its shallow wings and defective sight-lines. The original plan was based on the idea of extending the building on two sides and transforming the stage and auditorium into a single room; and that alone would have meant rebuilding the theatre, as it involved the removal of the proscenium arch which carries the weight of the dome and fly-tower. When structural changes had to be abandoned, Devine decided to try and make a virtue of the theatre as it stood by painting it; and as in the days before the first season, the company were up on ladders with brushes doing the job themselves.

17

THE LONG EXIT

IT is not possible exactly to pin-point the moment at which Devine began withdrawing from the Royal Court, but it was the simultaneous collapse of his health and his architectural dream in the winter of 1963–4 that finally changed the Court from a great adventure to a dead weight round his neck. 'If anybody mentions $2\frac{1}{4}$ per cent of the gross to me again' he said to Byam Shaw, 'I shall go fucking raving mad.' So far, this has been the story of his total commitment to the theatre: the remainder is the story of his attempts to escape from it.

On returning to Sloane Square after convalescence Devine told the Management Committee that the strain of running the organization single-handed had led to his illness; and he now needed an assistant who could take over full responsibility and free him from the day-to-day burden. The committee (with reservations from Duncan) agreed that it was an impossible task for one man, and set about appointing a Co-Director to take over from January 1965. It was easier said than done. Of the people with the required artistic and administrative skills, not many would be attracted by a subordinate position. And the Court's own A.A.D.s, poised for flight into glamorous jobs elsewhere, were all too well acquainted with the back-breaking labour of running the writers' theatre. Devine had omitted to equip the organization with a Crown Prince. Richardson, the most obvious candidate, was no office-worker and felt he had outgrown the Court which he regarded as a 'totem theatre'. Gaskill, having reluctantly left the Court to join the National Theatre, now refused the invitation to return. Michael Elliott likewise turned the job down: 'the E.S.C. had built its character on new plays, and I didn't see the new plays around to carry on with.' Devine, he says, appeared deeply depressed when they met: 'He had aimed at a kind of reform that would extend into the West End, but things in the theatre at large were much the same as ever; he felt he hadn't achieved what he wanted.' Finally the committee arrived at the stop-gap solution of appointing Lindsay Anderson and Anthony Page as joint directors of the post-West End season.

In the West End, too, Devine planned to take a back seat. The programme was to open with *The Seagull*, followed by Brecht's *St Joan of the Stockyards* and Michael Hastings's *The World's Baby*: all three starring Vanessa Redgrave under Richardson's direction. Devine, playing small parts, would be free to superintend the rebuilding and keep the interim administration ticking over. Almost at once there was a change of plan when Hastings's script was found unsatisfactory and shelved in favour of *The Way of the World*. It was a sign of the times that when the English Stage Company moved into the West End, it was without a single new English play.

The opening of *The Seagull* at the Queen's Theatre on March 12 was nevertheless a triumph which shone in bright contrast to the Moscow Art Theatre's subdued *Cherry Orchard* at the Aldwych, and raised the immediate prospect of a Broadway transfer. It was a personal triumph for Redgrave, who decisively implanted the figure of Nina as the play's emotional centre: and it was no less a triumph for the company, including Ashcroft, Paul Rogers, and Mark Dignam. Devine appeared as Dorn, which for many people was the finest performance of his career. Gielgud, with his long memory of the spotty boy who played Mercutio for the OUDS, pronounced it, 'amazing. He looked more handsome than I'd ever seen him in my life. Divinely sexy and attractive.' Strolling on in his panama hat, and observing the passionate follies of his companions with the detachment of one whose own appetites have been satisfied, he was indeed the image of a successful lady-killer in retirement. But the performance was also free from the usual accompanying cynicism. He played Dorn as a man who knows all about human egoism, and tries to do what little good he can in a generally hopeless situation: accepting Nina's gift of flowers with sincere chivalry, and submitting without protest when the jealous Polina snatches them away. 'How hysterical they are! ... And what a lot of love ... But what can I do, my child? What?' As Devine played that line, Dorn really wanted to know.

To his Royal Court colleagues, the performance was also an uncanny piece of self-portraiture. Take the speech in the first Act after Konstantin's play:

> I don't know, perhaps I know nothing about it, or have gone off my head, but I liked the play. There's something in it. When that girl talked about loneliness and afterwards when the devil's eyes appeared, I was so excited that my hands trembled. It is fresh, naive ... Here he comes ... I want to say all the nice things I can to him ...

'It was weird', Gaskill says, 'to hear him do that speech because he actually did say things like that. "It has *something*!" he would say, and his eyes would sparkle.'

Work on the Royal Court duly began in March, driving Devine from his tiny office in the Circle bar into temporary occupation of the No. 1 dressing room. A month later, he reported that Plan 'B' was going well, which may have brought some consolation to the Management Committee who were facing a £10,000 bill from the architect for services in connection with the abortive Plan 'A'. The new repertory policy, implicit in the 1963 programme, also took shape over the first months of 1964. Anderson and Page jointly declared that new plays should be presented 'only if they are deemed to be suitable for production and not solely because they happen to be new'; which, in practical terms, meant a steep increase in revivals. Whatever Devine thought of this safety-first approach, he sprang to its defence when it was queried by the committee's Devon contingent. If no new plays of merit were available, there was no alternative to reviving old ones. The losses on new plays had averaged £5,000 a production, and by no amount of planning could plays now be presented as economically as in the past. Up to mid-1964, the company had presented 150 new works, but there was no chance of maintaining such an output without additional revenue. He then prepared an estimate for the Arts Council, 'on the assumption that it was desired to keep the company on an established basis as England's only real experimental theatre, whose work would subsequently fertilize the theatre at large.' The estimate, embodying a suggested 5 per cent annual increase over the next five years, represented an attempt to escape the bugbear of one-year grants which inhibits subsidized companies from planning ahead. The Arts Council did not let that one through the net, but their grant to the E.S.C. did go up from £20,000 to £32,500 in 1965. 'The shoe-string we started with', Devine told the press, 'has turned into a boot-lace. With Wilson's assistance, may it blossom into a small rope.'

Returning to mid-1964, before such aid was in sight, it appeared that all the forces were conspiring to rob the Court of its independent role. In the West End, allied with Tennents, the company were doing well with a classic; in Sloane Square, they foresaw a future heavily dependent on revivals. As for internal organization, they had lost most of the original workshop staff when the builders moved in. As usual, the company were in the red.

In this situation, Richardson began rehearsing *St Joan of the Stockyards* with Redgrave in the title part mountainously partnered by Lionel Stander as Pierpoint Mauler. Richardson, with his rooted antipathy towards anything that smelt of Copeau, had decided that whatever form the production took, it would not be played in masks. However, when it became clear that the group scenes were not working, he did a quick *volte-face* and put the (verse-speaking) bosses into masks of blood-red grease-paint and the (prose-speaking) chorus of packers and wholesalers into half-masks, thus enlarging the gulf between them and the unmasked Black Straw Hats. In conjunction with Jocelyn Herbert's set, a stockyard backdrop surmounted by two gaunt revolving towers, the stage picture came over as an exemplary piece of Brechtian design.

St Joan of the Stockyards was an exciting spectacle; but what did not emerge from it was a coherent line of thought. Unassisted, Richardson might have arrived at a clear reading of the play; but he threw that chance away by calling in Page, Anderson and Devine to help him direct it. The cast were shuttled between the four directors who, Page says, had 'never sat down to discuss what the play was about. We didn't really have anything in common. Things got changed and actors got muddled, and there were terrible scenes in the stalls after some run-throughs. George came in, I think, because he was worried that it was going to be a disaster.'

Half way through rehearsals, Redgrave collapsed. As with Plowright in *Happy Days*, it was another case of the pregnant star; but more serious this time as the financial stakes were higher and the whole season had been built around the artist who had dropped out. As the whole machinery of West End bookings and advertising was under way there could be no question of cancellation. So, at short notice, Siobhan McKenna joined the production and gave it the *coup de grâce* with a ringing emotional performance in the style of Shaw's St Joan.

The show opened on June 11 to notices (mine included) which unfairly blamed the play more than the production: and houses were so poor that it was withdrawn after three weeks at a loss of around £15,000. That was the end of the Queens season, as Redgrave was unable to return for the third play.

Meanwhile, a split had developed between the Royal Court's two incoming directors. Like the rest of the A.A.D.s, they had been able to operate productively while Devine was there as a father figure; but once left to themselves, their temperamental differences came to the surface and Anderson resigned, leaving Page to run the season alone. One difference between them, ominous from Devine's viewpoint, was that Anderson's temperament was that of a group autocrat and Page's strictly that of a director of plays. The chance of Devine's taking a back seat diminished perceptibly with Anderson's departure.

So far, in spite of his flagging energy, it had been as busy a year as any other. Besides riding the company's upheavals in Sloane Square and Shaftesbury Avenue, he had directed *Play*, his most successful Beckett production, for the National Theatre during the run of *The Seagull*. His attachment to the National also involved membership of the Building Committee where he was instrumental in the switch in architects leading to the appointment of Denys Lasdun. He was one of the few members of the committee to strike up a personal friendship with Lasdun who initially felt at sea in the theatre, especially when this meant translating abstract directives into architectural terms. Because Devine was a craftsman and a builder, Lasdun says that he acted as a necessary bridge between the two sides. Like others before him, Lasdun found that while Devine had visions of his own, he was always looking for ways of getting things done in a manner that incorporated the visions and competing opinions of other people. 'Time and time again, he would put them in terms that I could understand.'

After the collapse of the Queens season, there was a two-month lull before the return to Sloane Square. Devine used some of this time to escape to Andrews Farm, where he got down to building a gazebo. But there was no real escape from affairs of the Court, with debts (including Elidir Davies's unpaid bill) overhanging the company's head and the question of the autumn repertory still unsettled. As director of the season, Page had proposed a division of plays into three categories: classics, twentieth-century plays and new plays. But just what they should be was another matter. 'To plan a couple of plays ahead seemed a miracle at that point.' Page had also set himself two irreconcilable objectives: to exploit the successful productions by transfer, and to engage a company to play throughout the season. Although Devine had shown this to be impossible, it is curious that when Page took over, and Gaskill after him, they both repeated the original experiment of trying to run a writers' theatre with a permanent company.

Two things were clear about the autumn season. Having been twice pushed out of the Royal Court nest, Page had had enough of the wilderness. 'I thought I'd bloody well been waiting, and I plunged in and did four productions, which was extremely greedy.' The second factor, was that Osborne had offered two new plays to the company. When the first of these, *Inadmissible Evidence*, arrived in March, that at least settled the question of how to open the season.

As September approached, the two factors converged. Richardson, formerly Osborne's regular director, was not available. Osborne appealed to Devine to direct the piece. Friendship apart, this was a natural choice. In *Inadmissible Evidence* the spokesman of British youth decisively parted company with the younger generation. It is a play of middle age, exploring the guilt and indecisiveness arising from conflicting loyalties, and showing a man inwardly cracking up under a professional façade. Devine knew this psychological territory inside out, and he loved the play. Nevertheless, he turned down the invitation so as to make way for the season's incoming director who had never previously directed an Osborne script or met the author. This turned out to be a shrewd move in more ways than one. Maitland, the disintegrating lawyer who shoulders the whole weight of the play, is physically and emotionally the most taxing of all Osborne's heroes, and the part seemed cut out for a heavyweight middle-aged star. But after prolonged auditions, the choice finally went to Page's candidate, the 26-year-old Nicol Williamson (with whom Page had worked at the R.S.C.). Williamson auditioned for Osborne and Devine, and as soon as he started reading, Page says 'there was just no more doubt.'

Single-minded concentration was the strength and the weakness of Page's régime. It sometimes yielded marvellous results on stage: it also meant that the mess would have to be swept up by somebody else. His phrase, 'It *is* John's play,' became a by-word at the Court, meaning, 'Would you get my laundry?' From Devine's point of view, this meant that although he was not directing the play, his attentions were required at late-night lighting sessions involving new equipment which Page did not understand. 'I don't think I am an administrator for that sort of theatre,' Page acknowledges: 'Devine needed the strain taken off him, and I probably asked him for much too much.'

For the time being, however, he was well rewarded. The renovated Court, with its red African wood stage, its squeak-free auditorium floor and a red plush Dress Circle, was ready for the planned opening; and was duly launched on September 9 with a production that hit the jackpot in all three of Devine's success categories. It was an artistic triumph; it was packing out the Court; and it was bound to transfer. It surprised no one when Williamson collected the *Evening Standard* Award for the Best Actor of the Year. By this time, the rest of the season was also taking shape with plans to follow *Inadmissible Evidence* with a Ben Travers revival and *Julius Caesar* (directed by Anderson) while holding the second Osborne play still in reserve.

Having piloted the company through their months of exodus and led them back to as big a welcome as they had ever received, Devine now informed the Council that he was retiring. His dreams were still unrealized: but at least the company were home and dry, installed in better premises than before and creating as much stir as they had done in the 1950s. He had done all he could to secure the survival of the E.S.C. as it stood. If it were to undergo any radical change this would have to be achieved by someone else.

As he put it in his retirement speech:

When a man begins to feel he is a part of the fixtures and fittings, it is time he left. I am deeply tired. The weight of this edifice has driven me into the ground up to my neck, like poor Winnie in Beckett's *Happy Days*. I should have passed the job on several years ago. I am getting out just in time.

It was three months between his letter of resignation and the public announcement of his retirement. During the interim his decision was kept within the company, some of whom did their best to talk him out of it. His answer to them was that he was worn out and that he wanted to write, but he was also on the track of another job. This was the directorship of the new Arts Centre at Sussex University, a project funded by the Gulbenkian Foundation whose representative, James Thornton, made the first approach to Devine.

The Arts Centre was an experimental venture. It was to be a building situated on the campus but operating outside the faculty system. Its official aim was to encourage the creative arts in the university and the surrounding region. The various arts would be practised side by side under the same roof, and there would be resident studentships for visiting artists to pursue their own work on the campus. The whole thing was based on the idea of a transaction between the professional artist and the intelligent young.

Long before the chance of this job, Devine's mind had been moving in the same direction; and the detached relationship of the Arts Centre to the rest of the university matched his own long-term position as a dedicated teacher who could never have felt at home inside the teaching profession. Also, with the theatrical disappointments of the early 1960s, his educational interests had intensified: and whenever it was objected that not many Court authors had reached the West End, he would point out that uncommercial authors like Arden were being played in universities throughout the land. What Sussex offered him, apart from an escape from the world of $2\frac{1}{4}$ per cent of the gross, was the chance to live and work in the midst of that public instead of waiting for them to come to him.

Devine's response to the project appears from a memorandum which he drafted in November. Taking as its first assumption that 'no more than the surface of this problem has been scratched up to now', this is at once a highly practical and rigorously undogmatic document, leaving everything open to question except the importance of the inquiry itself.

Over the short range, he advised an immediate start by erecting a temporary hangar on the campus and beginning activities there in the following term. There follows a list of first-year plans, aiming to weave a network of contacts with the outside community, and following the guiding principle of a confrontation between 'art' and 'life': for instance, by displaying sculpture in a natural environment and mounting exhibitions of fine art in parallel with industrial design. Alongside this, Devine proposed a list of fourteen artistic categories from which the artists in residence should be drawn: and a general research scheme aiming to examine the relationship between art and eight academic disciplines.

Theatre does not figure prominently anywhere in the memorandum. When the building did go up, as the Gardner Centre, what Sean Kenny designed was primarily a campus playhouse. But all that Devine specified was that 'certain large areas should be flexible in the use of space, so that these are not set spaces for set activities. This not only makes maximum use of the space available, but helps to avoid a sense of sacredness and remoteness.' He had come a long way from the drum-beating days of the Young Vic.

Even before the delivery of the memorandum, his appointment seemed a foregone conclusion. On a visit to Falmer to discuss the project and look over Basil Spence's parkland campus, he made one powerful ally in Professor Asa Briggs, the Dean of Social Studies; and shortly afterwards he heard from the Vice-Chancellor, Sir John Fulton, that his nomination was being put forward to the university Senate. This was followed by a Gulbenkian Foundation lunch, also attended by Fulton, intended to settle any last snags. With typical directness, Devine told the group that there were two little points he must make clear before matters proceeded any further: he could not participate in any form of organized religion, and he was living unmarried with Jocelyn Herbert.

It was now December and the euphoria of the return to Sloane Square had worn off. *Inadmissible Evidence* had been followed by Ben Travers's *A Cuckoo in the Nest*, and a modern-dress *Julius Caesar* which was withdrawn a week before the end of its scheduled run. There was no immediate chance of transferring *Inadmissible Evidence* to the West End as Williamson was committed to the Court's other productions: and huge obstacles were looming in the path of the second Osborne play. *A Patriot for Me* struck Devine as too big a piece for the Court; but the question of presenting it anywhere remained dubious in view of the censor's reaction. It had been hard enough steering *Inadmissible Evidence* through Stable Yard: but now, instead of line cuts, the Lord Chamberlain was stipulating the deletion of three central scenes. Osborne naturally refused: and the protracted correspondence and meetings of the following months developed into the biggest battle yet fought between the Court and the censor. Page, meanwhile, was immersed in directing *Waiting for Godot*, leaving Devine to shoulder the weight of daily administration.

Godot opened with moderate success at the end of December. The week afterwards, Devine attended the company's New Year lunch at the Savoy Hotel where his retirement was announced to the press. Blond made the announcement. Devine followed with a statement in which he summarized his theatre's achievements: 126 new English plays, the training of twenty assistant directors, a spirit of 'dedication to the essence of a work, and creative eccentricity.' As yet no successor had been appointed to follow him in September: whoever it might be, 'my only advice to him is: keep your best eye on the horizon, the other on your instruments.' It was an emotional occasion. The annual lunch was one of the rare times when the company and its critics met on social terms, and the atmosphere generally resembled a Christmas fraternization party between the lines. But this time the two sides found themselves genuinely united. For years they had alternately admired and grumbled at Devine, while always taking his continued presence for granted. Abruptly, they now realized what they were losing. Lindsay Anderson caught the prevailing mood and found words for it in a speech that had the practical effect of persuading Gaskill to change his mind and accept a second invitation to quit the National Theatre for Sloane Square as Devine's successor. 'The Lord giveth,' observed the abandoned Olivier, 'and the Lord taketh away.'

News of the retirement brought in a flood of letters from friends and colleagues of the past thirty years, expressing mingled feelings of congratulation, gratitude and loss. The most sadly ironic came from Norman Collins, who wrote:

> Everyone in the English theatre owes you a simply enormous debt. You have managed to do what no one else has done, or could have done. All in all, it can't be a bad thing seeing your name go down in history while you have still got the rest of your life ahead of you.

Among the mail that arrived at Flood Street that week, there was also a letter from Sir John Fulton announcing, in squirmingly embarrassed language, that the Sussex University job was off.

Religious non-conformity presented no obstacle to Devine's appointment; but the university drew the line at appointing a man who was openly living with a woman not his wife. The openness was the crime; for, as a Gulbenkian official subsequently explained, there would have been no problem if only Devine had kept his mouth shut. For the sake of keeping up appearances, the university rejected a man uniquely qualified to turn their experimental project into a national power-house. Even Devine, who had made a life study of the follies of the establishment, was unprepared for the abject timidity of this move. 'I could weep,' wrote Asa Briggs, 'that we didn't have you here.'

With the end of this, the last of his unrealized dreams, Devine resolved to leave the country when his time at the Court ran out and take Jocelyn to Brazil where he had been offered an appointment at the Theatre Conservatory in Rio. As a parting gesture he planned to write an autobiography, setting the record straight on the Vic Centre scandal and telling the story of the Royal Court. In 1961, when Faber & Faber first tried to commission such a book from him, Devine responded to the idea 'with horror and dismay ... It always makes me feel that it is a sign that it is dying if one starts to write a history of anything.' When Fabers renewed their offer in January 1965, he still felt that he would only be 'setting up a new neurosis' if he took it up: but with the collapse of the Sussex scheme he changed his mind and signed a contract with the publishers in April.

Meanwhile, in the standard Court phrase, Devine 'was around'. The figure in the mac with the bulging briefcase was still standing in the Upper Circle looking down at rehearsals, occasionally interrupting with a booming, 'Can't hear: speak up.' If an actor lost his voice, or there was a question of whether the theatre would foot a doctor's bill, or the technical crew were having fun with an inexperienced director, Devine was there, offering to replot the lighting, authorize medical expenses, save up any bad news until the day's work was finished; and generally cushion everybody's ego from avoidable assault.

That was the image he presented in the last phase: the horn-rimmed glasses, the mass of white hair, the sound of a pipe being scraped. He said he was part of the fixtures and fittings, but he was virtually a part of the bricks and mortar. There, at least, one would have expected him to have developed un-

shakeable self-confidence: but he remained, as he told Jocelyn
Herbert, a man born without courage who had to construct it for
himself. During a technical run-through of Desmond O'Donovan's *Spring Awakening*, the familiar figure appeared in the
corner of the Upper Circle and called down 'How's it going?'
O'Donovan's assistant, Peter Gill, involuntarily shouted back,
'"It's perfectly ALL RIGHT!" And the sound that came back
was something like, "Why don't you let Desmond speak for
himself?" but it was said by somebody completely crumpled. I
had upset somebody whom I didn't think was upsettable. He
could have said "Get out" or "How dare you:" but I had used an
authoritative voice, and he had been pierced.'

Against this, there remained the positive side of Devine's
undefensiveness. A few days before his last illness, he visited an
international camp for sixth-formers in the Cuffley woods. He
was speaking on censorship and putting forward his usual case
that it should be removed from the Lord Chamberlain's control
and made arguable in the courts. Somebody asked why there
should be any form of censorship at all. Devine was publicly
silent for a long time, and then said, 'I don't know.' It is remarkable that he should have been unprepared for such a
question; but even more so that he should have made no attempt
to disguise the fact.

Alongside his watching brief for the Page régime, he was still
actively pursuing new plays. One turned up from his young
assistant Peter Gill, *The Sleeper's Den*, which O'Donovan
directed one Sunday night before the *Spring Awakening* episode.
Besides an electrifying performance by Eileen Atkins as a dockland mother in the last throes of nervous exhaustion, the production offered a model demonstration of the Sunday night style:
Gill having specified a bare stage with the floor and door positions
marked out in white tape so as to convey the impression of
witnessing a final rehearsal before the arrival of scenery. Detail
of that kind appealed strongly to Devine the stage manager, and
he sought Gill out in the wardrobe where he had taken refuge,
too nervous to watch the show. This was Devine in the role of
Dorn. 'He just said, "Oh, son ... !" meaning "It wasn't *that*
good, but when are you going to write us something else?" It's
difficult to enjoy someone else's work, and he was usually a shy
man; but at moments like that he *flashed* with genuine generosity and pleasure. In your success was his success.'

Another house playwright who appeared at this time was David Cregan, a young Hertfordshire schoolmaster who arrived in the theatre via the Royal Court Studio, and exemplified Devine's belief that the company should grow its own writers as well as shopping for plays in the open market. Devine's plan had been that an acting company with 'certain skills' should be offered to the writer as an instrument, and he found Cregan's work sympathetic because (unlike Bond's) it took this offer up directly. Cregan wrote social comedy. Not only that: he specialized in tricks, physical gags, and surface animation of Devine's Vic School scenarios. Added to which, by his choice of social types, Cregan was picking up Copeau's old dream of a *commedia* drawn from modern life.

Cregan was not consciously following an approved house style, and was far from sure whether he was writing comedy at all. *Commedia* apart, his first play endeared itself to Devine for another reason. *Miniatures* (or *Mr Cregan's Profession*, as Devine called it) followed *Skyvers* as another expedition into the jungle of comprehensive education: this time from the vantage-point of the staff. The title reflected the play's cellular form. In place of continuous narrative there were close-ups of separate factions – gown-wearing traditionalists, redbrick casuals, graduates of technical, arts and physical training departments, all flung into an amorphous community, getting their lines crossed and inflicting incalculable confusions on the young.

Cregan was appalled when Devine told him he had written a funny play, and objected that he had never thought of *Miniatures* as a comedy. '"Ah," said Devine, "I wonder if it is. I've been playing it as if it is." After trying a line or two to himself, he said seriously, "I think it *is* a comedy. I think you *are* comic."' This little exchange followed a moment in rehearsals when Devine had asked the overwhelmed newcomer if he had anything to say; to which Cregan replied that he couldn't hear Devine's lines, and wondered if he could speak up. At this famous phrase, the company dissolved in silent mirth, and 'Graham Crowden whispered he had waited ten years to have someone say that.'

Miniatures had two Sunday-night performances with the kind of casting that is only possible on gala occasions. Lindsay Anderson played a tight-lipped second master conducting an intrigue for the compulsory wearing of gowns, and the theatre's casting director appeared as a one-line tea-lady. Nicol Williamson, as a deranged music teacher, was seen dismembering a record player and hurling the débris into the wings to illustrate the marvels of science. Impotently surveying this modern Tower of Babel was Devine as the headmaster, a man so unsure of his function that the act of picking up a cane threw him into a state of paralysis. Like his other late performances, it was ironically personal, bringing his own scepticism and administrative exhaustion into the character's service, and dropping the mask of his former authority roles. Tension, by now, had entirely vanished from his acting: he was playing to spectators, not nerving himself to confront a house.

By May, when *Miniatures* appeared, the plan for the remainder of the season was complete. *Godot* had been followed by an incoming production of Brecht's *Happy End*, thus freeing Nicol Williamson for the West End transfer of *Inadmissible Evidence*. And when new plays returned to the repertory, Osborne continued to dominate the scene, first directing Charles Wood's *Meals on Wheels* in the month before Page's production of *A Patriot for Me*. Devine was then to make his farewell to the Court by directing Vanessa Redgrave in *The Way of the World*.

Charles Wood was not a Court discovery. He arrived there on one of Oscar Lewenstein's options, having already made his reputation (with *Cockade*) as the first post-war playwright to tell the truth about the British Army. *Meals on Wheels* was a satire on the myths attaching to old age: a large theme limited by the fact that Wood had written the play for his home town of Bristol where it had been firmly rejected as *Muck on a Truck*. However, he was the kind of writer for whom the Court existed, and this was his first full-length piece. Also, it consisted largely of music-hall sketches and octogenarian cross-talk routines calculated to appeal both to Devine and to Osborne who cast Roy Kinnear as the central clown, and Lee Montague (a former Vic School student) as a pink-uniformed moral vigilante smothered in horse-brasses and bottle-top medals.

Devine was usually on hand during rehearsals, unobtrusively organizing the stage management and taking over the lighting and sound. But when the production reached its preview an audience of 'Friends of the Royal Court' received it with boos and slow hand-claps. Dreading what was to come, Kinnear and Montague hired a television set for their dressing room; they

loved football, and West Ham were playing for the European
Cup on the show's first night. Montague says: 'I've never done
this before or since. But because we knew it was going to be
disastrous we'd rush off stage as if it had nothing to do with us
and watch the football. We couldn't bear to think about the
show, because we *knew*. George Devine came in, and he knew
too. But he sat down between us and the set, saying, "Well,
there've been other disastrous first nights, don't worry about it."
Really cheering! And we were saying, "Thank you very much,
George," but wishing he'd go away so we could watch the game.'
It could have been a situation straight out of *Miniatures*, with the
well-meaning head blundering into the staff room at the wrong
minute.

Shortly before this collision with the new drama public,
Devine had faced a Stratford dining room where the ranks of the
Shakespearian establishment had gathered to honour their
patron's 400th birthday. He was there to propose a toast to
'the Drama', which he did by announcing that it had been worth
the train fare to hear himself pronounce so many distinguished
titles, and then demolishing his theme.

> I cannot stand the word drama. Every time I hear the word drama
> I become depressed. Drama conjures up for me all the dusty, fusty,
> moribund attitudes I deplore ... May I plead that this Royal
> Shakespeare Company, renowned for its lead in many fields, should
> replace this dead, sticky word with the more honest and resplendent
> word, Theatre.

With that out of the way, he got down to what he wanted to say.
The British theatre was on the brink of a momentous period.

> Within the next twenty years we will see theatre become an im-
> portant fact in the lives of more people than ever before ... We are
> moving towards the ideal situation in any civilized society where art
> is regarded as a social service, like health and education.

Two immediate reforms were needed: the abolition of censorship; and a raised standard of criticism, which was still trading in
the debased currency of personality journalism 'so wretchedly
promoted by the late James Agate'.

Perhaps Devine believed literally in his twenty-year prophecy.
More to the point, he was addressing a group of people who could
do something to make it come true. The second of his reforms

remains unachieved; but the first was carried through in 1968, thanks largely to his work at the Court and to his tireless battering away on public occasions of this kind.

At the time of the Stratford speech he had just suffered his most crippling defeat from the 'quaint old custom' of British stage censorship. Previously, by trading a few optional 'turds' for a crucial 'fart', the Court had succeeded in getting its plays licensed in not too unrecognizably mutilated a form. But no such concessions were forthcoming in the case of *A Patriot for Me*. The Lord Chamberlain acknowledged the play's 'evident merits' but the cuts demanded by Colonel Penn, the Assistant Comptroller, would have amounted to a neat removal of its heart. The play, as summarized by Lord Annan in the House of Lords,

> was based on the life of an intelligence officer in the Austro-Hungarian Army before the First World War, who gradually discovered his homosexual tendencies, indulged them and was blackmailed by agents of the Russian imperial secret service. On being exposed, he shot himself. I cannot conceive of any play less sentimental towards homosexuality ... and less likely to induce anyone to go into this practice.

Besides the usual list of unacceptable phrases, the censor disallowed the three scenes that establish what the play is about: the hero Redl's first night in bed with a man, a screaming row with his last boy-friend, and the drag ball scene for which, as Ronald Bryden correctly forecast, the play would go down in theatrical history.

Devine had lately emerged from eighteen months of negotiation with Stable Yard for the right to present a run of *Spring Awakening*. But, seeing that there was no chance of securing a licence for Osborne's play without emasculating it, he took the step which, up to this moment, he had invariably resisted: he turned the Court into a club theatre. In practice, this only meant that intending spectators had to fill up a form and pay 5s. for membership of the English Stage Society. But it was departure from his first principle that the company should conduct its experiments in the presence of the general public. Also the possibility of any London transfer was remote. This was a particularly damaging restriction in the case of *A Patriot for Me* which, as Devine pointed out when he first read it, was too big and expensive for Sloane Square. Consisting of twenty-five naturalistic scenes passing through the grand locations of the Austro-Hungarian Empire, and requiring over thirty actors, not counting the groups of soldiers, whores, flunkeys, waiters and ball guests, it was built for an environment like Drury Lane. If it had found such a stage, it would have formed the supreme example of Devine's Law: that theatrical impact is an equation between what happens and where it happens.

There was no way of doing visual justice to the piece on the Court stage. Nor, in spite of raising seat prices, was there any chance of making ends meet financially. Osborne himself re-solved the second problem by offering to take a 50 per cent share in production costs. As for design, if the theatre could not manage Drury Lane extravagance it could go to the opposite extreme of simplification; which it did with the engagement of Jocelyn Herbert for whom austerity of means was a basic aesthetic principle.

Most time-consuming of all, there remained the problem of casting. It was a question of finding a company of forty for a piece with which many actors were afraid of being associated. Casting bum-boys for the drag ball was almost as hard as casting the leads. Originally planned for April, the production was postponed for two months while the part of Redl rebounded from a succession of nervous British stars before it was finally accepted by Maximilian Schell. But the prize boomerang role was that of Baron von Epp, the drag queen hostess of the ball scene. There should have been no problem at all, as Osborne had written the part for Devine, who liked it and was available to play. But Page was not disposed to accept this *fait accompli*. Instead, he offered Devine a selection of crusty old generals and tried to find a high camp specialist for the Baron. Some thirty actors, including MacLiammoir, Coward and Gielgud all turned it down. Every day, meeting the casting director, Devine gruffly inquired, 'Well, who's been seen for my part today?' In the end, having run out of names, Page decided that casting Devine 'just seemed the best idea'. But even then, he asked the E.S.C.'s artistic director to go through the formality of an audition. 'I'm a bit worried about this,' Devine remarked to the casting director, 'I hope I've done this right. I've refused to read for Anthony.'

If he was hurt by this treatment, he did not show it publicly: and, with Dexter, the episode became material for a running joke. 'I've been rejected again.' 'Well, join the club. You rejected me, you can expect to be rejected by other people.' Such, under Devine, was the operation of theatrical hierarchy.

Patriot went into rehearsal at the end of May, casting difficulties in the ball scene having melted away with Devine's arrival. Dexter, walking into the Upper Circle one day, caught an early glimpse of the father figure *en travestie*. 'He was on stage in an old green sweater, flannel trousers, pipe, spectacles on the back of his head, and high-heeled shoes. He didn't exactly teeter; he lumbered across the stage, with the heels up in the air.' In this attire he was capable of swooping on a cigarette and saying 'Don't smoke on stage' without breaking the Baron's giggling rhythms. Not to mention dropping on late-comers like a ton of bricks. He remained the all-responsible boss, with one eye on the stage and the other on the rest of the building. But, as Page put it, 'acting now seemed a great luxury to him when it worked', and on this occasion he must have known that it was going to work like a dream.

Page was less sure of this. Like Dexter, he felt that Devine was nervous of homosexuality, and says that he stood outside the part for a long time: 'although he kept saying he wasn't embarrassed you felt he'd got cricket pads on under the crinoline.' Page, however, did not know about Devine's drag history: the line of breast-plated Wagnerian sopranos and rampaging Amazon queens familiar to the Motleys and to Vic School students. This was a side of himself that the public and his younger colleagues had never seen. Those, like Peggy Ashcroft, who viewed the performance as an eccentric whim, neglected the importance played by sheer fun in Devine's development as an actor. Having closed the gap between personality and technique, he no longer had to prove anything on stage and his acting relaxed into a joyful game. In this case, it was one which he continued playing off-stage. Page says he took the care of a prima donna over his wardrobe. The sumptuous hour-glass figure would appear, framed in the doorway of the General Office, startling the secretaries with a 'Haven't got the wig, but what do you think?' Ann Jellicoe, working in an adjoining office, witnessed another entrance when the door opened and out came Devine in wig, dressing-gown and white stockings. 'He looked visibly jolted, finding me there. "Oh," he said. "I'm just going to the Ladies." About twenty minutes later, the door opened again and IT appeared, in all this regalia and diamonds, with a train over the arm.'

Bookings for the production began two months before the opening of the eight-week run, and by the beginning of June the membership of the E.S.S. had shot up from 1,600 to nearly 4,000. Club performance may have run counter to E.S.C. policy, but the effect of restriction, as usual, was to bump up public demand. The scent of a possible clash with the authorities had aroused the English blood-sport instinct, and thanks to the censor there was no need for salesmanship.

However, the last thing the company wanted was a show-down with the Lord Chamberlain. As Gaskill shortly discovered with Bond's *Saved*, club performance was no safeguard against police action. Far from seeking attention for the production as a *cause célèbre*, the Court maintained the fiction that nothing unusual was happening: the society was not defying the censor, it was simply exercising its proper function of presenting a play to its members. Letters went out to reviewers asking for their co-operation: and at a press conference in May, Devine told them: 'I don't want to create a scandal about this play. I just want it to be seen. Anything you lot do to make the Lord Chamberlain look absurd will be detrimental to us.'

The production opened as planned on June 30 after a week of previews. As background material, the Court had circulated an essay on the nature of patriotism in the Austro-Hungarian Army, and until the first interval the play seemed thoroughly in keeping with this sober document; a leisured historical chronicle with no trace of any belligerent protagonist. Could this be an Osborne play? Then, to the sound of a harpsichord continuo, the curtain rose on what appeared to be a straight performance of *The Marriage of Figaro* in which one gradually realized that Susanna and the attendant coryphées and shepherdesses were all men. This shock was immediately capped by the sight of the hostess sweeping up the latest guest and making polite introductions. 'Colonel Redl, this is Captain Steinbauer – aren't you? Yes. She is.' It was a moment of blissful incredulity. The figure was unmistakably George Devine; and equally unmistakably Queen Alexandra. Osborne had specified ospreys in pompadour feathers, a pearl and diamond choker, and a beautiful fan; to these Devine added elbow-length gloves and an upswept red-gold wig set off by a sparkling coronet. Inset and unpainted within this bejewelled totem to imperial womanhood, the familiar square-cut features stood out in defiant contrast. The effect of the costume was to throw maximum emphasis on the face. And the face had changed. Without artificial disguise it had become a character mask suggesting an elated bird of prey, the nose as sharp as a beak and the neck emerging scrawnily from the pearls. When he lifted his head and stretched his mouth into an avid ellipse, you expected some tremendous squawk. Some details of the performance were based on the mannerisms of Hugh Beaumont. And Page, in a sense, was right about the cricket pads. It was obviously a man inside the dress – but a man who knew all about the manipulation of draperies, the proper use of the fan, and who asserted his sex by beating women at their own game. One can imagine a very different reading of the Baron – perhaps even more in keeping with Osborne's text – using these skills to convey snobbery and malice. There was no trace of these in Devine's performance, despite the ecstatic falsetto swoops and roguish flicks with the fan. His Baron may have been a leathery old queen, but he liked women.

Devine's decade at the Court ended as it had begun with the triumph of John Osborne. *A Patriot for Me* opened to critical acclaim, played to 95 per cent capacity, and picked up the *Evening Standard* prize for the best play of 1965. Despite Mary MacCarthy's sneer that the production had given employment to 'a large number of homosexual actors', the theatre received no complaints, by letter or in person, about the play's indecency. As expected, censorship prohibited any West End transfer but, to offset the £16,500 loss on the show, there was the probability of exploiting it on Broadway where the company were already contracted to revive Richardson's *The Seagull* (with Devine's Dorn) early in 1966.

During his run-out period Devine continued hacking out material for his book from the back-production files and attending Management Committee meetings where the affair of Elidir Davies's unsettled bill was still dragging on. Gaskill and his two assistants, Iain Cuthbertson and Keith Johnstone, were laying plans for the autumn programme; but the millstone of daily administration remained suspended round Devine's neck. There came the afternoon of a torrential storm; rain poured through into the temporary dressing rooms under the stage where a large part of the Hapsburg wardrobe was floating about.

Cuthbertson rushed into Devine's office announcing, 'Your stage is under water!' 'Isn't it remarkable,' said Devine, 'when anything goes wrong it's *my* stage. When things go right it isn't mine.'

His temper was shorter. People in the adjoining office picked up the sound of many a weary sigh and thudding script. But he was still teaching, lecturing, acting on television (notably, his heavyweight performance in David Turner's *The Bedmakers*) and entertaining friends from abroad, including Ionesco and Helene Weigel who arrived in August to head the Berliner Ensemble's season at the National Theatre. On the Saturday before their season opened, the Ensemble descended on Sloane Square to see a matinée of *A Patriot*, and in the reunion that followed Devine missed another engagement. This was the final run-through of *A Collier's Friday Night*, the first of Peter Gill's marvellous D. H. Lawrence productions, on the eve of its Sunday-night showing. Gill, who had never directed before, had taken the play to Devine in a panic, and received the typical reassurance, 'Look, if you do it, I'll come and see it.' Gill met him on the steps of the Court as the Germans were leaving. 'It's going rather well,' he said, 'I wish you could have seen it.' '"I'm sorry dear boy, I had all this," he said, waving them into the taxi; and he looked terribly tired.'

That evening he laced himself into the Baron's corset, descended the five flights of stairs from his dressing room to the stage, and went on to give his performance. On the way back he collapsed on the stairs with a heart attack and was rushed into St Geoge's Hospital. This time it was no warning but the real thing. He had seen it coming ('Actors have died on stage ... ') but he had not managed to get out in time.

At St George's he was placed in a huge casualty ward, an anonymous clearing house, restless day and night with new arrivals, deaths, and hovering priests. 'The most dreadful place in the world,' it seemed to Jocelyn, who at first even had difficulty in getting in to see him, as his doctor had quoted Sophie's name as next of kin. For the first few days he seemed to be responding to treatment. On the following Saturday, Osborne told the last-night *Patriot* audience that he was 'now recovering – by a very characteristic act of will'. Ashcroft, visiting the ward, was appalled to find him sitting up in bed writing letters. Then, eleven days after his admission, a blood clot hit a motor centre in the brain, paralysing the left side of his body. Richardson interrupted the filming of *Mademoiselle* and flew back from France to see him. Other friends, including Osborne, Penelope Gilliatt and Joan Plowright kept a round-the-clock vigil with Jocelyn and her three children, arriving in shifts to sit on the stone steps outside the ward, though all they could do was peer through the doors at the neglected end bed. To them it seemed that the hospital had given him up. Information was hard to come by, as Devine's own doctor had gone on holiday, but in the end Jocelyn succeeded in extracting an official opinion that there was little hope of saving him. Rather than sitting there waiting for him to die, she consulted a private specialist who gave her the option of using a new drug, propranolol, which could either arrest the damage or kill him outright. As the alternative appeared to be death anyway, she agreed to the treatment.

Its effect was positive. He was able to see a few visitors again. Anthony Quayle arrived with champagne and spotted a framed vellum document by the bed, signed by everybody who had worked at the Court. Desperate for conversation, he started congratulating Devine on this and what it stood for. 'What's the good of it', said Devine out of the corner of his mouth, 'when you can't fucking well move?' To Redgrave's wife, Rachel Kempson, he said, 'Tell Michael not to work himself into the ground.' And to Olivier's wife, Joan Plowright, 'It's done for me and I'm not sure if it's worth it. Don't let it happen to him. Get him out before it does it to him.'

In mid-October, two months after his admission, the hospital discharged him and he went home to the Flood Street flat with Jocelyn. His speech had returned almost to normal, but he remained paralysed in the arm and leg, and confined to a wheelchair. As those hospital statements suggest, the embolism had left his mind unimpaired. He was, and clearly saw himself, in the situation of a Beckett character: a perfectly functioning intelligence trapped in a ruined body and watching the process of its own extinction. He could not accept life on those terms. Although he and Jocelyn knew that heart damage is irreversible, he insisted on re-learning to walk and trying to regain the use of his hand. In much pain, he began working with a physiotherapist and practising exercises devised by Edward Bolton, his gym instructor. He also called in his secretary from the Court and started dictating the autobiography for Fabers.

The manuscript opens with a blunt record of the E.S.C.'s origins. There follows a famous passage which has been echoing through the English theatre ever since. I have already quoted from it on page 181. The remainder incomparably sums up the two sides of Devine: the sceptic who sees what is, and the visionary who sees what might be.

> I was not strictly after a popular theatre à la Joan Littlewood-Roger Planchon, but a theatre that would be part of the intellectual life of the country. In this respect, I consider I utterly failed. I feel I have the right to talk in this proprietory way about the English Stage Company, to which I gave nine years of my life and nearly died in the tenth. I was convinced the way to achieve my objective was to get writers, writers of serious pretensions, back into the theatre. This I set out to do. I wanted to change the attitude of the public towards the theatre. All I did was to change the attitude of the theatre towards the public.
>
> At the time of writing this, I happened to be asked to give some advice by my godson, Nicholas Hutchinson – son of Peggy Ashcroft – who wanted to enter the British theatre. He asked which theatre he should go to, and what I said to him might give a more explicit idea of what I feel.
>
> I said, 'You should choose your theatre like you choose a religion. Make sure you don't get into the wrong temple. For me, the theatre is really a religion or way of life. You must decide what you feel the world is about and what you want to say about it, so that everything in the theatre you work in is saying the same thing. This will be influenced partly by the man who is running it and the actual physical and economic conditions under which he works.
>
> Peter Hall has called the theatre a brothel. I don't agree. For me it is a temple of ideas, and ideas so well expressed it may be called art. So always look for quality in the writing above what is being said. This is how to choose a theatre to write in and if you can't find one you like, start one of your own. A theatre must have a recognizable attitude. It will have one whether one likes it or not.'

In November, Jocelyn gave a party for his fifty-fifth birthday. Christmas passed. He was seeing friends, resuming all his old closeness with Saint-Denis and forming an attachment to his grandson, William. Any return to a normal working life was out of the question, but at least he had not been snuffed out in institutional solitude. The end came on the morning of January 20 during a physiotherapy session. He had a spasm of chest pain and breathlessness. The doctor was called. Jocelyn got the oxygen mask over his face, and 'suddenly it was as if all the blood seemed to zoom into his face and head. And he died. I don't know what it meant.' 'Coronary thrombosis,' said his doctor: 'the last of a series of short sharp bangs.'

The funeral took place at Golders Green Crematorium in the pouring rain, and his friends stood outside under dripping umbrellas waiting for the previous service to end. Finally the door swung open and they were summoned inside by an usher-like figure who turned out to be Olivier. Sophie, in the last stages of cancer, was there with Byam Shaw and Saint-Denis; also A. P. Herbert with his family, and Lionel Hale from Devine's Oxford days. Beckett, arriving from Paris, joined a group from the Court who almost failed to arrive as neither they nor the taxi driver knew where the crematorium was. 'Hoop Lane,' Beckett told them.

It was a cold, awkward occasion. It brought together people from all parts of Devine's life, but failed to unite them. They came in uncomfortably in their wet coats, not sure where to stand, and there was nothing in the ceremony – as agnostic as Devine could have wished – to release the weight of private feeling. A short reading and a passage from Britten's *War Requiem*, and then out into the rain again.

Some of the unexpressed feelings came out at a memorial meeting when four of his friends assembled on the Court stage to talk about the man they had variously known as an apprentice, colleague and master. Edith Evans set the tone when she launched into recollections of the boy she met at Oxford with, 'I want to talk about Georgie.' Ashcroft followed; then Osborne, who read one of Dorn's speeches; and Plowright, who described how Devine had rescued her from the Vic School tunnel. It was instructive and deeply affectionate; and it left you feeling how fortunate they all had been.

Not long after Devine's death, Saint-Denis suffered another stroke. And within a month of the funeral, in the midst of designing a film for Polanski, Sophie died.

'If I had died at any time in the course of those ten years,' Devine said in a retirement interview, 'I would have got a longish article in *Encounter* and something in the *New Statesman*'s London Diary, and that would have been it. So far as I'm concerned, the intellectuals of London are a washout.'

He was wrong about *Encounter*, but the *Statesman* duly came through with a paragraph noting his services to the 'Angry Decade' and labelling him 'an accomplished actor of a somewhat old-fashioned kind'. The vagueness of the obituaries is not surprising, as so much of his work appeared inseparable from that of other people. Only an insider could have said the things that needed saying, as Osborne did in the *Observer* of January 23, 1966, describing him as 'the living lie to the common belief that a man who works much of his time inside the walls of a theatre is cut off from the mainstream of intellectual and cultural realities'. In the end, Osborne says, he was worn down by the 'grudging, removed attitude' of the English intellectual climate, but

> if I give an impression of George Devine as someone disappointed or embittered, I would be quite wrong. His disappointment was minimal, in fact, because his expectation was relentlessly pruned. This, combined with his prodigious, hopeful effort, seemed to make his stoicism heroic and generous, rather than a pinched, carping austerity. These were exactly the qualities he admired and saw in the work and personalities of writers as different as Beckett and Brecht. Perhaps it was a kind of reticence. Strength, gaunt lines and simplicity always excited him ... The two big subsidized companies – the National and the Royal Shakespeare – owe a debt to him that is incalculable. Their existence is due directly to him. Hundreds of writers and actors owe their present fortunes and favour to him. I am in the greatest debt of all.

For Osborne, Jocelyn Herbert and others both within and outside the Court circle, that was not it so far as Devine was concerned. There must also be a way of keeping his name alive within some ongoing theatre project. They settled on the idea of an annual award open to promising writers, designers or directors, and launched a £20,000 appeal to set it up.

Some of the money came from a charity performance at the Old Vic, which Olivier lent to the organizers for two evenings in June. The show, generally supervised and stage-managed by John Dexter, consisted of extracts from past Court productions reassembling all the original actors and directors who were available. Kenneth Haigh returned as Jimmy Porter, Olivier as Archie Rice, Robert Stephens as George Dillon, Jack Mac-Gowran as Beckett's Clov, and Guinness as Ionesco's dying king. There were scenes from resounding box office flops like *The Sport of My Mad Mother* and *Serjeant Musgrave's Dance* which had now turned into modern classics. Osborne came on with Jill Bennett in one of Redl's scenes from *A Patriot for Me*. He also joined in the crowd of cooks and waiters in the finale from Wesker's *The Kitchen*, which brought together a cast of over thirty, from all ranks of the profession, in the frantic dinner scene. Among its more conspicuous members were Olivier as the head waiter, Noël Coward as the restaurant owner, and Sybil Thorndike as an old waitress whe convulsed the house with the line: 'I'm not used to this way of working. I've never worked like this before, never.'

A record of this occasion exists in a so-far untransmitted television film which David Frost made of the dress rehearsal. Frost's payment and the sale of tickets, plus the appeal donations, brought the fund up to £18,000 which was then wisely invested by Blond. Since then, the George Devine Award has been annually awarded to a list of young artists including Edward Bond, E. A. Whitehead, Heathcote Williams, David Williamson and Mustapha Matura.

Another tangible memorial survives in the Olivier Theatre (the largest of the National Theatre's three houses), a focused open stage embracing much rectilinear detail within a fan-like design. Denys Lasdun, the architect, acknowledges that his plans were decisively influenced by Devine who insisted on the need for preserving the 'angularity of the situation' in opposition to a womb-like environment of perfect circles and bland curves. 'If anybody asked me why there is a jagged ceiling in the Olivier room, or why there is an angular counterpoint against the curve, it would come back to George Devine.'

His most obvious memorial, of course, is the Royal Court itself, still, amazingly, in business after twenty years and haunted by the presence of its first artistic director despite the passage of successive régimes and the splitting up of the old team. Dexter tells a typical story of returning there after ten years to direct Wesker's *The Old Ones*: arriving at a tricky spot in the text, he swung round to shout a question up to the vacant place in the Upper Circle. 'Your head always turns round to where he used to be. It still does.'

In that sense, it is artificial to cut off the story with Devine's death. He had built the company to last, and some of its later developments, such as its campaign in support of Edward Bond's plays, and its brilliant studio work in the Theatre Upstairs, are a straight continuation of his policy. At the same time, his death did mark the end of one chapter in theatrical experiment. It was followed by the fringe theatre explosion of pub shows, actors' collectives, and fly-by-night touring companies. For the fringe generation, the example of the Royal Court was something to be avoided. It did not create new audiences; and the effect of working inside the system was to alienate the successful artist from his origins and change him from an uncompromising David into a commercial Goliath. The lesson they took from Devine was not his practice of fighting the establishment with its own weapons, but his final message, 'If you can't find a theatre you like, start one of your own.' To the politicized wing of the fringe generation, the Royal Court even in its heyday represented a movement of middle-class transition, voicing the unstructured social protest of a set of disgruntled outsiders who promptly switched from Left to Right once they got in out of the cold.

To this reductive argument, one can only reply that it did not feel like that at the time, and that it is absolutely impossible to tax Devine's own work with narrow self-interest. He gave countless other people the opportunity of developing or betraying their own talents, without ever committing himself or his theatre to the positions they adopted. At Joan Littlewood's Theatre Workshop, as Tynan says, you heard the same tune over and over again: but 'George's band could play lots of tunes.' And if he became a prisoner of the Royal Court, it was so that the Court itself should retain its freedom.

'Theatre', he said, 'is a collective art,' and the task of recording his life has also meant telling the story of a succession of theatrical families – the Motleys, the Vic, the constellation of talents grouped around Gielgud and Saint-Denis, and the post-war classical establishment. Taken in sequence, these merge into a single story, chronicling all that was best in the English theatre over three decades. With the birth of the Royal Court, this tradition and the pent-up energies of the post-war generation came together in a great burst of renewal whose shock waves were felt on every stage in the country. Devine arrived at the Court partly through an accident of timing, partly through the logic of his own career; but, once there, he was supremely the right man for the job. Whether he achieved it more through striving or good luck, the fact that he seized this historic moment and gave himself over body and soul to keeping it alive, establishes him as the most important figure in our theatre since Lilian Baylis.

If I understand anything about Devine's character, he would greet that pronouncement with a sardonic shrug. Osborne says he was not a disappointed man, but he died confessing that he had 'utterly failed' in his main purpose. Time has confirmed this. In the years since his death there has been a tremendous pro-liferation of theatre building, expenditure of public money and experimental activity. As a direct result of his work, certain stereotyped and illiberal attitudes have been swept off the stage. But however great the internal changes, there has been no basic change in the theatre's relationship to the community. The great upsurge from the universities never happened. The West End remains its old self, as divorced as ever from external events. Audiences still comprise only a tiny minority of the population.

The hope, very strong in Devine's lifetime, that the theatre could occupy a central place in the country's intellectual life, has evaporated. Wherever the centre may be now, it is not located on any stage. Without the work of the E.S.C., my own life as a reviewer would have been immeasurably poorer, but it has also been a saddening experience to watch all that revo-lutionary energy slowly wasting away. Devine's memorial is not to be found in any lingering traces of what he called 'this great revolution that everybody talks about'.

When a theatrical leader dies his influence melts in-distinguishably into the surrounding atmosphere; and, as Osborne says, to attempt any statistical assessment of Devine's influence would mean following up hundreds of separate careers dispersed throughout the theatrical world from the Metro-politan Opera House to back-street agit-prop. The essential bond between the survivors, some impenetrably walled up behind their bank accounts, others running Marxist collectives, a few still working in the Royal Court, others who have sworn never to set foot in the place again, is that they remain united in allegiance to Devine as the man who once succeeded in containing them all under one roof. For them, and for audiences who shared in the Royal Court experience, he supplies a reason for continuing to act, buy tickets and write reviews. In his time, one had a glimpse of the theatre released from its bondage to the market place and revealed as a primary human activity. Once seen never forgotten;

and in times of reduced expectation, the memory of Devine is
something to hang on to. If it happened once, it can happen again.

For himself, his death was at once inevitable and absurd. He
knew that the Court was killing him, but the building had
virtually become an extension of his own body, and by the time
he tried to cut himself loose it was too late. But he was only
fifty-five, and was clearly on the brink of a new phase in his own
development; and if he had lived and found the right platform,
he might have carried through a second and greater upheaval in
the cultural landscape.

'If Devine had lived' has become a catch-phrase among his
descendants, sometimes in the manner of children longing for a
parent to return and sort things out. If Devine had lived, this
playwright would not have sold out his talent, that marriage
would not have gone off the rails, this dreadul policy mistake
would not have been made, that awful building would never
have gone up. In collecting interviews for this book, I have
noticed that some people still talk about him in the present tense,
or treat his absence as a ridiculous omission like a leading man
unaccountably walking out of a show. 'Where's Devine? He
ought to be on the divan!' 'Dead?' exploded Anthony Quayle,
'What do you mean, dead? We've got a lot of unfinished business.' That, perhaps, is a response his unsentimental spirit
would approve.

BIBLIOGRAPHY

Browne, Terry, *Playwrights' Theatre*, Pitman, 1975
Chekhov, Anton, *Platonov*, translated by Dmitri Makaroff with an introduction by George Devine, Methuen, 1961
Daubeny, Peter, *My World of Theatre*, Cape, 1971
Devine, Minos, *The Poet Preacher of Vere Street*, SPCK, 1938
Duncan, Ronald, *How to Make Enemies*, Hart-Davis, 1968
Findlater, Richard, *Michael Redgrave*, Heinemann, 1956
Gielgud, John, *Early Stages*, Falcon Press, 1939
Guthrie, Tyrone, *A Life in the Theatre*, Hamish Hamilton, 1960
Hayman, Ronald, *John Gielgud*, Heinemann, 1971
Komisarjevsky, Theodore, *Myself and the Theatre*, Heinemann, 1929
Landstone, Charles, *Off-stage*, Elek, 1953
Marowitz, Charles, Hale, Owen, and Milne, Tom (eds), *The Encore Reader*, Methuen, 1965
Marshall, Norman, *The Other Theatre*, John Lehmann, 1947
Motley, *Designing and Making Stage Costumes*, Studio Vista, 1964
O'Casey, Eileen, *Sean*, Macmillan, 1971
Playfair, Giles, *My Father's Son*, Bles, 1937
Purdom, C. B., *Harley Granville Barker*, Rockliff, 1955
Saint-Denis, Michel, *Theatre: The Rediscovery of Style*, Heinemann, 1960
Sicard, Claude (ed.), *Correspondance: Jacques Copeau, Roger Martin du Gard*, 2 vols, Gallimard, 1972
Thomas, Gwyn, *A Few Selected Exits*, Hutchinson, 1968
Thompson, Laurence, *Behind the Curtain*, Ward Lock, 1951
Whitbourn, Frank, *Lex*, Longman Green, 1937
Williams, Harcourt, *Four Years at the Old Vic*, Putnam, 1935
—— *Old Vic Saga*, Winchester, 1949

INDEX